Clarendon Press Series

LOTZE'S SYSTEM OF PHILOSOPHY

PART II

METAPHYSIC

𝔏𝔬𝔫𝔡𝔬𝔫
HENRY FROWDE

OXFORD UNIVERSITY PRESS WAREHOUSE

AMEN CORNER, E.C.

Clarendon Press Series

METAPHYSIC

IN THREE BOOKS

ONTOLOGY, COSMOLOGY, AND PSYCHOLOGY

BY

HERMANN LOTZE

ENGLISH TRANSLATION

EDITED BY

BERNARD BOSANQUET, M.A

FORMERLY FELLOW OF UNIVERSITY COLLEGE, OXFORD

Second Edition, in two Volumes

VOL. II

Oxford

AT THE CLARENDON PRESS

1887

[*All rights reserved*]

CONTENTS OF VOLUME II.

BOOK II.

Cosmology.

CHAPTER V.

THE THEORETICAL CONSTRUCTION OF MATERIALITY.

	PAGE
174. Matter homogeneous, or heterogeneous with common properties?	1
175. Limitation of the problem	2
176. Descartes and Spinoza on Consciousness and Extension	4
177. Schelling and Hegel; problems attempted by the latter	8
178. Kant does not connect his views of Matter and of Space	9
179. Why Kant explained Matter by Force	12
180. 'Force' involves relation between things	15
181. 'Force' as a property of one element a figure of speech	16
182. Kant rightly implies activity on the part of Things, not mere sequence according to Law	21
183. Kant's two forces a mere analysis of the position of a thing	23
184. Still a mechanical system of forces essential, and several may attach to each element	26
185. Force can only act a distance	28
186. Idea of 'communication' of Motion	31
187. Space no self-evident hindrance to action	34

CHAPTER VI.

THE SIMPLE ELEMENTS OF MATTER.

188. *Prima facie* grounds in favour of Atomism	38
189. Lucretius,—differences in the Atoms	41
190. Consequences of the Unity of an extended Atom	43
191. Notion of unextended Atoms—Herbart	47
192. Herbart's view modified—the Atoms not independent of each other	50

		PAGE
193.	Is Matter homogeneous or of several kinds?	53
194.	Homogeneous Matter not proved by constancy of Mass	56
195.	Connexion of the elements with each other in a systematic unity	58
196.	Plurality in space of identical elements merely phenomenal	60
197.	Self-multiplication of Atomic centres conceivable	63

CHAPTER VII.

THE LAWS OF THE ACTIVITIES OF THINGS.

198.	The square of the distance,—difficulties in the radiation of Force	66
199.	No mechanical deduction of a primary Force	70
200.	Alleged infinite attraction at no distance	70
201.	Herbart's view of the 'Satisfaction' of Force, not conclusive	72
202.	Philosophy desires one primary law of action	76
203.	Affinity would naturally correspond to the Distance itself	77
204.	Attempt to account for Square of Distance	80
205.	Can Force depend on motions of acting elements?	82
206.	Does Force require *time* to take effect at a distance?	83
207.	Causation and Time—Reciprocal action	86
208.	Idealism admits no special Laws as absolute	88
209.	Conservation of Mass	89
210.	Constancy of the *Sum of Motions*	91
211.	Absorption of Cause in Effect	94
212.	Not self-evident that there can be no gain in physical action	94
213.	*Equality* and *Equivalence* distinguished	98
214.	Equivalence does not justify reduction to one process	101
215.	'Compensation' in interaction of Body and Soul	102
216.	The Principle of Parsimony	104

CHAPTER VIII.

THE FORMS OF THE COURSE OF NATURE.

217.	Deductions of the forms of reality impossible	109
218.	Possibility of explaining natural processes in detail on the view of subjective Space	111
219.	Success the test of the methods of physical science	114
220.	Mechanism the action of combined elements according to general laws	115
221.	Mechanism as a distinct mode of natural activity—a fiction	118

222. The planetary system, light and sound	122
223. Electricity and Chemistry should not be sharply opposed to Mechanism	124
224. Motives for forming the conception of a Vital Force	128
225. Vital Force could not be one for all Organisms	130
226. Difference between organic and inorganic substances proves nothing about Vital Force	131
227. A 'Life-principle' would have to operate mechanically	132
228. Mechanical aspect of Organisms	135
229. Mechanical view indispensable but not exhaustive	137
230. Purpose implies a subject—God, the soul	138
231. Von Baer on purpose in 'Nature'	141
232. Unity of world determines all modes of action	144
233. The mechanical order need not exclude progress	145
234. Is there a fixed number of Natural Kinds?	150
235. Criticism of the question 'Is real existence finite or infinite?'	151
236. Development of the Cosmos—only its general principles a question for Metaphysic	157
237. Actual development of life a question for Natural History	158
Conclusion.	160

BOOK III.

Psychology.

CHAPTER I.

THE METAPHYSICAL CONCEPTION OF THE SOUL.

Introductory. Rational and Empirical Psychology	163
238. Reasons for the belief in a 'Soul.'—1. Freedom is no reason	165
239. 2. Mental and physical processes disparate	166
240. Disparateness no proof of separate psychical substance	168
241. 3. Unity of Consciousness	169
242. Unity of the conscious Subject	171
243. The subject in what sense called 'substance'	173
244. Kant on the Substantiality of the Soul	176
245. What the Soul is; and the question of its immortality	180
246. Origin of the Soul may be gradual	182
247. Ideas of psychical and psycho-physical mechanism	186
248. Interaction between Body and Soul	187
249. Idea of a bond between Body and Soul	190
250. The Soul not a resultant of physical actions	191

251. Meaning of explaining the Soul as a peculiar form of combination between elements	194
252. Consciousness and Motion in Fechner's 'Psycho-Physik'	195

CHAPTER II.

SENSATIONS AND THE COURSE OF IDEAS.

253. The physical stimulus of sensation	199
254. The physiological stimulus of sensation	201
255. The conscious sensation	204
256. Adequate and inadequate stimuli of sense	205
257. The connexion of various classes of sensation	207
258. Weber's Law	210
259. Hypotheses as to the reason of Weber's Law	212
260. The so-called chemistry of ideas	214
261. The disappearance of ideas from consciousness. The checking of ideas	217
262. The strength of ideas	219
263. Dim ideas	221
264. The more interesting ideas conquer	223
265. Association of ideas	226
266. Herbart's theory respecting the reproduction of a successive series of ideas	228

CHAPTER III.

ON THE MENTAL ACT OF 'RELATION.'

267. Simple ideas and their relations	232
268. The necessary distinction between them	233
269. Psycho-physical attempts to explain ideas of relation	234
270. Herbart's theory of the psychical mechanism	237
271. The truer view respecting simple ideas and ideas of relation expressed in Herbartian language	240
272. The referring activity as producing universal conceptions	241
273. Attention as an activity of reference	242
274. Attention and the 'interest' possessed by ideas	244

CHAPTER IV.

THE FORMATION OF OUR IDEAS OF SPACE.

275. The subjectivity of our perception of Space	247
276. How is the perception of spatial relations possible?	248

		PAGE
277.	Distinctions depending on Space cannot be preserved as such in the Soul	251
278.	A clue needed for the arrangement of impressions by the Soul	253
279.	The 'extra-impression' as a clue or '*local sign*'	254
280.	Does the 'local sign' arise in the same nerve-fibre as the main impression?	256
281.	'Local signs' must be not merely different but comparable	259
282.	'Local signs' must be conscious sensations	260
283–7.	On the local signs connected with visual sensations	263–276
288–9.	Local signs connected with the sense of touch	276–280
290.	How these feelings are associated with movement	280

CHAPTER V.

THE PHYSICAL BASIS OF MENTAL ACTIVITY.

291.	The 'seat' of the Soul	283
292.	The Soul not omnipresent within the body	284
293.	No reason to suppose that it has an action graduated according to distance	285
294.	No suitable place can be found for it on the hypothesis that it acts by contact only	287
295.	It must act directly and independently of Space, but only at certain necessary points	288
296.	Which these points are is determined from time to time by the activities which go on in them	291
297.	Our ignorance of the special functions of the central nervous organs	293
298.	Ideas of a '*Sensorium commune*' and '*Motorium commune*'	295
299.	The organ of language	297
300.	How the soul initiates action	299
301.	Reproduction of the right concomitant feeling	300
302.	Application of this view to the organ of language	303
303.	Phrenology	304
304.	The connexion of Consciousness with bodily states	306
305.	Does memory depend on physical traces left in the brain?	310
306.	Loss of memory	313
307.	Existence of the soul during unconsciousness	315
	Conclusion	318

INDEX 321

CHAPTER V.

The theoretical construction of Materiality.

174. THE elements of Real Existence have hitherto been spoken of only in so far as regards the positions occupied by them in Space and the changes in those positions; as regards the form and nature of that which takes up and changes its positions, we have been silent. This latter question, which at the point we have now reached we shall be called on to consider, is usually stated as the theoretical construction of Matter. If I were to give this name to the following investigations, it could only be with the reservation that I understand the philosophical problem which is commonly designated by it in a changed sense. For this Matter, the construction of which is required, is not a ready-made fact open to observation. Real Existence—as known to us in Space—consists merely of an indefinite number of individual objects variously distinguished by inherent differences in their sensible qualities. At the same time, however, we learn by observation and comparison of these objects to perceive a number of common properties in which they all, to a greater or less extent, participate. They are all alike extended in space; all alike show a certain tendency to maintain their positions against any attempt to change them; they all oppose a certain *vis inertiae* to any efforts to move them. These common properties of things, which are consistent also with the most manifold differences, may be classed together under the generic name Materiality, and Matter would then be a general term standing for anything which participated, to whatever extent, in the above-mentioned modes of behaviour. The problem of philosophy would be to determine what is the subject of which these are the attributes, and under what conditions there arise in their successive grades the forms of existence and of action which we comprehend under the name of 'Materiality.'

A general consideration of these questions must have regard to two possible modes of answering them. Conceivably the Real Existence which appears to us under forms of action so homogeneous, may be not merely of like, but of quite identical nature throughout, and may owe the differences which characterise it to subsequent accessory conditions. But it is equally conceivable, that Beings originally distinct, and such as cannot be comprehended in the totality of their nature under any one notion, should yet be bound by the plan of the world, in which they are all included, to express their own inmost and heterogeneous Being, where they come into mutual relations, in a language of common currency, i.e. by means of the properties of matter.

175. I shall not now attempt to determine, whether the present age with its more extended knowledge of nature has discovered grounds decisively favouring the first of these suppositions—what is certain is, that the ancients, who first propounded this view, proceeded on no such sufficient grounds. The conception of an attribute admitting of being applied to things differing from each other, they hastily transformed into the conception of a real identical subject underlying the varieties of phenomena. This example has unfortunately been very generally followed by Philosophy in subsequent times, and the days are still quite recent when the most strenuous attempts were made to construct this universal substratum, though even if it had been shown to exist, it would have been most difficult, if not altogether impossible, to deduce from it the different material bodies to the explanation of which it was supposed to be necessary. In any case, this universal matter could not have been adequately determined by reference to those pre-

dicates which constitute its materiality. For, all of them, extension, reaction, *vis inertiae*, denote merely the manner or mode in which a thing behaves or is related. They do not in any way touch the nature of that to which these changes of behaviour are attributed.

There are two ways in which it may be attempted to get the better of this difficulty. As we are under no obligation to lay claim to universal knowledge, so it may simply be granted, that Matter is a real determinate thing, but known to us and intelligible only in respect of its behaviour. This is roughly the point of view which is adopted by Physical Science. Science distinguishes that which is extended and operative in space from the empty environment in which it appears. But it leaves the original nature of this substratum undefined, or ascribes to it only such general characteristics as are forced upon it by the analysis of individual objects. By so doing, Science gives up the attempt to construct a theory of a universal matter, preferring rather to examine into the nature of phenomena singly, whilst assuming the existence of a common basis underlying them. On the other method, if we attempt to deduce the general properties of matter from the nature of the real thing of which they are predicates, we are met by a well-known difficulty. We convinced ourselves, when treating of ontology, that to look for the essence of a thing in a fixed quality and then to represent the modes of its activity as consequences derivative from this, was a method which could never be successful[1]. We saw, that all those forms of insight which seemed to explain the inner nature of things were only possible because they were nothing but forms of vision, appearances such as a consciousness may present to itself. What lay at the bottom of such perceptions, in external reality, always converted itself into some kind of activity or process or mode of relation. And however strong may be the impulse to attribute these living processes to some subject, we had to

[1] [Cp. Bk. I. Chap. 2, § 22.]

give up the attempt to explain the marvellous fact of active being, by representing its activity as the mere predicate of an inactive subject. Similarly, in the present case, it would be labour mis-spent to attempt to describe the reality underlying the forms of material existence previous to and independent of these its manifestations. There does however still remain something to be done, viz. to determine the place which this inaccessible substratum occupies in the sum-total of existence. At any rate we must be clear as to whether we mean to regard it as something absolutely original and specific, standing in no connexion with other forms of reality, or as itself, no less than its properties, an intelligible part of the order of the universe. The attempt to explain the origin of matter mechanically is now regarded as impossible; no theory of a universal matter can show how the existence of matter first became possible and then actual. All that can be done is to indicate the *manner* of its existence and its place in the order of the world. Not until the nature of matter had been thus explained, and so could be taken for granted, could the attempt be renewed to derive individual phenomena by mechanical laws from the universal fact of matter.

176. There has never been a dearth of such attempts; I shall content myself with a brief mention of only a few; confining myself to those which stand in the closest relation to existing opinions on the same subject. According to Descartes, extension and consciousness constituted together the two ultimate facts of perception, both being equally clear and neither admitting of being merged in the other. Having made this discovery, Descartes proceeded with a light heart to treat also the *res extensa* and the *res cogitans* as equally simple and clear. He considered that these were the two original elements of the world, and he maintained that they had no further community of nature than such as followed from their having both sprung from the will of the creator, and being involved in a relation of cause and effect,

which the same will had established. Doubtless, an advance was made upon this view by Spinoza, in so far as he conceived of conscious life and material existence not merely as springing from the arbitrary will of the creator, but as two parallel lines of development, into which, by reason of its two essential attributes, the one absolute substance separated itself. At any rate, it was established that the material world does not proceed from any principle peculiar to itself, and of undemonstrable origin: the Reality underlying the forms and relations of matter in space is the same as the Reality, which in the intelligible world assumes the form of Thought.

But I cannot convince myself that Spinoza got further than this point towards a solution of the questions now before us. Though insisting on the necessary concatenation of all things, even to the extent of denying every kind of freedom, he hindered the development of his view, by introducing barren logical conceptions of relation, the metaphysical value of which remained obscure. A logical expression may often be found for the content of a conception by enumerating a number of attributes co-ordinated in it. All that this really means is that every such determination a is imposed upon the single object in question by the given condition p, with the same immediate necessity with which in another case the determination b would follow upon the occurrence of q. But we cannot tell in what consists the unity of a substance, which apart from all such conditions exhibits two original disparate sets of attributes, leaving it open as to whether these are eternal forms of Being (*essentia*), and as such help to constitute the nature of the substance, or whether we are to understand by them merely two modes in which the nature of this substance is apprehended by us. The fact that in respect to the infinite substance every influence of external conditions must be denied, makes it all the more necessary that the inner relations which are contained in its essential unity, issuing as they do in such very different modes of manifestation, should be explained and harmonised. The striking peculiarity of the circumstance that Thought and Extension should be the attributes thus colligated, is not explained away, it is only hidden from view by the suggestion that besides these attributes, there are an infinite number of others, which though inaccessible to our knowledge are yet co-ordinated together in the nature of the absolute after the same incomprehensible fashion.

Again, every individual existence in the material world may be logically subsumed under the universal attribute which is called by the not very appropriate name extension, as species or subspecies; but, in the merely formal conception of absolute substance, there is nothing whatever to determine why out of the infinitude of possible modifications of the absolute substance which are logically conceivable, one should exist in reality and another should not—or, supposing it to be held that in the infinite unexplored totality of existence all these numberless possibilities as a matter of fact *are* realised, there must still be some reason why the events in the limits of our own experience take place in the order in which they do and not in another. Those two attributes of the infinite substance would, if left to themselves, be able to develope merely the system of all possible consequences derivable from them; but such is not the reality which we find before us; in order to arrive at that we need either a plurality of underived existences, or a simple plan capable of being the reason why of the possible consequences of those principles some occur often, others but rarely, and in all such infinitely various combinations.

Once more, it is true that no modification of the one attribute can be derived out of a modification of the other, and therefore thought cannot be derived from extension nor extension from thought. But the logical impossibility of deriving one from the other analytically cannot invalidate the possibility of their synthetic combination in actual reality, except on a view which treats logical subordination as if it were the same with dependence in fact, and confuses a condition with a cause. The necessary admission that in Being there are elements which cohere and mutually affect each other, though in thought they are incommensurable, cannot be replaced by the wearisome repetition of the assertion, 'ordo et connexio rerum idem est atque ordo et connexio idearum.' Whatever reference this proposition may be supposed to have, whether to the parallelism of the forms of Being in the totality of the world, or to the combination of physical and psychical functions in the life of each individual, as long as consciousness and extension have admittedly no common term, there can be no common term between the order and connexion of their respective modifications. Their alleged identity can only be understood in the restricted sense that always and in every case the modification b of the attribute B corresponds with the modification a of the attribute A, and that the change of a into α is followed always by a corresponding change of b into β. But there is no proof that the correspondence which is exhibited as a matter of fact between $a-\alpha$ and $b-\beta$ rests on any identity of nature; or, in other words, that the transition between two modifications of the one attribute is or expresses or repeats the same thing in a different form as the corresponding transition in the other. I cannot, therefore, discover that Spinoza has advanced the explanation of the material world in its relation to the spiritual. Instead of a metaphysical theory, what he gives is scarcely more than a logical classification. According to this, material and spiritual existences may be ranked under two disparate categories, which, both as real determinations in the nature of the absolute, and in all that is produced from it, are, not indeed by any inner necessity, but always as a matter of fact, combined. It is quite possible that we may not be able to make any advance worth speaking of beyond this point; but, in that case, we must admit that we have arrived at a result which is worth almost nothing, and we shall not feel bound to make any profession of enthusiasm on account of such a trifling addition to our knowledge.

177. I shall touch only briefly on the kindred speculations which our own idealist philosophy has developed more recently. Schelling contented himself at first, as Spinoza had done, with the recognition of that Law of Polarity, which as a fact constrains the absolute to develope itself under the twofold form of Ideality and Reality. He interested himself more, however, in showing the constant presence of these two elements in every phenomenon, and explained the manifold differences of things as arising from the preponderance of one or other of them. But it soon became evident (as would have appeared even more clearly if his demonstration had been successful) that he intended to regard this duality not as a mere fact, but as a necessary process of differentiation involved in the original nature of the Absolute. At a later period, he was dominated, as was Hegel, by the thought of a development within which the material world appears as an anticipation of the higher life of the Spirit. Of this development Hegel believed himself to have discovered the law.

It would be impossible, without going to extreme length, to give a representation of the governing purpose of Hegel's account, which should be at once faithful to the original, and at the same time adapted to our present habits of thought. I shall confine myself, therefore, to attempting to show that he has confused two classes of questions which ought to be kept distinct. After satisfying oneself that the purpose of the world is the realisation of some one all-comprehensive idea, and after being further assured that the arrangement of the forms of existence and activity in a fixed system is required as a means to this realisation, one may proceed to ask, what is the place of matter in such a system? what necessary and peculiar function is served by it? It would then be natural to speak first of matter in its most universal form, i.e. materiality as such; and we might hope to find that the same inner process of development, following which the original idea of matter breaks itself up into certain definite postulates of existence, necessitated by the correspondence of the idea with the whole sphere of reality, would be followed in like manner by the concrete forms which different objects assume in filling in the common outline, and that these would be similarly developed. No one now believes in the pleasant dream that this project is realisable, still less that it has been realised. Still, there is nothing unintelligible in the notion itself. What troubles us is the obscurity of the connexion between this project and the second of the problems I alluded to, that of showing how the postulates dictated by the Idea are satisfied both in existence as a whole, and in the complex course of actual events in particular. As regards the former point, it may be sufficient to bear in mind that the self-developing idea is no mere system of conceivable possibilities of thought, but itself living reality. The same reflexion cannot, however, as often it is wrongly made to do, serve the place of a system of mechanics, determining in reference to each concrete existence in Space and Time why precisely here and now this rather than some other manifestation of the idea should necessarily be realised.

178. More in accordance with the scientific views at present held is the teaching of Kant. I can remember how a few decades ago the student used to hear it said that of all Kant's epoch-making works the deepest were those which treated of the Metaphysical basis of Natural Science. While admitting the worth of what Kant has written on this subject, I cannot value it quite so highly. I lament, in the first place, the gap which separates the results of these speculations from those of the Critique of the Reason. The ideal nature of space which is asserted in the Critique is here left almost out of account; the construction of matter is attempted exclusively from the ordinary point of view,

according to which there is a real extension, and there must be activities adapted to fill it. I lament no less what has previously been observed by Hegel, viz. that there should remain such uncertainty as to the subject to which the activities thus manifesting themselves in Space, and so constituting matter, are to be attributed. That this subject is what moves in Space, and that it is the reality which underlies our sensations, these seem to be the only determinations of it which are not derived from what the properties of matter show themselves to be by their subsequent effects. Who or what this is that is thus movable or real remains unexplained. Taking into consideration the fact that Kant used to speak of things in themselves in the plural, it seems probable that his thoughts on this subject did not pass beyond the conception of an indefinite multiplicity of real elements, an obvious hypothesis, which was likely to recommend itself to him for the purposes of Physical Science. This view is confirmed by his mode of deriving the differences of individual existences from combinations of the two[1] primary forces in varying degrees of intensity, which is his invariable explanation of matter as a phenomenon. Now these differences of combination would have nothing to stand upon if they are not based on specific differences of nature in the real elements which they combine. Although, therefore, it is not explicitly laid down that the Real elements are originally distinct, still this interpretation is quite as little excluded, and it may be admitted that what Kant is endeavouring to explain is not a universal matter, but rather the universal form of materiality, together with the special manifestations which are developed within this form in consequence of the characteristic nature of the Reality which the form contains. But, supposing this to be admitted, we should still be at a loss to explain how this real existence is related to Space, in which it thus makes its appearance. If we refer back to the Critique of the Reason,

[1] [I.e. attraction and repulsion.]

we find one thing settled, but only in the negative. True Being can neither be itself extended, nor can the relations in which it is expressed be other than purely intelligible ones. The problem would then have been to show how the elements of Real existence are able to present themselves to our consciousness[1]—in which alone space is contained—in such a way that they not merely take up definite positions, but also have the appearance of being extended in Space. Kant never really handled this question. The forces of attraction and repulsion which he mentions can only be understood on the supposition of certain definite points from which they are put in operation by the ultimate elements. Moreover, if Space which is continuous is to be continuously filled with matter, differing indeed in degrees of density, but still such that no smallest particle of it can be absolutely driven out of Space even by the greatest pressure, and if matter is to an unlimited extent divisible into parts which still remain matter, there seems to be nothing left for our imagination but to conceive of extension in Space and impenetrability as original and fixed characteristics of the real substratum, which thus becomes the basis of further enquiry. But in that case, what we should have would be neither a universal matter nor the universal form of materiality. The latter would be merely assumed as the common characteristic in real elements otherwise diverse, in order that it might serve as a basis for investigation into the relations subsisting between different material existences. This result would not be very unlike that which is soon reached by the ordinary reflexion upon Nature. Different kinds of unknown elements are assumed, which owing to causes also unknown we come upon, each of them in numerous specimens, at different points in Space. At these different points each fills a certain volume with its presence; their presence is manifested by the changes of position which they originate, and by the resistance which

---

[1] ['Anschauung.']

they offer to any attempts coming from without to remove them from their occupancy or to lessen its extent. In other words, we think that there are many different kinds of matter which are distinguished for us by the different co-efficients which we are compelled to assign in each of them to the action of certain forces or inherent tendencies common to them all.

179. The application of this conception of force in order to explain the fundamental qualities of matter has always been regarded as the most valuable advance of Kant's Philosophy of Nature, though to some it has seemed to go further than experience would warrant. Kant himself does not appear to me to have allowed the motive clearly enough to emerge which led him to this view, though there can be no doubt as to what it was, and we may trace it thus. He mentions[1] Lambert's account of Solidity as a necessary property of all material existence. According to Lambert, it follows from the very conception of Reality, or, in other words, it is a consequence of the Law of Contradiction, that the mere fact of the presence of a thing in Space makes it impossible that any other thing should occupy the same position at the same time. Against this it was contended by Kant that the Law of Contradiction could not by itself keep back any part of matter from approaching and making its way into a position already occupied by some other part. This objection is not quite fair. We should not expect the physical impossibility referred to to be produced *by* the Principle of Contradiction, but only *in accordance with* that principle and *by* the fact of solidity which for practical purposes, we assume as an attribute of Real Existence. And why should we not make this assumption if there is nothing at variance with it in experience? It is no sufficient reason against doing so to urge, as Kant does in the course of his 'Proof' of this 'Precept No. 1' of his 'Dynamic,'

[1] [Kant. Metaphysische Anfangsgründe der Naturwiss. Dynamik. Lehrsatz I. Anmerkung. (Werke ed. Rosenkranz. 5. 344.)]

that to make way into a position is a motion; and that in order for there to be a decrease or cessation of motion there must be a motion proceeding from an opposite quarter, or rather a something which can produce such a motion, a motive force. For the view of atomism according to which the smallest particles of matter are possessed of solidity, though it would admit that motion makes its way up to the surface of a body, would not admit that it makes its way into the body; yet, according to this view, the effects of the impact communicated would not vanish without producing an effect at the surface of the solid matter, but would be distributed from one atom to another, or to several atoms, and so become imperceptible. Whatever difficulties may attend the explanation of the phenomena by this method, at any rate a closer investigation than has been entered on by Kant would have been required in order to exhibit them.

Again, what Kant adds in his note is not to me convincing. He admits that in constructing a conception it is allowable to assume any datum to start with, e.g. solidity, without attempting to explain what the datum itself is. This, however, he says, gives us no right to affirm that the hypothesis is altogether incapable of being explained by mathematics. It seems to him that such a view would only hinder us in the attempt to penetrate to the first principles of science. But supposing we were willing to go so far with Kant as to assume the force of expansion, to which he gives precedence, would this be more than a datum, which could be used certainly to explain subsequent manifestations, but was itself taken for granted and would not admit of being deduced from the nature of real existence as such? The point at which a man will declare himself satisfied in this matter really depends in each case on his individual taste. There could be no real necessity to follow Kant in assuming something more than solidity as a fact pure and simple, unless it could be shown that solidity itself is either impossible or inadequate. Now the question whether it is impossible must for the present be left out of account; inadequate, however, it certainly is. The fact that no visible body is of unvarying extension, but all are susceptible of compression or expansion, would, it is true, apart from Kant's assumption of a continuous *plenum* in space, form no immediate disproof of the solidity in question, though this obviously implies the allegation of unvarying volume. The atomic theory, postulating empty spaces between its solid elements, would have a different explanation for the varying size of substances. But all the phenomena of elasticity, in which bodies resume their former shapes so soon as the external agencies which determined them to change have ceased to operate, prove beyond question that there must lie in the very nature of real existence conditions capable of producing states of Being which as yet are not. The form and extension, consequently, which an object of sensible perception assumes, cannot attach to it as an original and fixed property, but are rather a varying state of its existence, determined by inner conditions inherent in its Being. Sometimes, the object is permitted to appear in its true form, sometimes it is hindered from doing so; in the latter case, however, i.e. where the inner states of Being are prevented from giving themselves expression, they make known their existence by the resistance which they offer to the adverse influences. These inner determinations may be spoken of as *forces*, in order to distinguish them from *properties*. It will then be seen not to be enough to ascribe solidity, as a property, though it were only to the smallest particles of matter. The atoms themselves must have certain moving forces attaching to them, in order to make the ever-changing volume even of composite bodies intelligible.

Thus we may say provisionally that Kant regarded as fundamental in this problem of Science that principle which we cannot dispense with even though we prefer the other principle; but which may very well help to explain that other principle. This solid matter was not a fact open to observation; it was not so even as applied to the smallest particles; it was an hypothesis. Hence, it could be denied, and every occupation of space not merely by large visible bodies, but by their smallest elements, could be regarded as a perpetually changing state produced by the force of expansion, according as its action was free or impeded. Stated in a few words the case stands thus. If every material existence, remaining always indivisible, occupied the same space at one time as at another, solidity might be predicated of it as an original quality which it must not be attempted further to explain. But, now, inasmuch as extension, though a *character indelebilis*, is not a *character invariabilis* of matter, the extension which a thing has at any moment is the result of conditions which though present at that moment may vary at other moments; one of these conditions lies in matter itself, and offers a resistance, though not an insuperable one, to those which come from without.

180. I wish to dwell for a moment longer on the difference to which I have referred between a fixed quality and a force. We have been long convinced that what we ordinarily call properties of things are really only modes which they assume, or manifestations which become known to us as the result of their interaction. Things do not have colour except as seen by us, and at the moment when in combination with waves of light they stimulate the eye. They are not hard, except in relation to the hand which attempts to move or pierce them. As a matter of fact, then, we should be at a loss to point to an indubitable instance of what we mean by a quality of a thing. All we can say is, that we are clear ourselves as to what we mean. By a quality is meant that which a thing is for itself and independently of any of its relations to other things. Hence, in order to exist, a quality neither requires these other things, nor is interfered with by them. A force, on the other hand, is not, like a quality, something belonging to things as such. In order, therefore, for a thing to be what it is, we do not attribute to it any force of being; though we do speak of its having a force of self-conservation, in opposition to certain conditions which we assume to be capable of changing it. Our conception of a force, therefore, involves the thought that the character of a thing is neither unchanging, nor yet on the other hand determinable to an unlimited extent from without. Rather, it implies that when the two things meet, they both undergo a real change, the change of the one depending on the nature of the other, but each at the same time by its own nature forbidding a change without limits or one which would amount to a surrender of its essential Being. If qualities attach to things in their isolation, forces can only belong to them in consideration of their relation to each other; they are, in fact, conditions which enable one thing to affect another and to place itself to it in different relations. It is in this sense that Kant speaks of the forces which fill space; they belong to the separate parts of matter, and are brought into activity by these parts in their mutual relations; their appropriate effects they either succeed in producing, or else show to be present by the resistance which they offer to other forces tending to hinder them. Here, however, it may be objected that Kant did not confine himself to the exposition of this process, but that taking this for granted as a universally presupposed fact, he imported into the discussion considerations of quite a different order, attaching to the term 'Force,' which he selected. I do not believe that Kant himself is liable to the charge here made against him; but the popular view of nature which was suggested by his doctrines, has given rise to a number of false opinions, and these therefore we shall now proceed to examine more at length.

181. It is no doubt most useful to be able to express the import of an intricate relation between several connected points, by means of a single word; at the same time, there is danger in doing this. After the word has been called into existence, not only are we able to combine it with other words, but we are led to suppose that every such grammatical combination has something real corresponding with it in fact. Thus, we speak first of all of force, and then of the force of matter. The use of the genitive in this instance, implying as it does that matter is possessed of force, or, that force is exercised by matter, has suggested these interminable questions concerning the nature of force as such, and its relation to matter of which it is a function. Such questions cannot be easily answered at once, when stated in this form. To understand, however, the *applications* of which this conception of force admits, we have only to observe the ordinary usage of Physical Science. Physics makes no mention of Force in itself, but only of its effects, i.e. of the changes to which it gives rise, or which it hinders. It is moreover against the Law of Persistence that an element should of itself modify its own states; the impulse to change must come from some other element. Thus, an element a is not possessed of a force p until a second element b is presented to it on which it may take effect. The force is really produced in a by the relation to b; and it changes to q or r if either the nature of the second element or the relation of a to it is changed. Now, observation shows that there is nothing impossible in the attempt to determine the nature of the elements, the relations in which they may stand to each other, and the changes which they undergo in consequence of these relations. We can understand how, when elements containing specific amounts of generic properties enter into specific forms of some general relation, there are general effects which follow and vary proportionally according to definite laws. The proposition, a is possessed of the force p, when all that it implies is fully stated, in the first instance merely conveys the assurance that whenever a is brought into a specific relation m with a given element b, changes of state will be experienced both by a and by b which will go together to form the new occurrence, of fixed character and amount, π. Having arrived at this result we may then go on to speak of this fixed determinate force in another way, as if, i.e. it were present in a in an ineffective and indeterminate form, its definite effect being supposed to depend on subsequent conditioning circumstances, e.g. the nature of the elements b or c which come into contact with a, the peculiarity of the relation m or n into which a is brought, the presence or absence of some third circumstance. To all these causes the actual realisation of the result π or κ might be ascribed. Even this mode of statement, however, expresses no more than a presumption as to what will necessarily happen in a given supposed case. It follows in accordance with the general law which connects the changes of things with one another, that the circumstances being such as they are, no other result could have happened. Each of the elements, in virtue of its own nature, contributes to this result, and it is an allowable mode of statement first of all to represent them as containing severally and individually all the required conditions, and then to rectify the error of such an assumption by adding that the force potentially inherent in each element cannot become active until the element enters into some specially determined relation. As a matter of fact, it is this special relation which gives rise to the force. If we desire a definition of force, we may say that it is that quantitatively and qualitatively determined result, which may or must ensue, whenever any one element enters into a specific relation with any other. It is only for convenience of speech that this future result, which under given conditions we are justified in expecting, is antedated as a property already present though inoperative in the element. This being understood, there can be no harm in thus speaking of a force as being asleep and awaiting the moment of its awakenment, according as the conditions, which together with the specific nature of the element constitute all that is necessary to produce the result, are present or absent. We shall perhaps make the matter clearer, if we adduce other instances besides those of physical forces with which we are more immediately concerned. Thus, it is the same conception of force which we have in view, when we speak of the powers of the mind, the revenue-yielding power of a country, or the purchasing power of money. In this last case, no one seriously believes that the current coin contains some latent property which gives it its value. The possibility of obtaining a given quantity of goods in exchange for so much money depends on highly complex relations which men enter into for purposes of traffic; and the value of the money changes not owing to any change in the substance of the metal, but to a change in some one of the conditions by which the value of the money is for the time being determined. There would be no power of purchase in money if there were no market in which to exchange it. Similarly we are quite justified in speaking of the Power of Judgment as a property of mind. When we make an assertion in regard to any given matter before us, which is what properly constitutes a judgment, it is certainly our intellectual nature that is called into exercise; at the same time, however, it would be nonsense to speak of a power of judgment, which belonged to us before we came to make use of it, or one which was constantly being exercised without reference to any distinct object-matter. It is impossible to say more than that we are constituted by nature in such a way that the mind, when it is acted upon by impressions from without, not only receives the impressions singly, but reacts upon them in that way of comparison of their different contents which we call judgment. It is only at the moment when it is exercised that the Power of Judgment is living and present, and this applies not only to the reality of the activity, but also to its nature and content; these likewise being dependent on the conditions which bring them into existence for the time being. We may say the same as regards the conception of force which obtains in Mechanics. Thus when we speak of centrifugal force, we do not mean that this force is possessed by Bodies as such, when they are at rest. We at once see that we are speaking of effects which may or must take place when bodies are rotating or being swung round. If we distinguish from these forces certain others, such viz. as the attraction which bodies exercise upon each other, and call the latter primary forces inherent in the bodies as such, all that we mean is that the conditions under which such forces arise are extremely simple and always fulfilled. In order for two elements to be drawn to each other by the force of attraction, all that is required is that they should exist at the same time in the same world of space. This one condition, however, is indispensable; it would have no meaning to say that an element gravitated, if there were no second element to determine the direction of its motion.

We shall not, therefore, attempt to determine what actual relation subsists between forces and the bodies which are their substrata, believing as we do that the problem itself results from a misunderstanding. No such relation exists in the sense that a force can in any way be separated from the body which we call its substratum. Its name 'force' is only a substantive-name employed to express a proposition, the sense of which is, that certain consequences follow upon certain conditions. What it signifies is neither a thing, nor any existing property of a thing, nor again is it a means of which a thing could avail itself in order to produce any given result. It merely affirms the certainty that a given result will happen in a given case, supposing all the necessary conditions to be complied with. Nor can we ourselves attach any meaning to those hastily-conceived maxims, which are popularly held to express the truth on this subject, such e.g. as that there can be no force without matter; and, no matter without force. These equally stale propositions merely add a small grain of truth to the old error in a more perverted form. It is rather true that there is no force inherent in any matter, and no matter which by itself has or brings with it any kind of force. Every force attaches to some specific relation between at least two elements. On the other hand no opinion is here expressed with regard to the question as to whether it is possible for two elements thus to be brought in relation without some force being engendered. It is dangerous to attempt to lay down propositions by the way with regard to matters of fact, merely for the sake of making a verbal antithesis.

182. If these considerations are regarded as conclusive, the term force will be understood, not indeed in the sense in which it is sometimes used, viz. as a Law according to which things take place, but as an assertion in regard to each single case to which the term is applied that we have in that case an instance of the operation of the Law. Thus understood, the term will not suggest any metaphysical explanation as to why the particular facts *must* fall under the general Law.

It is this sense which Physical science is content to adopt when making use of the term. For the practical aim of science, that of connecting events in such a way as will enable us on the basis of present facts to predict the Future or unriddle the Past, it is found amply sufficient to know the general law of the succession of phenomena and by inserting the special modifications of its conditions which occasion prescribes to determine the nature of the result. Science can afford to be indifferent as to the inner connexion by which results are made to follow antecedents. It cannot be maintained that this was all that Kant intended to be understood by his conception of force. He everywhere speaks as if he meant to explain extension not as a simple consequence of the existence of matter, but rather as due to the action of a force. This is a very different conception of force from that according to which it is regarded simply as the connexion of phenomena in accordance with Law. Clearly he means by Force something which is active in the strict sense of the word, something which, he believes, will produce real changes of state; whereas, the counter-theory, confining itself within narrower limits, asserts only that they follow each other in orderly succession. The popular view of nature which based itself on Kant's doctrine imported into the idea of physical force all those associations which are suggested by reflexion on our own conscious activity. In order for this doctrine not to seem to be at variance with the observed facts of the outer world, it had to be toned down, and, in spite of the manifold contradictions which the idea involved, the activity was regarded as Will or Impulse unconscious of itself. These latter-day developments of Kant's view I shall for the present leave to take care of themselves. It will, however, be understood after what I have urged in the ontological portion of my work as regards the relation of cause and effect, that this view which has been made to bear so heavily on Kant, is one in which I fully agree with him—I agree with him in the general recognition of an inner process and activity, in virtue of which things are able to be that which, according to the frequent expression of Physicists, it alone belongs to them of right to be, viz. interconnected points serving as the basis of ever-varying combinations, centres from which forces proceed and to which they return, points of intersection at which different converging processes meet and cross each other in fixed succession. I do not regret that Kant should have refused to put this view on one side. I regret rather that he should not have brought us to closer quarters with it. The general position for which I have already contended does not require to be further elaborated in reference to this special case of Physical causation. An element a cannot produce the effect p merely because there is a general law L, which prescribes that when a stands in the relation *m* to *b*, the result *p* shall follow. No doubt this result *does* follow in the given case, i.e. we who are the spectators see and know that it does so. But, in order for the change itself to take place, in order for *a* to give birth to an activity under these new conditions which it did not previously produce, it must undergo an experience through being placed in the relation *m* which otherwise it would not have undergone, and, similarly, the effect *p* could never be brought home to *b*, merely because the relation *m* existed between *b* and *a*. The existence of the relation *m* must have been *felt* by *b* before it could have been acted on. Hence, the results which arise in each case are not consequences of mere *relations* which subsist between *a* and *b*. These relations, as we call them, are really inner states of Being, which things experience as the result of their mutual activity. It is not to be expected that this theory of an unceasing activity of the inner life of things will be of much real assistance in the explanation of each separate fact of nature. It is a supposition, however, which it is necessary for us to entertain if we are to cease to regard the world from a point of view, which however useful it may be for practical purposes is full of inconceivabilities, the view, viz. that the elements of existence are without individuality and without life, endowed with reality merely because a network of relations is established between them by the agency of general laws. The usefulness of this latter point of view, if considered merely as a half statement of the truth, I shall not dispute, whilst at the same time I shall point out how far it is applicable and justifiable, and when and where it is necessary to recur to what actually takes place in the nature of things.

183. Out of the multitude of opinions which offer themselves for consideration at this point I shall make mention, first, of Kant's view, according to which there are two forces necessary to every material existence, the force of attraction, by which things are made to cohere, and the force of repulsion by which they are expanded; the two together forming a standing element in the countless attempts at explanation which have been made since Kant's time. I must confess myself that I do not feel much interest in these two forces. When the point is raised as to how it can be that a given matter has definitely fixed limits of extension, it is easy to see that there must be some reason why it is what it is—neither more nor less—i.e. there must be an attraction of the parts, which if it were allowed to work alone would reduce the extension to nil, and there must also be repulsion, which similarly, if it were the only principle at work, would make the extension infinite. This is simply a logical analysis which might be applied to the conception of any real existence which has a definite magnitude in space. The enquiry does not become metaphysical until it deals with two further questions; how, that is, these two mutually opposed forces are possible, both attaching as they do to the same subject; and what that is which produces and maintains them in such varying proportions as are required in order to give rise to the manifold differences of material things in point of extension?

The first of these two questions has been made a subject of investigation by Physics. It was considered that to ascribe to matter two equally original opposed forces would involve a contradiction in terms. The attempt was therefore made to assign the two forces to different subjects. The mutual attraction of the parts proceeded from the ponderable elements, the repulsion was regarded as confined to particles of imponderable ether; and thirdly, an interchange of activities between the two classes of elements was admitted, in order to explain those varying states of equilibrium between attraction and repulsion which the facts required. Whether this last result was secured by the hypotheses is for our present purpose indifferent. It may be admitted that the reasoning is logically sound, though the conclusion is only necessary, if, in compliance with the usage of language, both forces are conceived as original and essential attributes of the subjects to which they attach. How the whole matter may be regarded from a different point of view, for which the course of my argument will already have prepared the way, I shall now proceed gradually to unfold, ignoring provisionally arguments derived from the alleged ideality of space. Even if we adopted the ordinary view of the nature of space, it would not really become any less difficult to explain, why the mutual relation between two elements, belonging to the same world, should be one of absolute repulsion, when this fact would seem rather to show that the world to which they belonged was *not* the same; nor would it be less wonderful that two other elements, both of them, similarly, supposed to belong to one and the same world of extended matter, should be drawn towards each other by such an absolute force of attraction, as that if there were no counteracting principle, the whole possibility of their extension would be annihilated. Once grant that the world is a single whole, and not a mere confused aggregate of existences, and it will follow that its component elements cannot be governed by any abstract principles of attraction or repulsion, driving them continually out of or into one another, but must aim at the conservation of the whole order, which, in accordance with the intention of the whole, assigns to each one of them its place at each moment of time. The force which proceeds from the collective mass of the elements, is one which determines the position of those elements and which, while it seems to reside in each individual element, really sets itself against any deviation from the law imposed on all. It sets limits to the nearness or remoteness of objects as regards each other, appearing in the one case as the force of repulsion, in the other, as that of attraction; in both cases acting as a corrective wherever there is a tendency in the object to oppose the requirements of the whole. I wish to see the order of our thoughts on this subject reversed. We are accustomed to regard the position of a thing as the result of certain forces acting upon it. The first consideration, as I think, on the contrary, is precisely the position which a thing occupies, as determined by its nature and character, in the world-system, and the first and only function which a thing as an individual has to perform, seems to me to be to retain this position; while attraction and repulsion we may represent to ourselves as the two elements into which this self-conservation of things admits logically of being analysed. In reality however what happens is that the self-conservation assumes one or other of these forms according as the needs of the moment give occasion to it. We must postpone the consideration of the question, as to what takes place in the inner nature of things when the place in which they find themselves at any given moment is out of harmony with the place marked out for them. As a phenomenon in space, the tendency to return to an equilibrium must necessarily appear in its simplest form, either as the approximation or as the separation of two elements. Hence it is possible to refer all physical processes to motive forces consisting of attraction or repulsion. But it is not the case that on all other occasions things are empty of content, and that these forces attach to them merely for the time being. Rather, like the gestures of living beings, the forces are merely the outward expression of what is going on within.

184. Thus far, no doubt, the statement of our views has conveyed the impression that we regarded the world like a picture having fixed outlines, within which every single point invariably occupies the same position and clings to it with equal tenacity. Such a picture would be little in accordance with the facts. We have long known that the world is never at rest and that the picture which it presents is for ever changing. Yet, the whole case is not stated even when we have grasped this truth. Admitting that the picture of reality is what it is at any given moment in virtue of its essential connexion with the arrangement that prevailed the moment before and that which is to prevail the moment after, the forces emanating from the different points of space must still derive their power to act on each separate occasion from the law which pervades the whole. The connexion between the whole and the part is peculiar to each case, and is very different from a mere instance of the operation of law in general, such as is known to us by observation and makes it possible to us to apprehend the process of the world as the result of innumerable individual forces working by invariable rules. I have, however, already[1] endeavoured to show that this plan or idea cannot be made real in this off-hand way of itself and without means; rather indeed that it presupposes uniformity of action on the part of the elements, so that under like conditions like consequences flow from them, quite independently of the place which each occupies in the universal plan. Hence, even assuming that the world is ceaselessly in a state of flux, our view that the permanent tendency of each thing is to maintain the place which belongs to it in the system of the universe, and that this is what gives to it its force, does not exclude the opposite or physical view according to which the course of events in the world is explained as due to varying combinations of constant forces. I may add that the supposition of a number of forces attaching to the same elements at the same time, but acting in different directions, does not seem to me to be liable to any of the objections which are commonly urged against it. No doubt, it would be unintelligible as applied to two elements working in isolation, but it is not so as applied to elements between which a connexion has been established owing to their belonging to one and the same world. We may learn to comprehend this by the experience of our own lives. Our actions are conditioned by many different systems of motives, which operate on us at the same time. The satisfaction of our physical wants may e.g. be incon-

[1] [E. g. § 67.]

sistent with the social good. What family-affection requires of us may conflict with our duty as citizens, and within this last sphere we find ourselves parts of many different institutions whose claims it is not always easy to harmonise. A like interpretation must be given of the world in which we live. When we speak of a systematic connexion between things, we do not mean a single uniform classification in which we could find any given member by following out one principle of division. Rather, there are many cross-purposes at work, each of which requires that the elements should be distributed exclusively with reference to its own satisfaction. Each element may be stationed at the intersecting point of several different tendencies which unite and divide the world. As long, therefore, as two elements are considered as belonging to such a world, there is no reason why their mutual activities should not be regarded as the result of a plurality of forces acting simultaneously, and differing entirely in the effects they produce in response to each change in the circumstances of the environment; owing to the different points of view under which they bring the same set of circumstances, and to the consequent variety of the reactions set up.

185. There still remains to be considered the question as to whether it is allowable to speak of forces which take effect from a distance, or whether those are not right who regard the possibility of a thing's acting where it is not as inconceivable. I cannot help adding to the two conflicting views which are held on this question, a third one of my own. It seems to me that *motion* can *only* be an effect of forces acting at a distance; to speak of action when the elements are in close contact, I regard as a contradiction. Let us suppose two spherical bodies of equal diameter and density to be placed so as exactly to contain each other. If, then, the nature of the materials of which the bodies are composed is such as to admit of their reciprocal action, and if we are to disregard all possibility of effects taking place

at a distance, it will follow that every point *a* of the one body will produce an effect on the point *b* of the other body, with which it coincides. Now, I do not dispute that the two elements may be affected in a very real way by reason of this coincidence at the same geometrical point. But, whether the effects thus produced are such as to intensify or such as to diminish the condition in which the elements find themselves, i. e. whether they tend to attraction or repulsion, in no case can these inner occurrences result in motion. *a* and *b* being already stationed at the same point of space cannot by any attraction be brought nearer; nor could any force of mutual repulsion, however actively manifested in other ways, avail to part them asunder, there being no reason why the initial movement tending to separate them should take any one direction rather than another.

Nor need we confine ourselves to bodies perfectly coincident in extension. No matter what form the two bodies assume, they would never be able to affect each other's motions, if there were no distance intervening between them; for those parts of the two bodies which were coincident would admit only of being affected *internally* by their mutual action, and thus there would be no external motion. It makes no difference as regards this conclusion, that effects are spoken of as taking place between *contiguous* bodies, and that the ambiguity to which this mathematical conception so easily lends itself, is made to yield a perplexing solution of a difficulty which is one of fact. If we confine ourselves to the case in which the two bodies are spheres, their volumes can only meet at one point. Now, we must be sure that what we have in view is a real contact of the bodies in question, and we must banish from our minds all thought of there being *any* distance, even an infinitesimal one, intervening between them. As long as we have any such idea we have in principle admitted the action of force at a distance, though without any reason restricting the distance to an infinitesimally small one; a conception which, besides other difficulties, it is, to say the least, not easy to explain on physical principles. It is equally inadmissible to substitute for a *point* of contact an infinitely small *surface*, or, supposing the contact to be between flat surfaces, to imagine that the layers which are in contact and which thus produce the effect, can have any, even the smallest conceivable degree of thickness. It must be taken as settled that the bodies which are in contact have their boundaries common or coincident, in the first case, in a point without extension, in the second, in a surface without thickness. Whatever way we may try to turn these ideas, the fact will always remain, that real elements which occupy the same position in Space will exercise no effect as regards the production of motion, and such effect as does take place will spring only from those parts of the bodies which are really separated from each other by intervals of Space. As for a contact which does not involve either separation or coincidence at the same point in Space, the idea is intelligible enough as applied to the whole volume of each of the two bodies brought into contact, but it has no meaning as applied to a possible interaction of single points such as we have been here considering.

This same observation holds good as regards the attempt to substitute, instead of forces operating between different elements, a reflexive power of expansion or contraction, in virtue of which a thing assigns to itself a greater or less space of its own accord. If the 'thing' here spoken of is understood as a material existence extended and divisible, this power of self-extension belonging to the whole must in every case be capable of being finally referred to the reciprocal repulsion of the parts, these being already distinguished in Space. If, on the other hand, the thing is held to be endowed with this power in consequence of a real metaphysical unity prior to its multiplication in Space, we shall then have to face another enquiry, which is for the most part overlooked in these attempts to construct a theory of matter, viz. this, How did this reality first get form and extension in Space—that form and extension which are always presupposed, in order that forces of the kind mentioned above may be furnished with points to which to attach themselves? This question we propose to consider in the next chapter.

186. All that the above demonstration proves is that mere contact of elements cannot produce motion. If, however, it should be found to be equally inconceivable that effects should take place at a distance, we shall be compelled to deny that motion is a result of force in any shape whatever, and our task will then be limited to the attempt to conceive of physical effects as taking place owing to the supply of motion already in existence being perpetuated. But it soon appears that the expression, *communication* or *distribution of motion*, though enabling us to picture to ourselves results which are constantly passing before our eyes, does not give any tenable conception of the process to which the results in question are due. Take, e. g. the familiar instance of the effects of impact on inelastic bodies. Suppose b to be a body in motion and a a body at rest, then, when b strikes against a, we say that it communicates to it a certain part of its own motion, and this, no doubt, is an extremely convenient way of signalising the new fact which has taken place, in consequence of the two bodies having been brought together. We cannot, however, seriously suppose that the motion produced the result by changing its place. If we may repeat what has before been said[1], it is for ever impossible to conceive that a state q, by which a real thing b is affected, should loose itself from b, and pass over to a; yet this is such a case; before the motion could transfer itself from the limits of b to a, it would have to traverse, no matter in how short a time, a certain space intermediate between the

[1] [§ 56.]

two, and during this time it would be a state which was the state of nothing. The absurdity of this notion is here even further increased by the fact that it is only by a free use of language that we are able to speak of motion as a *state* at all. Motion, in fact, is not a quality permanently attaching to anything; it is an occurrence merely, or a change which the thing moved undergoes. Hence, the very conception of a motion, which is itself set in motion in order to pass from one thing to another, is *ipso facto* impossible. But what should we have gained, supposing that this inconceivability were a fact? If the motion has passed over to a, it is now where a is, but that would not make it a state of a, nor would it explain why it should ever move a. Inasmuch as it was possible for the motion to become detached from b, either wholly or in part, why should it not continue on its course according to the same law of Persistence which it followed whilst on the way from b to a? Why should it not leave a at rest, and again become a motion belonging to no one as before, and so on *ad infinitum?* It results, therefore, that this theory fails to give any reason for the motion of the body which receives the impulse, and it gives only an obscure reason for the decreased motion of the body from which the impulse proceeds. Of course, it will be argued that both these facts are due to the impenetrable nature of bodies, which makes it impossible for one of them to find a passage for itself through the space occupied by the other. But this impossibility taken by itself rather suggests a dilemma than furnishes us with a solution of it.

If two bodies cannot both occupy the same position in Space, and if nevertheless it is this at which one of them aims, the question arises as to how these two conflicting propositions are to be reconciled. How they are reconciled as a matter of fact we see before us; we see motion originated in the one case, and a corresponding decrease of motion in the other. But we cannot suppose that this happy solution comes to pass of its own accord because it is an ingenious idea; it must rather be the necessary consequence of what the bodies are in themselves, and of what they pass through at the time. If, further, we bear in mind that in order adequately to estimate the result, account must be taken of the mass of the two bodies, we shall be led back to the conclusion that this impenetrability, which the communication of motion requires, is an effect produced by the conflicting tendencies of various forces, which thus give rise to motions in opposite directions, so that bodies at rest are supplied with motion which before they were without, whilst the bodies set in motion lose some of their velocity owing to the resistance of the bodies at rest. But it is impossible to represent such a repulsion as arising when the bodies are in contact, and not before. For, if at the point of contact there is no interpenetration of the two surfaces, the contact instead of being a real one becomes a mere geometrical relation; it can have no influence on the bodies themselves, but only on the limits by which they are bounded. If, however, we suppose that the bodies *do* interpenetrate each other at the point of contact, it will follow from our previous conclusions that the forces proceeding from the two bodies can only affect each other's motions at those points which are still separated by an interval of space. Nor can it be said that the motion q, which is communicated to a body at rest a by a body in motion b, determines what would otherwise be undetermined, viz. the direction of the two bodies at the moment of their divergence. For, from the mere fact that the mutual repulsion takes place at the moment that the body b, whilst tending in the direction q, comes into immediate contact with a, it could only be argued, in opposition to all experience, that b would pass through a in its former direction q with accelerated speed, whilst a would begin to move in the direction $-q$. It seems to me, therefore, that under these circumstances we cannot but conclude that even the communication of motion is an effect dependent on the action of moving forces, and that, in this case as in all others, forces can only produce motion when the bodies are removed from each other, while, contrariwise, they are powerless to produce it when the bodies are in contact.

187. All this reasoning would be to no purpose, if there was really any insuperable difficulty in conceiving of forces as taking effect at a distance. But I must say for myself that it quite passes my comprehension to understand on what grounds it can be maintained to be the most self-evident of facts that a thing can only act where it *is*. What, we may ask, is the meaning of the assertion, *a is* at the point a? Can there ever be any other evidence or manifestation of a thing's Being, than by means of the effects which are transmitted from a to the point p, where we ourselves are? Of course, it will be instantly objected: 'No doubt, the effects of a and the directions which these follow in the course of their transmission to us, are the only sources of the *knowledge* which justifies us in concluding that a is at the point a; the fact itself, however, is independent of the means by which we come to know it.' But what conception can be formed of this fact itself, if we abstract all the effects which the given form of existence a emits from the point a, where it is stationed? Is the existence of a in general a conception which has anything definite corresponding with it? and how can the limitation of a to the point a be understood, if it does not give rise to any effects at that point distinguishing that point from all other similar points of Space, where a is not present? It is an illusion to believe that the mere *being* at a certain place can give a thing any determinate character, and that it acquires *subsequently* to this the capacity to produce the effects which seem to be diffused around that point. We ought rather to say, on the contrary: Because, in the disposition and systematic arrangement of the world as a whole, and in the world of Space which is its counterpart, a is a meeting point for relations of the most various kinds, and acts upon the other elements as these relations prescribe, for this reason and for no other, it has its fixed place amongst them; or more correctly—it is this which justifies us in making use of the common forms of speech, a is at the point a and acts from thence.

This, however, will form the subject of further investigations. Putting this question as to the relation between real existence and Space for the present aside, we shall make use of a very simple idea to expose the fallacy of the doctrine here referred to. Let us suppose that at the commencement of their existence things were stationed each at some one point of Space, e. g. a and β: what reason would there be why the interval $a\beta$ between them should prevent them from mutually affecting each other? 'It is obvious and self-evident that it would do so;' it will be replied,—'the body set in motion does not feel the impulse to move, until the impelling body reaches it. There can be no sense of vision until the nerves have been touched by the moving particles of the ether. That which is incapable of transmission has no effect, and is for us as if it had no existence.' These instances, however, may be met by others. The stone falls without requiring first to be impelled; an electric repulsion takes place to all appearance quite independently of any connecting medium. If anyone wishes to refer these phenomena to the communication of motion already in existence, he may do so; but he will be appealing not to observed facts, but to his own hypotheses; he will be employing without any just reason the particular form which one class of effects assumes, as if it were the universal form which must necessarily be assumed by all other effects. And yet even these hypotheses, which aim at the avoidance of all distant effects in the case of large bodies, cannot help interposing Spaces between the infinitesimal particles of the media which are held to explain the transmission of the impulse. There could be no presumption in favour of the above interpretation unless it could be shown that contact in Space was as obviously a condition favourable to the action of force, as separation in Space is maintained to be unfavourable to it. But this is not true with regard to contact in Space. For, it cannot be concluded that anything must of necessity happen from the mere fact that two elements touch at the same limit, or are stationed at the same point of Space; nothing can come of the contact of the elements if they are not fitted by Nature mutually to affect each other, and when this condition is wanting, spatial contact cannot produce it. As for the assertion that elements which have this capacity to affect each other, require contact in Space in order to make its exercise possible, it rests on that arbitrary selection of instances mentioned above; with those in whom it has become a cherished prejudice it is ineradicable, but it is not in itself necessary, nor capable of being shown by the evidence of undoubted facts to hold good universally. We ourselves, it is true, are not endowed with any capacity for producing effects at a distance. The objects on which we attempt to bring our activity to bear, we, no doubt, set in motion by means of a continuous succession of intermediate effects, which serve to bring us and them together. But this is not enough to make us conclude that two elements, between which there is an interval of Space, belong, as it were, to two different worlds separated by a gulf which nothing can bridge over. We are compelled, in order to understand their subsequent effects, to conceive of them both as subject to the same laws; a fact which we are accustomed to consider as self-evident, without enquiring into the presuppositions which it involves. This fact obliges us to regard, without exception, all things throughout Space as interconnected parts of one world, and as united together by a bond of sympathy to which separation in Space acts as no hindrance. It is only because the elements of the world are not all of the same kind, and, instead of being simply co-ordinated, are related in the most various ways, that this unfailing sympathetic *rapport*, by means of which all things act on each other at a distance, is not in all cases equally apparent, but differs in degree of intensity, and is in some cases widely diffused, in others contracts itself within narrow and scarcely perceptible limits.

CHAPTER VI.

The Simple Elements of Matter.

THE confused notions which the different theoretical constructions showed to exist in regard to the true nature of Matter, led us in the first place to examine into the conception of the forces, the operation of which gives rise to the changing qualities of material things. There remains now to be considered the question as to the form in which the real thing, from which these forces themselves emanate, takes up its position in Space. The subject to which we shall be introduced by this question is the antithesis between atomism and the theory of a continuous extension in Space.

188. What appears to be the evidence of immediate perception on this point must not be misrepresented at starting by a slovenly mode of statement. Of a single continuously extended Matter it tells us nothing; all that it presents to us is a vast variety of different material objects which for the most part are separated from each other by clearly defined limits and are but rarely blended and confused together. This multiplicity of things is all that can be affirmed at starting—many, however, even of these things the naked eye at once perceives to be composed of parts existing side by side, but differing in kind. Others, which appear to be extended in Space with unbroken continuity, are seen by

means of the microscope to fall asunder into a distinguishable variety of divergent elements. It is not proved by this, but it is made probable, that the apparent continuity of the rest merely conceals a juxtaposition of discrete elements. But, what *is* proved for everyone who has eyes to see is, that substances composed of atoms may produce on the senses the impression of perfect continuity of extension. The frequently-urged objection, that a combination of discrete parts would never account for the coherent surface and the solid interior structure of material bodies, does not really require any *metaphysical* refutation. The sharp edge of a knife, when placed beneath a microscope, appears to be notched like a saw, and the surface, which feels quite smooth, becomes a region of mountains. Spots of colour again, even if seen only from a short distance, take the form of a continuous line. These recognised facts are a sufficient proof that the nature of our sensible organs makes consciousness of what intervenes between successive vivid impressions impossible for us, when the intervals are either empty of all content, or such that they only faintly affect us. Though, therefore, the appearance of continuous extension, no doubt, may correspond with a real fact, it arises none the less certainly and inevitably from a sufficiently close approximation of discrete parts. Now, what induces us to adopt this last hypothesis in explanation of the whole is this, that even substances which seem to be continuous admit of being divided, to an apparently unlimited extent. For, as the parts which spring from this division retain unimpaired the same material qualities which belonged to the undivided whole, it would seem that they cannot owe their origin simply to the division of this whole; but that they existed before it, and formed it by their combination. Later on, I shall give reasons for suspecting the soundness of this conclusion; but, at first sight, it is convincing enough, and in all ages it has given rise to attempts to exhibit the parts of Matter as elements whose metaphysical unity of nature expressed itself in terms of Space as indivisibility.

I shall offer some remarks—not intended to be historically exhaustive—on the forms of Atomism which thus arose. Two points I shall mention here in advance. First, let it be remembered that this hypothesis of a multitude of interconnected points admitting of changeable and precisely determinable relations and interactions, is the only practical means of satisfactorily explaining the extremely complex phenomena for which an explanation is sought; and that in contrast with this explanation, the bare general supposition of the uniformity of Matter, not less than the special one of its continuity in Space, has never led to any fruitful solution of the facts given in experience. To prove this would be only to repeat what has been so clearly and convincingly stated by Fechner (cp. his 'Doctrine of Atoms'). Taking it then for granted that the real world of nature is presented to us primarily under the form of an infinite number of discrete centres of activity, I shall confine myself merely to a metaphysical investigation into the nature of these centres. This is a question which Physics is not practically called upon to decide, nor is her certainty about it at all equal to the ingenuity with which she avails herself of the advantages which the hypothesis offers to her. Again, I am entirely at one with Fechner in regard to his second conclusion. I believe with him that the atomic view of the Physical world is peculiarly adapted to satisfy the æsthetic needs of the mind. For what we long to see exhibited everywhere and in the smallest particulars, is precisely this, organization, symmetric and harmonious relations, order visible throughout the whole, and a clear view of the possible transitions from one definite form into another. The demonstration of this point I likewise do not repeat. I wish only to say that I have never been able to comprehend the reason of that tendency, which for a long time past our German Philosophy has shown, to look down upon atomic theories as of an inferior and superficial character; whilst the theory of a continuous matter was opposed to them as quite incontrovertibly a truth of a higher kind. If there were proofs at hand to establish the necessity of this latter conclusion, they should have been set forth in a more convincing form than they have yet received. There is, however, really nothing to admire in the theory of continuity, either when considered in itself, or in regard to the results which have been derived from it. It seems as if a mystical power of attraction had been given to it merely owing to the mathematical difficulties in which the whole conception is involved.

189. The following are the chief characteristics of general interest which distinguished the atomism of antiquity, as represented by Lucretius. Theoretic knowledge of the changes of things would be impossible for us, if we were restricted to observation of the co-existence of qualities, and the modes of their succession; there being no fixed standard, by which to estimate their relationship, opposition, and quantitative difference. We cannot be in a position to deduce from such conditions any conclusion of real value, unless we are able to exhibit the states which succeed each other as comparable forms of a homogeneous existence and occurrence, or unless, at any rate, we can show how effects disparate in themselves can yet be annexed to comparable relations of comparable elements. The conviction that this was what had to be shown, led by steps of reasoning which can easily be supplied to the attempt to refer the varieties of sensible phenomena to differences of shape, size, combination, and motion, in certain absolutely homogeneous and unchangeable elements. The working out of the theory in detail was extremely defective and rudimentary. It was not so much that it was left unexplained how the sensible appearances which attach to these mathematical groupings can arise out of them, but the impossible assertion was made that the sensible qualities *are* nothing but these very mathe-

matical determinations themselves. Setting aside, however, these imperfections, the general conception of Atomism is one of the few Philosophical Speculations of antiquity which have hands and feet belonging to them, and which, therefore, live on and lead to ever fresh results, whilst other theories, with perhaps more head, find a place now only in the History of Ideas. The hard and fast line of distinction that was drawn between the complete identity of the several parts of Being, as opposed to the varied diversity of their relations, excluded all original differences from the ultimate elements themselves; these latter, however, if they had been so completely identical, could never have served as a basis for the manifold appearances which spring out of them; they had, therefore, at any rate to be assumed to differ in size and shape.

But this admission was no sooner made than it was seen to be inconsistent with the uniform oneness of all existing things. Hence, these differences were held to obtain merely as facts, which in the order of nature as it now exists cannot be reversed, but which are not in themselves original, having come into Being only at the commencement of the present age of the world's history. At any rate, I think I have shown that Lucretius distinguishes between the multiform atoms, which are the unchanging causes of the *present* order of phenomena in the world, and those infinitesimal and essentially uniform particles, from the combination of which the atoms are themselves ultimately formed. He supposes that there are different ages of the world, during each of which the combination of the atoms for the time being is dissolved by the stream of change. It is only the *combination* of the atoms which is dissolved; the atoms themselves do not change, but are combined afresh. At the *end*, however, of each age the atoms likewise are reduced back to their homogeneous first elements, and these latter being again united so as to form new atoms, are what constitute the material substances out of which are met the demands for the phenomena of the next succeeding age. We see here a recognition of the metaphysical difficulty mentioned above, though not a solution of it; it still remains that the form which the atoms are to assume is determined by an arbitrary cause.

The further elaboration of the system presents little that can interest us. The common nature of what is real, which was declared to be the true substantive existence contained in all the countless atoms, might, one would have thought, have suggested the hypothesis of an inner relation existing between them, and from this might have been developed the conception of forces by which they mutually affect each other; forces, which would assume different modes of operation, according as the ultimate component particles of the atoms were differently combined. But no use was made of this thought. The communication of motion by impact remained as the sole form in which things affect each other; and the resistance which they oppose to the falling asunder of their parts was no less inadequately explained than the invincible tendency of the ultimate elements to combine in the form of an atom.

190. Passing over the various forms which Atomism assumed after it had been revived by Physical Science, I shall mention only the last of them. As long as extension and shape were ascribed to the atoms, no matter whether all were supposed to be the same in these respects, or, some to be different from others, it could not but appear that a question was being solved in reference to the larger bodies by the assumption of the smaller ones which was left unsolved as regarded those smaller ones. It was impossible to go on for ever deriving each atom from atoms still smaller; some point of space must at last be reached which is continuously filled by the Real thing. But here a doubt suggested itself. How can the continuous substratum be indivisible, if the space which it occupies is infinitely divisible? That a portion of space should be held intact

against all attempts to encroach upon it, would seem to be conceivable only as the combined effect of activities proceeding from points external to each other, and prescribing to each its fixed position in relation to the rest. Such active points, however, would inevitably come again to be regarded as so many discrete elements, from which the whole is formed only by aggregation. It seems to me that the regression into infinity which would thus result, could not be escaped from by any appeal to the metaphysical unity of the essence which forms the real content of an atom, and which preserves it from the division of its appearance in Space. This distinction between the real essence and its appearance in Space would be a meaningless rhetorical phrase if it did not suggest questions far deeper than any of those with which atomism is concerned and quite indifferent to it.

Atomism considers extended and tangible matter as reality pure and simple, not as a mode in which Reality manifests itself, and which requires a process of intermediation to connect it with Reality. Now it is most difficult for many reasons to apply to this extended Real thing the conception of unity. I do not mean to maintain that the question is at once decided by the fact that in order for a form of matter to remain unaffected by all external forces, it would have to be credited with a simply unlimited power of resistance, such as would be very little in harmony with the first principles of our knowledge of mechanics. I do not say this; for in the last resort there would be nothing to prevent us from conceiving of the atoms as elastic; and then each atom would really undergo a change of form proportioned to the force acting upon it; only that there would be an accompanying reaction, sufficient to restore to the atom its original outline, and preserve it from disintegration. No doubt, in a sense it is true that the atom would require to have an unlimited power of cohesion in order to admit of this process. But there is nothing in it inconsistent with what we know about mechanics in other respects. The force inherent in an atom would not be indifferent to all external influences; rather, it would react with a degree of intensity precisely corresponding with the original stimulus.

But another requisition must be complied with if the metaphysical unity of an extended real thing is to make itself felt as an actual fact and not be a mere name. Essential unity of nature cannot contain parts, which are affected by experiences peculiar to themselves, and not shared by the rest. Every impression by which the point a of any such unity A is affected, must at once be a state or impression of the whole A, without any process of intercommunication being required, to transmit the impression from a to b, or to the other points contained in the volume. At all events, if the parts of A are so different that what each experiences has to be transmitted to the rest, I fail to see in what would consist its essential unity, or how, since a system of discrete elements would necessarily proceed in precisely the same way, there can be any difference between the two. Before proceeding further, I must guard these statements against a possible misunderstanding. I cannot find that there is anything incompatible between the essential unity of A and the existence at the same time of different modes of its Being $a\beta\gamma$, which are necessitated by different influences acting upon A simultaneously: I only wish to maintain that both a and β are equally states of the whole A, and therefore that they are neither of them produced by influences which merely affect themselves, but are both modified by the fact of their contemporaneous existence in the same essential unity. Let us suppose a and β to be motive stimuli affecting two points a and b in the same atom. The result would not be two separate movements of these two points, which at some later period merged in a common result; but in the point a, which was the part affected by a, the whole Real thing would be present in the same complete fulness as in the point b, which is affected by β. The immediate effects of both impulses would be felt equally at both points, and the resultant ρ would be but one motion which would at once lay hold of the whole extended substance. Further, since every change requires for its occurrence a certain space of time, and according to the law of Persistence, leaves a trace of itself behind, it is quite intelligible that a primary stimulus a should not till after some interval show itself as the condition of the next stimulus β; and that a new impression of the kind a should make itself felt in modifying the states connected with it before it modifies those that are connected with β. When this happens, we are accustomed to say: 'only one *side* of the whole Being of the thing was affected; the other remained untouched.' But by the use of this figure derived from Space, we express most inappropriately our better and truer meaning. At each moment, the whole essential Being is both acting and being acted upon; only it belongs to the nature of this indivisible unity that the several activities which external conditions elicit from it should, as they succeed each other, exhibit the most various degrees of mutual dependence, and should be some more and some less closely associated together.

Let us apply these legitimate ideas to the case before us. What we should be entitled to say would be, not that the atom A responds so immediately to the stimulus a by producing the result a that there is absolutely *no* intervening interval of time, but rather that the reaction in it does always follow upon the stimulus, at however infinitesimally small an interval of time; so that what takes place here too is that A is first affected on its receptive side, and only *afterwards* and in consequence of this on its side of reaction. This imagined splitting up of the substance into parts has nothing in common with the false notion of there being *in fact* any such separation between them, as would be the case, if we meant that an impression a produced upon an atom is confined to a point a, from which point it does not pass on to the remaining points b and c, until after some lapse of time. In such a case, there would, as I have before remarked, be nothing left to distinguish the pretended unity of this A from the communication of effects which takes place in every assemblage of discrete and independent elements when brought into active contact. If we are serious in supposing this unity to exist, we must assert that every motion communicated to a point a in an atom, *is* also literally a motion of the point a^1 at the other end of a diameter of the atom. The motion, consequently, would have to be transmitted all along the intervening line $a\,a^1$ in absolutely no time at all; and the ordinary rule according to which the intensity of a force varies with its distance, would have in this case to be suspended; the effect produced upon the remoter point a^1 must be as strong as that produced upon a. These consequences which, as it appears to me, are inevitable, cannot be reconciled with the ordinary principles of Mechanics. But if they are to be avoided, either the unity of the atom or its extension must be given up.

191. Physical theories in favour of the latter of these two alternatives have assumed a variety of forms. Though they have not been expressly based on the above-mentioned arguments, which have led me to infer that extension is not a predicate of a simple or single substance, but the appearance assumed by many different elements when combined, they have originated in a general feeling that the very thing which it was intended to explain in composite bodies by means of the atoms, could not be consistently assumed as already existing in the atoms. The extension of the simple elements was not a fact given in experience; nor was there any necessity for assuming it. All that was required was, certain points in space, from which forces of attraction and repulsion could operate with a certain intensity. The unextended atoms, as the vehicles of these forces, served quite as well to explain phenomena, as they would have done on the almost inconceivable hypothesis of their extension. Hence, since all that was needed was a working hypothesis, it became the custom for Physicists to describe the atoms simply as centres, to and from which Forces and Operations are transmitted, leaving it unexplained how these real points are distinguished from the empty points of space which they fill. This omission may easily be supplied. A real thing could never by being extended in space produce an effect which it was not in virtue of its nature capable of producing when in relation with the other thing in question. At most, the space which it occupies could only prescribe the sphere of operation, within which capacities due not to extension but to the inherent nature of what the thing is, are exercised. If, further, it is impossible to conceive of motion as produced under conditions of actual contact and if distance is necessary to the operation of force, actual reality becomes independent of extension in space, and the elements, though they have indeed positions in space, are without either volume or shape.

This point of view grew up not merely as a conclusion arrived at by Physics; it is an ancient possession of Philosophy. Herbart refers back to Leibnitz; for myself, I prefer his own definite exposition to the doctrines of his forerunner, which can only be arrived at by a somewhat dubious interpretation. Herbart's ontology starts from the assumption of countless simple substances without parts or extension, which form the elements of the world. His construction of matter could, therefore, only lead to Atomism; and, he tells us quite clearly what are the original subjects from which the activities formative of matter proceed, and as to which we found Kant's explanation unsatisfactory. Herbart distinguishes his own theory from the theories of the Physicists, by calling it 'Qualitative Atomism.' He gives it this name, not only to show that his simple substances owing to their qualitative differences are endowed with distinct concrete natures, and not merely substantiated abstractions of a single homogeneous reality; he uses the term in a far more important signification than this to imply that from the inner experiences to which these differences of nature give rise, all those Forces and Laws of relation are derived, which the common modes of speaking and thinking in Physical Science represent, without any further attempt at explanation, as predicates inherently attaching to the ultimate elements. Being, as I am, quite at one with Herbart in regard to this general conception, I regret that owing to a certain ontological doctrine, which I do not myself share with him, he should have been deprived of the fruits of these conclusions in constructing his theory of matter.

The entire independence which he ascribed to each of the essential elements prevented him from holding the doctrine of a pervading connexion, in virtue of which the states by which one is affected become the immediate condition for what is experienced by the rest. Another of his assumptions, the origin of which I am ignorant of, led him to regard contact in space as the only cause capable of disturbing the mutual indifference of the elements and forcing them into active relationship. As, on this view, it was impossible for the essential elements to act on each other from a distance, Herbart became involved in the hopeless attempt to show how points unextended, though real, are brought into contact in order that they may act upon each other, but yet not absolutely into contact, in order that their combined effects may endow a multiplicity with an extension which attaches to no single one of its component parts. It is a view which requires to be changed only in a single point, though this no doubt is a vital one. The simple elements of reality, on which the constitution of the world primarily depends, must be regarded as conditioned, not independent, and therefore as in unceasing relation to each other. By making forces which act at a distance emanate from the simple elements, elements not empty but of a definite internal character, we can frame an intelligible picture of the forms of matter, as systems of real unextended points, limited in space, and endowed with forces of cohesion and resistance in very various degrees.

192. Now, at this point we might stop, if it were not for another assumption which these theories commonly contain, that viz. of an actually extended space, in which the real elements take up their positions. The contrary conviction, in support of which I have contended, compels me to introduce some further modifications into the view which I have first stated in order to arrive gradually at the idea which I wish ultimately to establish. I continue for the present to make the assumption of an indefinite number of individual existences; an assumption from which the explanation of the variety of phenomena must always make its first start. Not much need be added to what has been already said as to the general relation of these existences to space. These simple elements, having as such no connexion with space, stand to each other in a vast variety of relations, which only for our modes of apprehension assume the forms of position and distance in space. It is for Psychology to supplement the suggestions which have been already made by telling us how this mode of apprehension is originated; here, we are only concerned with the ideas which we must form of the nature of Real existence, in order to make intelligible the particular mode in which it presents itself to our subjective consciousness.

In the first place, then, to repeat what I have already mentioned, it is requisite that we should reverse one of our ordinary ways of thinking. When a certain element a is in a certain position a, we think of this fact as if it was something in itself, as if it was in virtue of this that the element had the power to produce effects on other things in certain definite ways. But, according to all the results at which we have so far arrived, we ought contrariwise to say:—That the element a 'is in the position a,' can only mean for it, that it has received so many and such impressions from all the other elements which belong to the same world to which it belongs, that, if we regard the whole mass of existing facts of that world under the form of space no place except a corresponds to that which is assigned to a in the universal order. Hence, the position which an element occupies must always be regarded by us as the result of the forces that determine it, and in so determining it are in a state of equilibrium. This conclusion the Science of Mechanics only half admits. It admits, no doubt, that during every moment that an element remains at rest, the forces working upon it must be in a state of equilibrium. But the conception still remains possible that an element might occupy a position in space without any action of force whatever, and that forces arising subsequently might find it there and act upon it.

Further, I have abundantly shown that by this systematised arrangement of unextended points, which I believe to be what constitutes the world as a whole, I understand not the order of a rigid classification, but an order which, incessant as is the movement of things, and manifold and various as are the forms which the sum of conditions at each moment assumes, maintains throughout a continuous and unchanging purpose. The position, therefore, which an element assumes, when it appears in space, does not simply indicate the place which it occupies from all eternity in a classification of the world's contents, but, rather, the place which, at that moment, was the only point at which the changing conditions to which it is subject came to a changeable equilibrium. It would be too simple an explanation of what takes place, to suppose that when two elements a and b make their appearance at two points of space in close proximity, a and β, they have been accredited to these positions owing to the special sympathy of their natures or the intimacy of their interaction. Rather they may have been quite indifferent to each other, and yet have been forced into this juxtaposition, simply because the demands made by all the rest of the elements and their motions can find no better satisfaction than in the momentary proximity of these two elements, though it may not answer to any vital connexion between the elements themselves. Reflexion upon this constant motion of the world will cause us to modify our previous view, or, at all events, to define it more accurately. The position a of an element a, though always no doubt it expresses the balance of the several forces for the time being affecting a, may also at the same time be the expression of an unavoidable want of equilibrium between the present state of a, and that state to which its nature gives it a claim in the totality of existence; an expression, therefore, of a discordant Tension, which remains until, in the course of events, the causes which occasioned it again disappear.

I make these remarks, in order to give an idea of the complex kinds of relations which here present themselves, and in order to remove the impression that there is any correspondence between the appearance of the world in space at any given moment and an intelligible order of things, in which the position of each element would correspond with the conception which permanently represents its nature. But I hasten to add that this reference to a disproportion of states, in the above-mentioned sense, must not be mixed up with any secondary associations of 'that which is out of place,' or 'which contradicts the purpose of the whole.' Whether anything of this kind ever happens, whether, i.e. there is anything in the world's course which can be compared with discords in a musical progression, we shall not here enquire. The disproportion of which we have been speaking is primarily nothing but the impulse to a change of state which arises in the course of events, and which tends to or accomplishes the transition to new positions according as it is impeded or unimpeded. Turning now from these general considerations, we will apply ourselves to the solution of certain special questions, which acquire from our present point of view either the whole of their significance or a different significance from that which is commonly assigned to them.

193. Let us start as before from the supposition of a given plurality of active elements; remembering at the same time how frequently it happens, as has been proved by experiments, that apparently different properties are really only the result of different combinations of a single homogeneous substance. The question will, then, obviously be, must we, in order to explain the facts, assume the existence of a multiplicity of originally distinct materials? or, shall we explain even the characteristic differences between the chemical Elements as mere modifications of a single homogeneous matter? The eagerness which is now shown in favour of the attempt to explain away these differences seems to me to be based to some extent on a false principle of method. For practical purposes Science is, of course, always interested in reducing the number of independent principles upon which to base its explanations, and in making calculable the course of events by subordinating the complex derivative premisses to a few primary ones. But not less certain is it that Science cannot desire any more complete unity than actually exists, and until the point is decided by experience, a unity which remains still unknown must not be presupposed as certainly existing except in cases in which without it a contradiction would be introduced into the nature of the subject-matter.

Now, our idea of Nature implies three things. (1) A system of universal laws, which determine the sequence of cause and consequence. (2) A multitude of concrete points to which these laws may attach and so find their application. (3) Lastly, a purpose to realise which these actual existences are combined together. Every theory of Science admits the two first of these postulates; the last is, no doubt, the subject of conflicting opinions. But wherever the thought of a purpose in nature is cherished, it stands to reason that there can be but one, and that all seemingly independent tendencies must be really subordinate to this unity and appear as moments in its Being. Not less necessary is the unity of the supreme laws which govern the connexion of events. These consist not so much in the rules to which various forces variously conform, as in the universal truths of mathematics, to which any self-consistent world, even though it were quite otherwise constituted than the existing one, would always have to submit throughout its whole extent alike. It is impossible to conceive an order of nature, unless it can be determined according to the same rules of measurement in every instance what results may be deduced from the presence of active elements in given proportions, and from their reciprocal interactions in calculable degrees of intensity. On the other hand, the actual existence, which has to furnish these laws with cases in which they will apply, has to fulfil no requirement but the primary one of being manifold. Nor is there the slightest reason why a theory which takes no exception to the doctrine of an original plurality of homogeneous atoms should regard with suspicion the hypotheses of original differences of quality. No further likeness of nature need be attributed to the atoms than such as is required to enable them to combine together in the same order of things. It must be possible in so far as they affect each other by way of interaction, to exhibit their natures as combining in definite degrees of intensity certain universal modes of activity. But there appears to me to be no necessity for regarding the group of specific coefficients which these general modes of action are found to take in any particular element, as attached to a substance of like nature throughout, or, more strictly, as attached to what is merely the substantiated abstraction of reality. The group may equally well be regarded as the expression of a specific quality, so far as such expression is allowed by the mutual intercourse of the various forms of matter.

Practically the importance of the difference between these two views would consist in this, that the latter would altogether exclude the possibility of one chemical element passing into another, whilst, according to the former view, this would be at any rate conceivable. It would indeed be more than conceivable. It would rather be inexplicable that throughout the endless process of combination, dissolution and transformation to which the parts of matter are subject, no element should ever lose its identity or merge its own individuality in that of some other. If the essential character of each element depends merely on a peculiar arrangement of homogeneous particles, it may be conjectured that the same course of events which gave birth to one of the forms thus composed, might again produce the conditions which would lead to its being either dissolved or transformed into some other shape. But if it was meant that it could be shown that there are certain forms of combination which having once originated can never by any possible conjunction of forces be dissolved, it would still be open to ask, Why at any rate there is not, through a further composition of the simpler structures, a constant increase in the number of these irrevocable combinations? Finally, if it is to be regarded as an eternal fact that these combinations are all alike indestructible and at the same time incapable of further development, it would be difficult to say in what would consist the difference between this view and that which assumes an original difference between the elements. As regards the practical explanation of nature there would be no difference between the two ideas; it would be a difference merely of theoretical view. The probability of all reality being homogeneous in essence, unless confirmed by future experience, could only be maintained upon considerations of a different and more indirect kind.

194. To this class of considerations belong the views commonly held in regard to the mass of matter, its constancy, and its influence in determining the character of different kinds of effects. It is now quite superfluous to recur to what was once a mistake of frequent occurrence in philosophy, by pointing out that the idea of mass is not exclusively associated with that of weight and heaviness; but, that, as applied to the reciprocal action of any two material bodies, the term expresses the intensity of the force which each contributes to the common result. Let us suppose that we have formed two bodies from m and μ numbers of units of the same matter, and have observed their behaviour to a third body c in regard to a certain effect of the kind p. If having observed this, we then find that two other bodies, both demonstrably formed from the same material, behave in the same way towards c as the two first in respect of the same effect p, we rightly conclude that they also contain m and μ number of units of the same matter. Suppose, however, these two latter bodies exhibited divergent properties, so that their consisting of the same matter was open to doubt, and yet that, in regard to p, they were affected towards c precisely as those two substances had been which we had ourselves formed from a demonstrably common matter, it would no doubt be a natural and obvious conjecture that their behaviour was also due to the presence of m and μ units of a homogeneous substance, though this likeness was hidden in their case by secondary differences of quality. At the same time, this conjecture would go beyond the facts. All that the facts teach is that in respect of the effect p, the two bodies in question are *equivalent to m* and μ units of the before-mentioned matter; not that they actually *consist of* them. There is nothing to prevent them from being in all other respects different in original quality from each other, and from c, and yet being capable of a special interaction of the kind p between them and c, in which their contribution to the common result admits of a numerical expression m and μ, as identical or comparable with that of the two bodies first considered. If now, assuming them to have the above specific quality, we proceed to consider their interaction with a fresh body d resulting in a different kind of effect q, we shall not be justified in assuming that the proportion in which they contribute to this result is the same, viz. $m : \mu$, as that in which they contribute to produce p. Rather, it is conceivable that in their new relation to d, bringing into play as it would new forces, they would be like where they had before been unlike, and unlike where they had been like; or, in a word, that in regard to the effect q, they would assume the quantities m_1 and μ_1, different from the previous quantities m and μ. In point of fact, at any rate at first sight, this is how the several effects p, q, r, produced by the reciprocal action of the bodies in question, are related, and it is never certain that a which in regard to p is greater in quantity than b, will still remain so in regard to q.

Whether these differences can be intelligibly explained on the hypothesis of a homogeneous matter, as secondary effects due to different modes of combination, must here be left undecided. Owing to the extreme variety of the phenomena to be taken into account, such a conclusion could only be established, if at all, in the distant future. On the other hand, it is of course always possible to express each of the new quantitative determinations that arise, e. g. m_1 and μ_1, by means of the old ones, i. e. by $k\,m$ and $\kappa\,\mu$, and so by assigning for each kind of special effect a specific co-efficient to bring the fiction of a homogeneous mass into harmony with the given facts. In a metaphysical point of view this would decide nothing. The possible qualitative difference between the parts of matter is as little made to disappear by this reduction, as corn and meat cease to be two different things after their value has been expressed in the common term of money. The doctrine then which I am maintaining is not open to any general objection on these grounds, though it cannot be applied to explain the particular facts. It, at any rate, does not oblige us to think of the different elements as differing without any principle. Belonging as they would to one and the same world, their qualities would be mutually related members of a single interconnected system, within which they would be combined in different directions, in different senses, and with various degrees of intimacy. Stationed at the meeting-point of many opposing tendencies, an element might on one of its sides display a greater degree of force than its neighbour, on another an equal degree, whilst on a third side its force might be less; and, if we knew the purpose of the whole system, which we do not know, we should be able to deduce from the mass which an element exhibited in the production of the effect p, the specific coefficients which belong to it for the actions q, r, &c., and to exhibit those coefficients as a series of mutually dependent functions.

195. I have made these observations, still proceeding on the assumption that a plurality of individual elements is what forms the ultimate constituents of the world. We shall see, however, that they have equal force, if viewed in connexion with a result established by our ontological investigations, according to which these multitudinous elements are but modifications of one and the same Being[1]. To hold this latter opinion, seems at first to be equivalent to repeating the very view against which we have been contending. It appears as if we could have no real interest in establishing the fact of difference amongst the elements, if this is not to be regarded as ultimate and irremovable. But the doctrine here maintained is essentially distinguished from the doctrine of Physics. I understand by this absolute Being, not a Real existence infinite in quantity and of like nature throughout, which has no other inherent capacity than that of falling into countless homogeneous parts, and which only is in a secondary sense, by means of the various

[1] [Cp. Chapters vi. and vii. of Book I.]

possible combinations of those parts, the ground of a diversity existing in the content of the world. I conceive it rather as a living idea, the import of which, inaccessible in its essence to any quantitative measurement, is no mere homogeneous aggregate of ideas, but a self-articulated whole of variously interwoven parts; each one of these parts, as well as the several elements which compose it, acquiring a determinate quantity according to its value and position in the whole.

Let us give an illustration. If this idea could be expressed in terms of our thought, it could only be so by means of a number of propositions which would be towards one another in those extremely various modes of dependence in which the different parts of a scientific system are connected together. But these propositions would be meaningless, if they were not again composed of words—words of which the meanings while different and unchangeably fixed, are still not immeasurably different, but so precisely determined in relation to each other that they admit of being joined together in very various syntactical combinations, to serve as vehicles by which the Idea is articulated into its parts. With these words I compare the elementary materials of nature. In themselves they are nothing; they are merely forms of a common principle underlying the world, a principle, however, which maintains them as constantly uniform activities, so that in every case in which they occur and enter into mutual relations they observe the same laws of behaviour. But, although thus involved from all eternity in a network of relations, they still remain different as regards each other, and incapable of being referred to mere division and re-combination of a uniform substratum. The mathematical mode of regarding the question which favours this latter view, and which has very extensive rights in the treatment of nature, is still not the only way of conceiving its unity, nor does it penetrate to the ultimate ground of things. Merely, within the limits of our observation, this mathematical connexion of things, secondary though it is, presents itself first. That whole world of quantitative and numerical determinations is itself based on an order of things, the synthetic connexions of which we could never have arrived at by any logical analysis. We have called this order 'systematic,' and now we may replace this imperfect expression by another, that of the 'æsthetic' unity of purpose in the world, which, as in some work of art, combines with convincing justice things which in their isolation would seem incoherent and scarcely to stand in any relation to one another at all. Or, lastly, we might prefer to use the term 'dialectical unity,' in memory of a late phase of our German Philosophy, which was thoroughly alive to the truth of this doctrine, but failed, as it seems to me, because it believed itself able to apply to details of fact principles which can only in a rough way prescribe a general direction to our thoughts.

196. This transformation of our views introduces us to a further question, which to Physical Atomism appears to be no question at all. It is assumed that a countless number of individual atoms fill the world. Now, be they the same or be they different in kind, whence comes their plurality? If they are regarded as starting-points to be assumed, beyond which we cannot go in thought, no doubt their dispersion throughout space can also be included in the number of facts to be taken for granted, which we must recognise without attempting to explain. But, to us, who have conceived every qualitatively distinct element as one of a connected series of acts emanating from the supreme principle of the universe, it is necessarily perplexing to find that the instances in which each element occurs are scattered over a countless number of different points in space. Nor is this an enigma merely from our point of view. We can, no doubt, by an act of thought easily represent to ourselves the same content a a thousand times over, and we can distinguish the thousand creations of our imagination, by localising them at different points of space, or by enumerating them according to the different moments of time when they first suggested themselves to us. But how, strictly speaking, can it be conceived that, in actual fact, the same a occurs several times over? Must not the mere fact that there are several, make it necessary that a should be in one case something different from what it is in another, though it ought in every case to be the same? What constitutes the objective difference between them, which makes a truth of fact of the logical assumption that they are so many like instances of a general notion or a common nature? We remember what a stumbling-block this question was to Leibnitz. It seemed to him to be impossible that two things should actually occur, unless their duality was based on a difference of nature between them. He would not even allow that two leaves of a tree could be exactly alike. This difficulty scarcely attracts any attention now. I must say, however, that it seems to me to have been somewhat too hastily passed over by those who have followed in the footsteps of Kant. What Thought could not achieve, was held to be made possible by spatial perception. It was in and through space that it was clearly shown how things could be at once like and manifold; they might differ in position, but be perfectly identical in the nature which occupies the position.

Certainly, this is clear enough; but I cannot see in this clearness a solution of the difficulty. All that it does is to bring the problem itself vividly before us; but for this phenomenon, indeed, the difficulty would scarcely have been suggested. Now, if science admitted to an unlimited extent the possibility of things acting upon each other at a distance, it might no doubt be granted that one atom is never subject to precisely the same sum of external influences as another. And, if it were further granted that the atoms experience changes of inner state corresponding with these external influences, it would follow that an atom *a* would be in some way different at each moment of its existence from a second and otherwise similar atom, since its internal states at any moment are not an extraneous appendage to its nature, but an actual constituent of what it is at that moment. But this mode of statement would still involve the latent supposition, that though the states by which an atom is affected change, yet through all this change the atom itself remains as a constant quantity, which would have maintained itself in its position even if there had been no forces acting on it, and which only becomes distinguished from other atoms of the same kind as itself owing to external influences which *might* not have been operative. Thus we are brought back to the question, What does it really mean that an element occupies a point in space? and how can it be that in virtue of its position it is distinguished from other elements, seeing that all points of space, both in themselves and in their effects on the elements, are precisely alike? I have tried to give an answer to this question. Its very terms are meaningless from the point of view which regards space as something actually existing by reference to which things are determined. Things do not first find themselves in certain positions, and then become enabled to take effect, but it is the kind and degree of the effects which they already exercise upon each other that makes them occupy those positions for the perceptive consciousness, which seem to us to be those which originally belong to them.

This answer, however, does not at once remove our present difficulty. In order to find a reason why these qualitatively-distinguished elements should assume the form of a scattered multitude of individual atoms, it seems as if we should be compelled to suppose that in the intelligible world, which reflects itself in space, that action or thought which we designated as the nature of an element, must repeat itself as often as its phenomenon. Is such a repetition less unaccountable than the easy hypothesis of a plurality of atoms with which Physics is content? I feel myself able to answer in the affirmative. It is merely owing to the effect of constant association with the forms of space, that when we come to represent to ourselves these 'repeated' actions, we conceive them as falling into a number of disconnected groups separated from one another by empty intervals just as the parts of space are separated by their lines of distance. There is really no such relation between them. Just as in our own inner experience the self-same principle or the same conception recurs in the most various connexions, and exercises a limiting or determining influence of many different kinds on any other of our thoughts with which it happens to be associated, just so the idea, which determines the qualitative nature of an element of matter, serves in the order of the universe as a point of intersection for the different tendencies which make that universe into a connected whole; connected, as I must again insist, not merely as a rigidly classified system, but as an eternally progressive history. We are, therefore, not called upon, nor are we interested to maintain that there are distinct special existences corresponding in number with the functions which the same idea must fulfil when thus associated with others in these various combinations. The number of scattered atoms is merely the number of the separate appearances which an element assumes to our perception of space owing to the manifold relations in which it is involved with other elements.

197. The extremely paradoxical nature of this conclusion shall not prevent me from mentioning also a certain corollary which follows from it. We have now arrived at a point of view from which the atomic theory can no longer satisfy us, not even after that transformation of its fundamental idea, to which it seemed not to be disinclined. So long as the unextended points, from and to which forces proceed, points which have indeed positions in space but no volume, were conceived as having, not less than the extended atoms had previously been conceived as having, an obstinately indestructible nature, there could of course be no mention of a further division into parts; since that which was to be divided was, as its very name implied, indivisible. This mode of representation no longer holds good. If the single real idea which determines the nature of a qualitative element necessarily manifests itself under a number of distinct forms, and if there is no limit to the multiplication of the relations which it may assume towards other ideas, why should it be specially attached to just those points in space where it happens to be active at any given moment? Why should not the positions which it may occupy also admit of being multiplied indefinitely, seeing that none of the manifestations of the element have any other claim to a separate existence except such as depends on the mandate of the whole order which assigns to them this and no other position?

Not that I have any desire to return to the notion of a continuously extended, infinitely divisible matter, nor to that other notion, according to which the real atom, at least in its spatial phenomenon, is quite continuous in the sense that it is equally present at every point within its own narrow volume. I would rather not in any way depart from the results of Atomism most recently arrived at, according to which an atom is conceived as developing its activity from a geometric point. But I can see no reason for regarding the amount of force which is thus diffused—a force which is now no longer in any sense an indestructible metaphysical unity—as eternally attached to this one point. Rather, it would admit of partition in space, just as it is itself only a partial manifestation of a single identical function of the whole. In proportion as new combinations of phenomena were required to exist by the course of the world, each centre of activities would have the power of breaking itself up into several centres, which would then assume different positions in space according as the new conditions to which they were subject prescribed. These conditions may be very different. Their effect may be not merely to compel the new centres of activity to combine with atoms belonging to other elements, but also to cause an increase in the volume of any particular atom by forcing its constituent elements to expand and fall asunder. There would thus come to be differences in the density of the atoms. Owing to this constant process of inner dissolution, new points of departure for effects would be multiplied, and there would arise the appearances which were formerly believed to be only capable of being explained on the hypothesis of a continuous and real extension in space, and which are only accounted for at the cost of a permanent improbability by those who believe, with ordinary atomism, that all things are ultimately analysable into real existence and empty space. In this way we should be brought to the idea of an infinite dynamic divisibility of unextended atoms, an idea which, it is to be hoped, will seem less frightful than the barbarous name by which, in order to distinguish it from the traditional theories, I believe that it may most briefly be described. It will no doubt have been taken for granted that the degree of intensity, or, to put it shortly, the mass of each of the parts will be diminished, while the sum of these masses remains the same. I have nothing to say against this addition, but the principle on which it is made will require further discussion in our next chapter.

CHAPTER VII.

The Laws of the Activities of Things.

OF the inner movements of things we know nothing. Still less do we know what are the constant modes of co-operation which the order of the Universe requires them to assume. Hence, experience alone can discover to us the motive forces into which the course of natural events can be analysed and the law according to which each of these several forces may be conceived as taking effect. But a sufficiently careful and comprehensive observation has long since established certain general results, which deserve, by way of supplement at any rate, to receive an interpretation in connexion with metaphysical views, and which suggest the question whether they are really nothing but the expression of what has been observed to take place, and not rather of necessities of thought to which experience has directed our attention only subsequently. I shall attempt to investigate this point, though well-knowing beforehand that my labours are not likely to produce any considerable result. They will serve merely to draw attention to the ambiguity of those speculations, philosophical no less than scientific, which will never cease to be directed to this unpromising subject.

198. In the first place, it is universally admitted that the intensity of the effects which a force produces at a distance, is dependent on the interval between the elements between which it operates. And to this conclusion the doctrine which is here maintained must also lead, though it remains to be seen later by what steps. If the positions of things in space are merely expressions of the forces which are already acting upon them, *a fortiori* every impulse to further activity will depend upon these interactions between the elements and on the distances in which those interactions manifest themselves. This merely general characterisation is not, however, enough to determine precisely the nature of the connexion between forces and the distances of elements. But the other assumption, which is asserted with almost as much assurance as the last, viz. that the intensity of the effect is in an inverse ratio to the distance, has nothing to recommend it if we exclude the familiar instances furnished by experience, except the inadmissible idea that space acts as an obstacle which cannot be overcome except by a partial sacrifice of force.

Other preconceived notions combine with this one to produce an impression that this decrease of force is a fixed law, holding good in all cases in which forces act at a distance. That a force, emanating from a certain starting-point, diffuses itself through space, is not merely our mode of expressing the fact that its effects differ in degree at different distances. Unfortunately, we believe ourselves to be describing not only a fact but an actual process by which the necessity of this difference is explained. As the force is transmitted to larger and larger spherical shells it seems as if its tenuity must increase in the same ratio as the area which it occupies, the ratio of the square of the distance from its starting-point. This coincidence of a simple geometric relation with a general law which we see illustrated in the effects produced at a distance by gravitation and by electric and magnetic agencies, is too tempting not to invite often-repeated attempts to establish the closest connexion between them. None of the assumptions, however, which are required as links in the connexion can be admitted. A force cannot be supposed to proceed from a point c, without at once being regarded as an independent fluid medium. That its tenuity should increase with its increasing extension, would no doubt not be altogether inconceivable. But still we should have to discover to what the motion of the fluid was due. This could only ultimately arise from a new force, a force of repulsion, exerted upon the fluid by the thing present at c. We should have also to show what becomes of the force thus diffused, if it meets with no object on which to take effect, and further from what source the constant supply of force at c is derived. These questions cannot be evaded by supposing that the force does not *diffuse* itself around c, but is, as it were, a permanent atmosphere already diffused around it. To deny the fact of the movement of radiation, would be to take away the only justification for the principle that the density decreases with increase of distance, whilst it would contribute nothing towards the explanation of the effect eventually produced. Let us, then, suppose that a given force whilst proceeding from c, meets in the point p with an object which it is to act on. How is this action possible? and how can the force impart to the body motion in any particular direction? All that could be concluded from the arrival of the force at p, would be that it was now present at that point—not, that a body situated at that point must, owing to the action of the force, be set in motion. But, even granting that it were thus set in motion, what direction could the motion take? The motion as such could stand in no relation to the point c; for, if the activity of the force is made to depend on this process of its diffusion, it follows that it only acts at p just as far as it is there; it makes no difference whether it was there always or whence it came there. Supposing it then to coincide exactly at p with some real element, it could not impart any motion to that element, for there would be no reason why it should prefer one direction to another[1].

[1] [Cp. § 185.]

If, on the other hand, we suppose that at the first moment of its beginning to exercise its activity, the force *is* separated from the element by ever so small an interval, we are making action at a slight distance serve as an explanation of action at any and every distance, though we cannot bring the former under any definite law, and must therefore fail in the attempt to deduce the law of the latter.

Even if these difficulties could be got rid of, it would still remain a question whether the resulting motion will take the direction $c\,p$, or the opposite one $p\,c$. For this process of radiation would be just the same for an attractive and for a repulsive force. Each smallest particle of the fluid would, in such a case, still have to exert attraction or repulsion upon whatever it might meet with at the point to which it had come, as a property peculiar to itself and not admitting of further explanation. But, if that were so, there would be no longer any occasion for confining these effects to the parts of the force which come *before* p in the line $c\,p$; the parts on the other side of p, which lay in the course of this line when produced, or which had come there, would exercise an influence on the element at p, of the same kind though in a contrary direction. The ensuing motion would then be the result of these different impulses; at any rate it could not correspond with the simple law which it was hoped could be deduced from it. Finally, the attempt may be made to get rid of these difficulties, by supposing that the radiating force imparts its own motion to the element which it lights upon, and determines by its own direction that which the element in its turn is to take. Putting aside, however, that this is a transition from one idea, that of a force acting at a distance, to another, the idea of communication of already existing motion, all that would be explained by this method would be the centrifugal effects of repulsion; every case of attraction would require a centripetal pressure, such as has, indeed, often been assumed, but has not hitherto had any intelligible explanation given of it.

199. On these grounds I not only hold that these attempted deductions have failed to establish their own special conclusions, but the spirit in which they have been undertaken seems to me to be inconsistent with itself. Of course, many of the occurrences which take place in the world are of a compound character, and arise from mechanical combination of others. It is possible that gravitation and other similar phenomena which seem to us to be the expressions of the simplest primary forces, may really be compound results produced by forces still more simple. An elaboration of experience so advanced as to show this to be the case would really have succeeded in furnishing us with a genetic theory of the Law of Gravitation. If, on the other hand, these and all effects of a like kind are regarded as the expression of simple and primary forces, we must not attempt, as is done by these theories, to give a mechanical explanation of their origin, by referring them to a diffusion and attenuation of force. The only proof that can be expected of these elementary processes and their Laws is the speculative one, that they have a necessary place in the rational order of things. The *Ratio legis* might be given, but not the machinery by which it is carried into effect. The treatment, then, of this problem belongs, without doubt, to Philosophy, nor do I complain that there should have been such innumerable attempts to solve it, though unfortunately I know of none that has been successful. I do not therefore continue my own investigation with any hope of arriving at a result that can be final, but merely in order to bring out more clearly some of the distinctive features of my general view.

200. Owing to the doctrine which I have already expounded in regard to the nature of forces, I do not feel touched by an objection which Physicists have urged against the absolute validity of the Law of Gravitation, an objection which, if it held good, would render untenable the whole of this doctrine which speculation so obstinately attempts to deduce *a priori*; where the distance = o, the attracting force must according to this law, it is said, be infinite. I will not now stop to enquire whether this result is altogether inadmissible. It would be open for those who maintain the ordinary hypothesis of a continuously extended matter to urge that contact takes place only between points, lines, or surfaces without thickness, and consequently that the masses whose distance = o, must in every case themselves = o also. If the hypothesis of unextended atoms conceived as points be preferred, we should certainly have to ascribe to them an infinite power of resisting separation, in case they had once got united in the same point by attraction. But all that would be necessary would be to take care that such a case never arose. It would be easy indeed so to alter the formula of the law, that in case of all observable distances, even the smallest, it should correspond as nearly as possible with the results of observation, while in the case of vanishing distances it should still not imply the infinity of the force of attraction. But, I think we can achieve the same end, without introducing a modification of the law such as would be purely arbitrary and incapable of ever being proved. All the several forces which Physics is led by experience to assume, stand in our view merely for the various components into which the single power of inter-action inherent in the nature of things admits of being analysed. It is not therefore at all surprising that a law which expresses with perfect precision the operation of one out of this number of components should nevertheless yield infinite degrees of intensity or other inapplicable values if the component is supposed to continue its operation isolated and uncontrolled. These cases of isolated action are precisely those which are never met with; they express merely what would occur under certain imagined conditions, but what under existing conditions, never does occur. Hence it is not necessary to modify the formula of the well-known law of gravitation, considered as simply claiming to indicate the variations of the attractive action; in this sense the formula may be perfectly precise; only the limiting case never occurs for which alone it would yield such problematical values. In proportion as the elements which are attracted approach each other more nearly the tendency to repulsion will be found to grow even more rapidly, and if any one of the proposed modifications of the law could be shown to hold good in actual experience it would not be a more correct expression of the attraction taken by itself so much as of the total effect in which attraction and repulsion are already united. Moreover, it is easy to see that without this supposition this partial law expressing mere attraction would yield results which would be not so much inconceivable as merely inapplicable in our view of nature. Let us suppose two elements a and b between which there is attraction but never repulsion, to approach the point c from opposite sides. They would then at the moment of meeting have not only an infinite attraction g, but also infinite though opposite velocities $\pm v$. Now as the velocity last reached, v, has arisen by the summation of all the accelerations which have been increasing infinitely up to the value g, we cannot but regard the infinite quantity v as greater than the infinite quantity g. Hence, if there were no repulsion, g could not prevent the two elements from passing with opposite velocities through each other's midst and thus distance would be restored between them and the amount of their attraction would become finite again.

201. A special objection to the received views has been urged by Herbart. He will not himself admit the operation of forces at a distance; but for those who do admit it, he holds that the only legitimate assumption is this, that the intensity of each force is diminished in proportion as it is satisfied by the attainment of its result. That a repulsion, therefore, should decrease with the distance which it has produced, requires no explanation. On the other hand, the force of attraction, which becomes always more intense in proportion as it has drawn its object nearer, remains a paradox for him. This objection is plausible enough if the object is to explain the observed effects of the law by reference to its inner meaning; but I cannot think that the particular psychological analogy, to which it owes its conclusiveness, will admit of this general application. I entirely agree with Herbart that there are inner processes in things, from which the forces moving them are derived, and I will concede to him that in both the cases which are here brought together—psychical endeavour and physical motion—the impulse to what is done lies in a difference between a thing's actual state of being and some other state, which, if it could be realised, would be more in correspondence with its nature. But I dispute the conclusion which is so hastily drawn from these premisses. Herbart shows himself in this matter to be influenced by his main conception, according to which each changing state of a thing is a disturbance of its original nature, so that the only manifestation of activity which can fairly be attributed to real existence, is that of self-conservation or recurrence to the *status quo ante*. In that case, no doubt, supposing M to be this permanently fixed aim, and q the state which is a departure from it, the result to be achieved at each instant would correspond to this difference $M-q$. Strictly speaking, it does not at once follow from this, that the intensity of the force which exerts itself to recover the former state, must vary directly as the amount of divergence represented by q, and inversely as the result already obtained. All that would be measured by $M-q$ is the extent of what is required in order to attain the given end. But there would be nothing to prevent the force from continuing to operate with unvarying intensity until this difference had been made to disappear, just as a labourer in filling up a pit does not at first work more rapidly and afterwards with less energy, because the space to be heaped in was at the beginning larger and has since become smaller, but he works throughout at the same pace.

Even, however, admitting this assumption, insufficiently proved as it is, I doubt the relevancy of the analogy which would make the occurrence of a physical effect correspond with the satisfaction of psychical impulse. If, taking an imaginary case, we compare a supposed quantity M, of which we have an idea, with a smaller given quantity q, no doubt we know that $M-q$ expresses the amount which must be added to q, in order to make it $= M$. In this case, M, though not present before us in external reality, was as adequately represented by its idea as q was, and the estimation of the difference between them was thus made possible. If, however, we experienced a state q, and this were merely a manner or mode of our consciousness, some form perhaps of feeling, this feeling would not be able by itself to produce in our minds the idea of the absent M. Knowledge of the character and extent of the difference between q and M could only arise if we had had a real experience of M as well, and it were to enter into our consciousness in the form of a feeling or the remembrance of a feeling similar in kind to q. Although, therefore, the disturbed state of our feelings may depend upon the difference $M-q$, yet this difference only exists primarily for the comparing mind of an onlooker; it is not a real element in the experience of the being who is affected by the state q, at any rate not unless there is some remembrance of the state M. It cannot therefore be the obvious standard by which such a being, with a sort of preference for what is reasonable and just, determines the intensity of the effort which it has to make. However far, then, we may go in assimilating the inner states of things to processes of mind, so long as we do not believe that the physical operations of things are regulated like acts of our own by rules drawn from experience, as long as we believe rather that there is a necessity imposed on them to come to pass as they do, the difference between an actual and a better state of things cannot be the determining reason by which Physical effects are regulated.

On the other hand, there is no reason, we at least can see none, why the order of the universe which prescribes to all things their nature and mode of working, should not have attached to q a blind and unpurposed activity, which was as a matter of fact measured by the difference $M-q$, though the individual thing which was affected by the difference was itself unconscious of it. But, as there is nothing to hinder this supposition, so there is nothing to make it necessary; it remains a possible though but an arbitrary assumption that the course of things is nothing but a constant effort to attain to an equilibrium and to reproduce a state M which can only be effected by getting rid of their present state. There is equally nothing to prevent us from admitting the claims, though not the exclusive claims, of the opposite view, according to which the attainment of a state q means a change in the condition of things, which tends to reproduce itself in a more emphatic and intensified form. That other theory, the watchword of which is 'disturbance,' has thought only of pain; and then it seems quite natural that the self-conservative activity directed to the removal of pain, should decrease in proportion as it succeeds. It has taken no account of pleasure, which just as naturally creates a stimulus to the intensification of the state which was desired and is pleasant. For it is not true, except in those cases in which the source of enjoyment lies partly in the body, that pleasure is dulled with satisfaction. The body, no doubt, is forbidden by the habits of its action from contributing to the intensification of feeling, and interrupts it by weariness and satiety. It will not, however, be maintained that the pursuit of knowledge and its results, or the aspiration after beauty and goodness, is lessened by approximation to the ideal.

But we will leave these analogies, which decide nothing.

The general conclusion to which we come is this: there is a blind tendency in each thing, owing to its place in the all-embracing order of the world, whenever it is in any given state q, to produce an effect. The character and extent of this effect are not regulated by any law inherent in the nature of substance or force, and binding things without regard to the purport of this universal order. It is this order and this alone, which, in accordance with its own aims, connects reason and consequent, and it is as able to determine that the force of reaction should increase with the attainment of results, as that it should diminish in proportion as they are attained.

202. It is easy to see the consequences that follow from this conviction. As we do not know the idea which is endeavouring to realise itself in the world, it is from experience only, as I have before remarked, that we can derive our knowledge of the recurrent operations of things according to general laws. We cannot, therefore, take it amiss that Physics, following the lead of observation, should assign to the different forces, the assumption of which is found to be necessary, laws of action of the most various kinds. These Laws Physics regards merely as expressions of the facts, without attempting any metaphysical interpretation of them, and every idea of this kind, serving to clear up a group of interconnected phenomena, and enabling us to infer the future from the present, deserves respect, as an enlargement of our knowledge. Philosophy is altogether in the wrong, when she depreciates results obtained in this way, merely because they do not penetrate to the ultimate truth; but she is certainly within her right, when, starting from her own point of view, she attempts to supply the interpretation which is still lacking to those results. Whatever may be thought of space and of existence in space, if once the intensity of interaction between two elements is made to depend on the distance separating them, and just so far as it is made to depend *only* on this, it seems to be impossible that different forces could be determined by this cause to act in different ways; the same distance, it would seem, could only make itself felt by the elements and determine all their reciprocal effects in the same way. It is this which has prepossessed philosophers in favour of the view that the different modes of action which Physics assumes, when it makes different forces dependent on different powers of the distance, cannot have a primary right of existence, but that there must be one fundamental law for the relation of action to distance, and the deviations from it which experience compels us to admit must be due merely to the complexity of the circumstances. By an easily understood transition, this fundamental law then came to be identified with the Law of Gravitation, this being a Law which is obeyed by many familiar effects, differing from each other and occurring under apparently very simple circumstances. I cannot myself share this prepossession, except with great reservations. It is necessary first of all that a certain asumption from which all such attempted explanations start, should be clearly stated. That assumption is made by thinkers, by whom perhaps in their ultimate essence all things are mysteriously merged in the unity of an infinite substance and a single creative plan, when they afterwards leave out of sight the continuous operation of this single principle, and explain the whole course of the world merely from the permanent qualities and the changing relations of individual existences, and the consequences which, by common logic, seem to follow from these two premisses.

203. Upon this assumption we are not justified, according to all that has preceded, in regarding the interval of distance itself as that which determines the amount of force exercised between two elements, a and b. This is due only to the inner states of the elements which correspond to the distances between them. Every mode of treating the question must admit so much as this. Even if we adopt the ordinary view of space as objectively existing, the distance of things will still only be distance *between* them; the distance and its measure is, therefore, a reality *prima facie* only for an observer who is able to represent to himself the space which must be traversed in order to pass from a to b. If a and b are to be guided by it in what they do, it must be possible for them and not for an observer only to take note that the distance between them is in one case d and in another case δ; thus in order to act they must first be acted upon by the very same condition which is to regulate their activity. This would lead us—supposing the merely phenomenal character of space to be assumed—to the conclusion, that every actual distance between a and b is nothing but the manifestation in space of the sum of the effects which they experience at the moment from one another and from the whole, and which are also the cause of their effect upon us. The universal order is, however, neither according to our view, nor according to the ordinary view, a rigidly classified system, such that each element persistently occupies the place which corresponds with its conception. Such a system no doubt exists, but its parts which are in a constant state of chaotic flux, are every moment falling into relative positions which do not correspond to the permanent affinities of their natures.

We know what this means in terms of ordinary spatial perception; it is not the elements which are by their nature most fitted for active intercourse which are always the nearest neighbours; the action of some third or fourth element may separate those which are coherent, or bring together those which are indifferent. It is indeed impossible to give a picture of what things undergo or experience in their inner nature when they enter into those changing intelligible relations with which we are familiar in spatial perception as distances of greater or less extent. As objects of such perception, i.e. as distances, these relations seem to us obviously to imply a greater or less amount of estrangement or of sympathy in the things, and upon this the degree of their reciprocal action is naturally supposed to depend. Yet our previous investigations have shown that we cannot account for the manner and degree in which things act upon each other from the mere fact of their being outside one another; it is only from what they get or experience from this fact, or from the way in which it *connects* them, that we can do so. We cannot, therefore, say that the distance between things itself exercises an influence on the intensity of their force; it is merely the mode in which the greater or less degree of their metaphysical affinity is manifested to us, varying as this does with the different combinations into which they are brought by the course of events. Throughout this process the things remain what they are, and continue to act upon each other conformably to their natures. At the same time, the different degrees to which they are temporarily displaced from their position in the system, cannot but have some influence on their behaviour; a change in the closeness of their metaphysical affinity involves a corresponding change in the amount i of the intensity p with which they stimulate those mutual actions for which their nature has fitted them. If these very abstract considerations have so far inspired any confidence, we now stand before a conclusion which seems certain, and before an alternative which we are quite unable to decide. No reason can be anywhere discovered why this metaphysical affinity should correspond to any but the first power of the distance, which is the distance itself. On the other hand, after what has been said above, it seems quite as possible that the effect of this affinity should vary directly as that it should vary inversely, with the distance. The two formulæ—

$$i = pd \text{ and } i = \frac{p}{d}$$

would be the only formulæ in which this point of view could result, and they would be of equal validity.

204. In making use of these expressions, I wish it to be borne in mind that as I understand them they have not the same meaning as any of those quantities to which the ordinary mechanical view of Physics leads us. We do not use i to designate any kind or degree of outward performance, but merely the intensity of the stimulus with which, in virtue of the relation at the time being subsisting between two elements, one of them excites and is excited by the other to any or all of those possible forms of reciprocal activity which spring from their affinity, their difference, or generally their respective places in the system. As regards what follows from the stimulus a fresh and specific determination is required to decide whether it is to be attraction or repulsion, and yet another to decide its amount. The first requirement, however, may perhaps be assumed to be already fulfilled by the coefficient p. For though we have hitherto spoken of this merely as a quantity, it is dependent on the nature of the interacting elements, and therefore, strictly speaking, could only be a concrete number. On the other hand, as regards the amount of the initial motion, I can see no reason why it should not be considered as simply proportionate to the stimulus i, which is its motive cause. I shall not, therefore, make any further comparison between the formula $i = pd$, which would indicate a sort of metaphysical elasticity, and what we meet with under the same name, though generally under highly complicated conditions, in the sphere of Physics. As regards the second formula, I do not see how the desired result, viz. dependence upon the square of the distance, could be shown necessarily to follow from it.

I will however mention the assumption which would have to be made in order to bring this law into ultimate harmony with the other or metaphysical view. I cannot esteem as of any value for such a purpose the appeal to the reciprocity of all effects, which some distinguished authorities have introduced into the discussion. If $i = \frac{p}{d}$ is the intensity with which one element is attracted by another and at the same time tends of itself towards it, I cannot see any reason for supposing the result to equal the product of the two activities; like every other resultant, it would be the *sum* of them; it is only the intensity of the effect, not the function of the distance upon which it depends, that would be affected. Perhaps, however, it will be urged, that the effect of a force depends not merely on what the force intends to do, but also on how much it is able to do, i.e. in the case before us, not merely on the amount of mutual excitation, but also on the conditions which promote or check the satisfaction of the demands. To put the matter shortly and clearly; the distance d between a and b indicates a degree of estrangement between them, and their willingness to act upon each other is therefore inversely proportional to that distance. But, the weaker will is not only weaker, but has opposed to it the greater obstacle, in the shape of the greater distance which weakened it. The active force, therefore, which can be exerted, is found by multiplying the effort by the reciprocal of the resistance to be overcome; and accordingly is inversely proportional to the square of the distance. Such a mode of expression could indeed only serve to indicate briefly the essence of the idea; in real truth, the distance d even if it were a really extended space between a and b, could not be regarded as an obstacle to the effect. According to the view which we have maintained, it could not actively condition the incipient process, except in so far as it was represented within the elements a and b by means of that hidden state of excitation which we found ourselves obliged to assume in all cases. But perhaps it is precisely to this inner state of things that an argument of this kind may seem to be most rigorously applicable. It may perhaps seem incredible that when two elements a and b are separated by the distances d

or δ, they should in both cases alike, though not excited to action to the same degree, yet in spite of this difference aim at producing one and the same effect. It may be thought that the *object* of their effort as well as its integrity would vary, and vary proportionately to the degree of their excitation. The amount of the actual external result would then be found by multiplying i into a quantity proportional to i, and would thus vary inversely with the square of the distance.

I shall not attempt to decide whether there is anything of value in this suggestion: I wish only to point out that this new way of characterising an intended result, as one which increases in proportion to the stimulus, is just one which cannot be decisively established, if nothing is assumed but individual elements with their natures and the relations subsisting between them. There is no universal Metaphysic of Mechanics, capable of showing that every time any two existences combine in a relation, they *must* have so combined. Whenever any such relation occurs, it is a matter of fact, which, from a Metaphysical point of view, can only be regarded as an effect of the all-embracing M, i.e. the idea of the whole. It must be this idea which is present and active in all individual elements, assigning to each its mode of manifestation in relation to the rest, which otherwise would not flow necessarily from the mere conception and the nature of the elements. But, as we do not know the content of this idea, we cannot affirm positively that it imposes a necessity on things to assume these forms and no others; and hence, the whole attempt to establish the existence of a single, original, and only legitimate law for the operations of all forces is entirely fruitless.

205. Nothing is left to us, but to accept with thanks the empirical rules which enable Physics to express, in conformity with observation, the effects actually produced by the several forces on each occasion of their activity. Philosophy should not turn away from assumptions, unless they are inherently absurd, and those made by Physics are seldom that. Thus, no one has ever attempted to explain an increase or diminution in the intensity of force as depending on mere Time; where observation seemed to confirm such a view, the Time was in every instance occupied by actual occurrences, each of which contained in itself the efficient cause of that which was to follow; these processes, then, and not the mere lapse of Time, must have determined the varying intensity of forces. On the other hand, there is no reason on philosophical grounds to deny that the amount of force which results from the interaction of two elements, depends to some extent also on their motions. For according to our view motion is not merely a change of external relations, which takes no effect on the things themselves; as those relations depend on inward states of the things, so the rapidity with which they change them is also an inward experience, and one which at every moment may help to determine their subsequent behaviour. Besides the degree of intensity which a force would have, corresponding with the distance at the moment between the two elements from which it proceeds, there would thus be a positive or negative increase of the force, dependent on the rapidity with which the elements travel through the space which they at present occupy. But it is not expedient to continue the discussion on this point; for while the hypothesis has been employed by Physicists only with extreme reserve, in regard to the interaction of electric currents,—a case in which it seemed to be required,—there would be no limits to its application when treated, as we should have to treat it, as a general principle. Once admitted, the dependence of force upon velocity of motion, and upon its successive accelerations, would apparently have to be regarded as a universal characteristic of physical action.

206. Connected with this question is the other one: Do forces, in order to take effect, require Time? Stated in this form, indeed, as it occasionally is, the question is ambiguous.

It is a universally admitted truth that, every effect, in its final result, is formed by the successive and continuous addition of infinitesimal parts which go on accumulating from zero up to the final amount. In this sense succession, in other words, expenditure of Time, is a characteristic of every effect, and this is what distinguishes an effect from a mere consequence, which holds good simultaneously with its condition. Vain, however, would it be—as we saw in our investigation of Time—to seek to go further than this, and to discover the inscrutable process by means of which succession of events in Time comes to pass at all. The question we are considering was proposed on the assumption of the diffusion of force in Space. Supposing it were possible to instance a moment of Time in which a previously non-existent force came into Being, would all the various effects which it was calculated to produce in different places, both near and remote, be at once realised? Or, would a certain interval of Time be required, just as it is in the case of Light, which transmits itself to different objects rapidly, but not instantaneously, and must first come into contact with them before it can be reflected by them.

It is not necessary to embellish the question by introducing conditions which make any decision impossible. There is no need to imagine either the sudden appearance out of nothing of some new body in the world, or the disappearance of one already existing, and then to enquire, whether the addition of gravity, as in the first case (the new body being likewise supposed subject to the law of gravitation), or the subtraction of gravity, as in the second, would make itself felt by distant stars immediately, or not till after a measurable interval? The action of force in its beginnings may be illustrated by examples nearer to hand. Each smallest increase in the velocity of two elements, which are working upon each other—whether by attraction or repulsion—at a distance, by the very fact that the elements are brought nearer to or are parted from each other, brings about an increase of attraction or repulsion, in other words, a new force, though no new vehicle of it. Similarly, the electrical actions of bodies, depending as they do upon a condition which is not always present, furnish an example of a beginning of force in Time. It makes no difference that this condition itself does not come into existence at once and with a permanent intensity, but only by degrees; at any rate, a moment can be assigned for every one of its degrees before which it did not exist, and from which its effect must begin. Having regard to such cases the question that has been raised can only be answered in the negative; there could be no possibility of an affirmative answer, except on that supposition of a diffusion of force which we found to be impossible[1]. But even on that supposition, it is the passage through space which, strictly speaking, would have to be regarded as the first work of the diffused force; the work done upon its arrival at the distant object would be only second and subsequent, for its presence as force would not be felt by the object until it had come into the necessary contact with it. It must not however be supposed that after the force has come into Being, a blank space of time t is required to pass before the motion begins to be transmitted; nor again, that after the force has reached its object, and so secured its control over it, it should require a similar space of Time t, in order to take effect. If this space of Time t were really blank, everything would remain at the end of it as it was at the beginning, and the effect might just as well be expected to occur at the end of some other space of Time $= n\,t$; if, on the other hand, any positive change in the phenomena takes place during this time, this change is a link, by means of which C, the imperfectly realised condition of the result F, is completed and perfected: that part of C, however, which was already present has, at the moment of its coming to be, immediately produced that corresponding part of F which it was adequate to produce.

[1] [Cp. § 198.]

207. It will be objected that real events are, as I stated above, not related to each other in the same way as conditions to their consequences, because the result in the former case always follows the cause which produces it; but for this succession, events would be transformed into a system of cotemporaneous parts, which would differ only in the different degrees of their dependence upon the first of the series: C and F, therefore, though it is true there could be no blank interval of Time between them, would always come into contact in the order $C\ F$, not in the order $F\ C$. This true remark again suggests an enigma, the insolubility of which we have already admitted. For succession in time could never arise from these contacts which occupy no time, however often repeated, between members which follow out of one another; we should still have merely a systematic order if C and F did not each fill a certain extent of time of its own; if they did, then, it seems, F would have to wait till C had completed its interval of time. But even this is not a way out of the difficulty. Suppose C and F both to consist of a series of parts following each other in unbroken succession, e.g. $c_1, c_2, c_3, f_1, f_2, f_3$. Are we then to suppose that the occurrence of F is conditional on the completion of the group C? that it cannot, i.e. commence, until c_3 is reached, and that nothing of the nature of F takes place until this term is realised? There are facts enough which seem to confirm this view, and indicate that the result F is attached to a specific determination of C. A closer examination will, nevertheless, not fail to show that the force C, all the time that it seemed to be increasing in amount without producing any effect, was really already occupied with the removal of hindrances which stood in the way of the occurrence of anything of the nature of F. When, at last, the amount c_3 is reached, this removal is completed, and from this point its first positive and visible effect commences, though not absolutely its first effect. As regards this effect, again, we do not believe that a finite amount of it, f_1, arises *suddenly* so soon as C is ended. Rather, each smallest addition which is made to B, involves a correspondingly small addition to F; but between these two occurrences there is no blank interval of Time; f_n corresponds to c_n immediately. But the assumption we have made as regards C itself involves the same difficulty. If C remains unchanged during the whole space of Time t, which it is supposed to fill, there is no better reason why F should follow at the close of that time than at its commencement. If however we assume, as was assumed, that C traverses the series $c_1\ c_2\ c_3$, then, as the order of the series is supposed to be fixed, each term must be the condition of the succeeding one, and as in the previous case, if they are to form a succession in time, two adjacent terms can neither have any blank interval of time between them, nor can they be simultaneous.

The conclusion to which this points is clear. The whole nature of Becoming is unknown to us, and we cannot reconstruct the origin of it in theory. In this quite general sense, it is true to say that every operative condition and every force draws its consequences and its effects *after* it. But in order to do this, it is not so much the case that they need a lapse of time, as that they *are* this lapse of time itself; only because they are themselves in a process of becoming can they convey that same process to their consequences. But there is no measurable interval of Time between the condition c_n and its true and immediate result f_n; there is nothing but the enigmatical fact of their contact, a fact which cannot be ignored any more than it can be explained.

If we now leave these general considerations, and return to the subject which first suggested them, that of forces acting at a distance, it must follow from the doctrine which has been stated, that, at the same moment that the force which is active in the element p passes from c_2 into c_3, there will be a similar transition in the element q, no matter how remote it may be, from f_2 to f_3, provided that c and f are causally connected through that inner sympathetic affinity upon which all action depends. Moreover, just as c_2 in the element p can only change into c_3 continuously, that is, by passing through all the intermediate values, in exactly the same way in the element q, f^2 will pass by succession into f^3. But the idea that a lapse of Time is required in order that p should transmit its force to q at all, is barred, among other considerations, by that of the reciprocal action of the two elements, which is universally admitted to be a necessary assumption. No force could be diffused from p towards q, nor could any force even originate in p, unless it were awakened and solicited in p by q; on the other hand, q could not produce this excitation, unless it was invited by p. No action, therefore, could ever take place between p and q, if it were required that a force should first proceed from p to q; for the only thing which could excite this force to set out from p would be the stimulus of another force starting from q; and this stimulus it would never have, because q would be waiting for an invitation from p. This connexion of mutual affinity between the elements, the source of their action upon each other, does not at one time or another *come into* existence through a diffusion of forces in space; it always *exists*, thus rendering it possible that changes of state experienced by one element should involve corresponding changes in another.

208. Owing to the boundless complexity of the manifold conditions which meet in the course of nature, we cannot expect to be able to explain every event directly from the joint action of the forces which combine to produce it. Hence, the desire has often been felt to discover certain customary rules by which, at any rate, the course of the natural world is regulated. It was hoped that in cases where knowledge of the special connexions between things is wanting, we might thus be enabled to establish equations expressive of general conditions with which the results, however unknown may be the manner in which they are brought about, must certainly correspond. Experience itself also leads us to the same ideas, whether, as some believe, it is from this source that they are derived exclusively, or that they are preconceptions which experience merely confirms, and which, as it then seems, we must have arrived at independently.

Opinions are divided between these two alternatives. The Realistic view inclines to treat general principles of this kind either as designations of mere matters of fact, which might have occurred differently, or else their universality is explained by what is called their self-evident truth, though its opposite is not regarded as strictly inconceivable. On the other hand, the Idealist view, which is that which we here adopt, can recognise no supreme law except the one unchanging purpose underlying the multiplicity of phenomena, and seeking for its realisation in them. At the same time, the Idealist, being unable to express the nature of this purpose, or the laws to which it requires that things should conform, cannot regard these universal principles, in so far as they are borne out by experience, as more than habits of nature on a great scale, valid within the circle of our observation, but not infallible as regards the far larger sphere of reality which lies beyond the limits of Time and Space to which our investigations are confined. Hence, instead of establishing any positive truths, the duty which lies before me is the less grateful one of calling in question the unlimited validity of principles, the limited validity of which is one of the most important and unfailing aids to scientific enquiry.

209. One of the simplest of these truths appears to be the invariability and the conservation of mass. Though not especially, or, at any rate, not invariably confirmed by the appearances of every-day life, this doctrine receives such universal support from the systematic view of science, that it would be superfluous to adduce any detailed arguments for its certainty. But now that it has been fully established,

I cannot see in it any necessity of thought the late discovery of which need cause surprise. It may indeed be self-evident for a theory which regards the world as composed of individual and mutually independent atoms. Out of the absolute void, which would be all that would lie between these atoms, obviously no new real existence could arise; the principle that out of nothing comes nothing, would hold good absolutely. But this point of view we have been compelled to abandon. In order to conceive reciprocal action, without which no course of nature is intelligible, we were led to regard the individual elements, not as self-conditioned, but as depending for the beginning, continuance, and end of their existence on the determination of the one Being, from which their nature and capacities of action are derived. Now, it is certainly a tempting conclusion, but it is no necessity of thought, to go on to suppose that this one Being at least is a sum of reality which cannot be increased or diminished, and which changes only the forms of its manifestation. And we ourselves inclined above to this idea, when we admitted it to be natural that each individual qualitatively-distinguished element, i. e. each activity of the one existence, when conformably with the plan of the world it splits itself up into various elements, should have a diminished intensity in each of the parts so arising.

But all this world of quantitative determinations has no significance outside that complexity of things and processes which the one and only true reality creates to express itself. It is only their meaning and function, and the value which they thus acquire, that give to the individual elements and forces the particular magnitudes they possess and exhibit in comparison with others. But what lies beneath them all, is not a quantity which is eternally bound to the same limits, and can only represent the same sum in different ways, however variously divided. On the contrary, there is no reason why, if it is required by the Idea which has to be realised, one period of the world should not need the efficient elements to be more, and another less, and why in the former case each part of the whole should not also exert itself with a greater degree of force on the rest. The history of Nature would then resemble a musical melody of varying strength of tone, the swellings and varyings of which do not spring from nothing, nor yet from one another, but each in its place results from the requirement of the whole. I do not mean to affirm that this actually *is* what takes place in Nature. Quite conceivably it may be part of the hidden purpose of the supreme Idea, that all its requirements should depend for their realisation on a fixed sum of real elements, and that the production of variety should be restricted to different adaptations of the same material. Still less ought we to be surprised if the course of Nature, so far as we can observe it, shows this to be practically the case. For, as far as we can see with clearness, we find Nature moving in a cycle, which makes it certain that forms once in existence will maintain themselves in existence. The only phenomena which suggest a progress wholly new, a progress which would go nearest to proving that the materials as well as the results are changed, are those which come from an antiquity so remote as to preclude exact investigation. It would, therefore, be mere folly to call in question the principle of the conservation of mass, so long as we confine our view to the world of accessible facts, and to what we may call the retail dealings of the physical elements in it. But it is the business of Philosophy to be constantly reminding us how limited is that section of the universe which is open to our observation, and that the whole which comprehends it is a reality, though not one which we can make an object of positive knowledge.

210. Similarly, the attempt has been made to conceive of *the sum of motions* in the world as a constant quantity. The general state of knowledge at the time when this idea was first entertained, did not admit of its being substantiated or even rendered probable by evidence derived from experience. For, as long as the effects which things exercise upon each other were explained as due merely to communicated motion, the conclusion could not be evaded that contrary velocities of elements tending in opposite directions would neutralise each other either wholly or in part, and consequently that motion disappeared from the world without any compensation. And ordinary experience seemed to confirm this conclusion by an abundance of examples, which no one knew how to explain in any other way. On the other hand, it was seen that living Beings were centres from which fresh motions were initiated at every instant, which could not but be taken for really new beginnings. So that neither was there anything in experience which was inconsistent with the indefinite multiplication of motions. Nor, finally, did experience suggest at all that this increase and diminution must balance each other, so as to maintain a constant sum of motion. Such a conception originates in an hypothesis as to the general character of the course of nature. Such an hypothesis was furnished by the idea of a system, having no object but the maintenance of itself, and furnished with fixed resources to this end: one of these means was the sum of motion, as it once for all exists, which in the economy of nature might not be spent, but only differently dispensed.

Recent physical speculations tend to revert to this same idea. So many apparently fixed qualities and conditions of things have been already demonstrated to be a ceaseless process, that it may be doubted whether there is such a thing as Rest at all, except in the indivisible moments of reversal in the minute oscillations with which all things are vibrating. Philosophy can have no motive for objecting to the assumption of such eternal motion as a matter of fact; it is a mere prejudice to infer, that because from our point of view an element must be first supposed at rest in order that the results of varying motions which condition it may be understood, this quiescence must have been prior in reality, and that the impulse to motion is an addition for which it has to wait. At the same time, it is only as a fact, and not in any other light, that we can regard this perpetual motion. It implies, not merely that motions already in existence may be communicated, but also that fresh motions must be produced in cases where two motions are opposite, and their communication could only result in the neutralisation of both. This elasticity of things, without which it would be impossible for them to counteract the self-annihilation of motion, is only conceivable if there are inner states of their being capable of developing the forces from which motions spring. It is possible, though not probable, that effects produced at a distance—against which there exists an unfounded prejudice—are conveyed in this way by means of motions transmitted from point to point of some connecting medium. But, even in that case, not only the conception of force, but also in a special sense that of force producing effects at a distance, is still indispensable, in order to explain each one of those countless communications of motion, the sum of which is usually held to compose the effects of force at measurable distances. If, however, force alone gives a sufficient reason for expecting that the motion will be replaced, which mere communication would permit to be lost in its antagonism, it cannot be supposed that force itself is the constant quantity which is in request; its intensity varies with the distance, though this is itself determined by force. The constant element in the course of Nature can only be an inner connexion between the circumstances which give rise to the operation of forces, a general law governing all combinations and connected successions of effects. It was thus that that most comprehensive principle, the one which dominates our whole estimate of physical processes, that of the Conservation of Force, first suggested itself, in respect to which I proceed now, though only so far as the connexion of my views requires, to offer the following considerations.

211. The simple principle, that out of nothing comes nothing, requires to be more precisely defined by the addition that even from something no result can follow, so long as that something, the event B, is only the condition or occasion of what is to take place, and remains just the same after the consequence F has been produced as before. On the contrary, B must be sacrificed, either wholly or in part, in order to produce F. This is the difference so constantly referred to between a causal *nexus* of events and the merely formal connexion of conditions and consequences. Our ontological discussions proved to us that, in the simplest case of causation, at least two factors, a and b, must enter into a relation c, and that the result which takes place consists in this, that a becomes changed into α, b into β, c into γ. Every effect, therefore, is the effect of two elements acting upon each other, neither of which can inflict upon the other a change in its condition, without paying a definite price for it by a corresponding change in its own. If a wishes by acting at a distance, whether in the way of attraction or of repulsion, to change the place of b, it can only do so by displacing itself in the opposite direction to a corresponding distance. There is no reason for excepting any single operation of nature from this general law; it holds good even in those cases of communicated motion when the process cannot be observed in all its details. It is not possible for a motion of one element, after imparting a certain velocity to a second, to persist unchanged in the first, ready to produce the same result again, and so increase its effect to infinity; its influence is exhausted in proportion to the degree in which it has been exerted.

212. Certain corollaries, of different degrees of certitude, arise out of this general conclusion. If we assume that the course of nature includes occurrences differing in kind from each other, and not admitting of being represented as mere quantitative or formal modifications of a single homogeneous process, we shall not be justified in asserting that every occurrence, A, calls into existence every other, C, or admits of immediate application to its production. It would be quite conceivable that there was no way from A to C except through the medium of a third, B, A and C remaining unsympathetic to each other. If therefore it cannot be said that there is necessarily any reciprocal action between every A and every C, it is equally clear on the other hand that if such a relation does take place, a specific amount of A must be sacrificed in order to produce a specific amount of C. Nor is it logically necessary, or self-evident, that every connected succession of two occurrences A and C must be convertible. No doubt, whatever is lost to A in the process of producing C, testifies to an effect of C upon A; but this effect is merely to impede A, and it is not a matter of course that every C which is able to do away with an A should therefore be able to call into existence an A which does not exist. That none the less it seems natural to us that this should be so, is due to the assumption which unconsciously we make to ourselves, that the economy of nature has no other object than self-conservation. In a process which implied progress, the order of events might easily be so determined as that A should lead to C, but that there should be no way back from C to A.

It cannot therefore be asserted *a priori*, and as a self-evident truth, that all the processes in Nature must be mutually convertible backwards and forwards; how far this convertibility extends can only be learned by experience. But, even in those cases in which it holds good, it is still by no means certain that the same amount c of C, which was produced by the amount a of A, and which therefore caused a to disappear, would now reproduce exactly the same amount, a, as was spent in its own production. That could not be unless it had been previously proved that there is in Nature no tendency towards progress; if there is progress, there can be nothing to make it impossible that each stage in a series of occurrences, $a\ c,\ c\ a_1,\ a_1\ c_1,\ c_1\ a_2$, should contain the condition of an advance in the next stage. This assertion is at variance with ordinary ideas; as, however, I do not intend to apply it to explain the actual details of the course of Nature, I shall merely repeat by way of justification what has previously been suggested, viz. that the nature of being and process is not limited by any premundane system of mechanics, but that it is the very import of this process which determines all the quantities in which the elements make themselves felt, and the consequences which their relations entail.

Finally, if, proceeding on the assumption of the unlimited convertibility of mutually productive activities, we suppose that a and b enter into a varying relation c, the sum of the effects which one is able to exercise on the other will be, within certain determinate values of c, a constant quantity. As each intermediate amount of c is reached, the capacity for action continues as regards that part of the possible total amount which it has not yet produced; on the other hand, it has lost so much of its force as was required to produce the result thus far achieved; this loss can only be made good by restoring the elements to their original state, that is, by doing away with the results already obtained. If we call this capacity for future action potential energy[1], in contrast with kinetic energy[2] which is active at the moment, the sum of these two forces, when the two elements are related as above, forms a constant quantity.

In the same way a sum of money M, so long as it remains unspent in our possession, has a purchasing power, and loses this power in proportion to the purchased goods which it acquires. Its original purchasing power can only

[1] [Spannkraft.]   [2] [Lebendige Kraft.]

be restored and applied to other objects by re-selling the goods. This example throws light upon the difficulties raised above. It would be impossible for us to know *a priori* that the potential force which the possession of the money would imply, could put us in possession of other objects by being itself got rid of; this exchangeability depends, in fact, on highly complex relations of human society. Nor should we be any more justified in taking for granted that the goods, G, by being similarly got rid of, would put us again in possession of the money; and as a matter of fact, this convertibility, which in like manner presupposes the connexion of human wants, has its limits; for it is well known that by buying goods and selling them again, we are equally likely to gain and to lose. It is not the case, then, that in the conversion of trade every quantity reproduces the same quantity as that by which it was produced. It is of course obvious, and need not be urged as an objection, that this result is due to conflicting circumstances, and to the influence which the nature of human business has in determining the relation of M to G; it is to these dealings of men with each other, not to any essential peculiarity of M and G, that the fact of their standing in any relation is due. But this is the very point which I would urge against the over-confident procedure of natural science. It does not appear to me self-evident that a perfectly adequate ground can be found for the mutual relations of the elements of Nature either, merely by considering their fixed characters M and G; here, too, their exchangeable value may depend partly on some larger commerce of the world. At the same time, I have no doubt as to the practical truth of the principle of the Conservation of Force, within the limits of our experience. Merely in the interests of Metaphysic I felt compelled to speak of these difficulties, and I wish now to make mention also of some accessory notions which have formed round this general principle.

213. We are often told with enthusiasm how it has at last been shown that all the various processes of the natural world are produced by a single indestructible force never varying in its intensity, and that nothing changes except the form in which the ceaseless transformations of this force are presented. It is especially the important correspondence between mechanical work and heat, which, by a somewhat hasty generalisation, has given rise to this idea of a transition of forces into one another, and of a universal primitive force to which they are all subordinate. The satisfaction thus given to that feeling which compels us to comprehend the infinite multiplicity of things and events under some single principle, seems to me to be illusory. Lichtenberg once contrasted the early ages of the world, when mankind was equally ready to believe in God and in ghosts, with the present age, which denies both; he feared compensation in a future when all that would be believed in would be the ghosts. Something like this seems to have happened in the case before us. For after all we are only doing honour to a ghost, when we dream of an absolutely nameless primitive force, which, formless in itself, and consisting of nothing but an unnamed number of constant amount, assumes, as a trifling addition that needs no explanation, the changing names under which it is manifested. If, however, we reflect upon and realise the fact that this original force never exists in this naked and nameless shape, but is continually passing from one to another of the forms which it assumes, we are again admitting that what really gives to each phenomenon its character is the concrete nature of that which embodies the quantum of force, either wholly or partly, for the time being. The same reflexion would show that what makes the succession of changing phenomena possible, is a unity of meaning which pervades and connects all those concrete forms of being with one another. Finally, it would appear that the persistence of quantity through all this play of forces is only a mode in which the already existent reality manifests itself, and cannot be the source from which that reality with all its various forms originally springs.

The latter view, which would reverse the true order and mistake the shadow for the substance, scarcely needs any further refutation; more serious are the objections which may be raised against the general assertion which we admitted above, that the conservation of the same sum of force is as a matter of fact the rule of experience. In as far as we can reduce two physical processes A and C to comparable primary occurrences consisting in comparable velocities v of comparable masses m, so far it may be shown that C which is produced by A, contains precisely the same amount of energy which A, by producing it, has lost. Where, however, the two elements do not admit of this exact comparison, and we have before us merely the fact that the specific amount a of A produces the specific amount c of C, and, it may be, *vice versa*, it is an essentially arbitrary course to conclude that c and a contain the same amount of energy, merely distributed in each case in a different form. All that can be said is, that a and c are *equivalent*, not that they are *equal*. It is possibly a just expectation that all the various processes of external nature will admit of being ultimately referred to variously combined motions of infinitesimal elements, and as regards these particular processes, the arbitrary interpretation referred to might be defended on this ground; but the general conception which underlies the principle of the conservation of Force must without doubt apply to one case in which no such expectation can be entertained; I allude to the interconnexion of physical and psychical processes.

Whatever effect is produced on the organs of sense by an outward irritation I, whether it is simply received, or transmitted, or diffused, or changed, there must always be left over from the physical process a residuum i, to which the psychical process of the sensation s will succeed immediately; nor can we doubt that the strength of the sensation will change with the changes in the strength of i. Again, no matter what constitutes an act of will W, or how it may act upon other states of consciousness, or be limited by them, there must be ultimately a part of it w, from which the first motion, f, of the body and all its consequences take their rise, and in this case we do not doubt, any more than in the other, that the extent of the physical effect is determined by the varying intensity of w. Now according to all ordinary views of what happens in such cases, the mere fact that there is an i or w, considered as an opportunity or occasion, is not enough to entail the existence of s or f. In order that the reaction may vary with the varying amount of the stimulus, the stimulus must be perceptible by that which it affects, in other words, must produce in it a change of state of definite amount. In the two cases before us, as in all others, it will be found that no effect can take place, i. e. neither that of the last physical movement upon the sensitive subject, nor that of the last mental excitation upon the first nerve-element which it acts upon, without a corresponding loss; here, too, the productive energy is consumed, in whole or in part, in bringing about the result. But never will it be possible to refer i and s, or w and f, physical and psychical processes, to a common standard; the members of each of the two groups may be compared with each other, but the unit of measurement in the one has nothing in common with that in the other. Granting, then, that here is compensation for physical energy by psychical or for psychical by physical, still in such a case as this there ceases to be any meaning in saying that one and the same *quantity* of action or work is maintained throughout; all that is open to us is, to speak of an equivalence of two activities, such that a specific amount $s\,\mu$ of the one, measured by the unit μ, corresponds to a specific amount $i\,m$ of the other, measured by the unit m. No one, however, can say whether these two activities are equal in quantity, nor which of them is the greater.

214. These considerations suggest certain others. In the first place, we may attempt to generalise from what has been discovered as regards these processes; in all cases, we may say, the simplest fact, the fact which first meets us in experience, is this relation of equivalence between two processes or forces. We do not first discover that two forces are equal and like[1], and therefore produce equal and like[1] effects; but what we do first is to observe that they balance each other, or, that under the like circumstances they produce the like motions. From this equivalence which has been found to obtain between them in certain special cases we infer their quantitative equality; at the same time we assume for the elements to which the forces in question belong, the qualitative identity which enables us to apply to them the same standard of measurement. I have no motive for entering here into all the indirect reasons and proofs which show in what a number of physical processes this assumption holds good; I would refer especially to the idea of homogeneous mass and of its conservation understood as it has been above. Confining myself to the metaphysical aspect of the question, I wish merely to point out that the principle of the conservation of Force, or, as I prefer now to say, the equivalence of different effects, does not impose on us any obligation to reduce all processes in Nature to the single class of material motion. So far as the principle applies to this latter class it is only a special instance of that more general correspondence, existing between heterogeneous things as well, which we express by this wider term of 'Equivalence.' Far, therefore, from being a monotonous transmission of the *same* unchanging process, it might be that the course of nature is for ever producing unlike by unlike; though the equivalence which the sovereign purpose of the world has established between these several disparate activities, would make the 'incidental view' practicable and fruitful,

[1] ['Gleich,' cp. note on § 19.]

according to which we reduce the concrete varieties of phenomena to mere quantitative values of a single, abstract, uniform principle, just as we determine the value of the most different things by the same artificial standard of money.

I know well how stubbornly this view will be contested. The very analogy we have used will appear defective; the prices of things, it will be said, only admit of comparison because the things all serve more or less to satisfy human wants which themselves admit of comparison; and this implies that the effects of the things on us, and ultimately therefore that which is the source of those effects, must be homogeneous. I on my side am not less stubborn in the defence of my own view. I do not deny that in so far as different things have like effects upon us, we are able by means of an artifice to ignore their specific differences for the time being, and to regard them as differing only quantitatively; but the things themselves are not therefore like because they admit of this justifiable fiction. Even if all qualitative differences are pronounced to be mere appearances, yet the difference of this appearance still remains, and belongs no less to the sum-total of reality; the utmost, therefore, that we can do will be to exhibit the external world as a mechanism of homogeneous parts which produces in us these appearances; but by no process of Mathematics or Mechanics would it be possible to deduce analytically concrete magnitudes from abstract ones, or magnitudes of different denomination from magnitudes of the same denomination. The process of the world is no mere combination of identical elements, but a synthesis of elements differing in quality and only connected by unity of plan.

215. But are we really correct in what we have laid down with regard to physical and psychical processes? Is it true that in this case also, the activity which occasions the result must necessarily be sacrificed in the process? Long before the principle of the Conservation of Force had excited its present interest, I had pointed to this conclusion; but it is not self-evident except upon the assumption which we adopted above, viz. that isolated elements can only be influenced by one another if they are capable of acting upon one another, and that no one element will adapt itself to another without requiring compensation for its amenability. But, it may be said, if all the elements, a and b, must be regarded as moments of the one M with no independence of their own, why should not the change of a into a suffice to give the signal, which is simply followed by the change of b into β, according to the theory of Occasionalism? Why should any special effort be required in order to bring about an affinity between the elements which already exists? Still it is clear that if what this theory demands is conceded it cannot apply exclusively to the interaction of physical and psychical processes as an exceptional case. The same consideration would apply also to all that takes place between the elements of the external world. Even the atoms would find in M a constant bond of union, and what was experienced by one atom would be the simultaneous signal for changes in another, which would follow like premisses from their conclusion, without involving any self-sacrifice on the part of the first. If, however, we find that this sacrifice does as a matter of fact take place, as it certainly does in the external world, though it can scarcely be proved by experience in the case of physical and psychical processes, all that remains to us is to suppose that this fact too, is a constituent element in the purpose which finds or ought to find expression in the real world; at the same time, we must not represent it as a condition imposed by some inscrutable necessity, without which the world as it is would not be possible. My only object in making this remark was to repeat, that if all conditions continued to exist simultaneously with their consequences (which is what would follow from the principles of Occasionalism), the world would appear again as a merely systematic whole, from which all change was absent. If, however, Becoming, the alternation between Being and not Being, is the very characteristic of the real world, it appears to me that the absorption of the cause in the effect is quite as necessary to that world as persistence is necessary to the conception of motion. For those signals which we spoke of could themselves have no signals for their occurrence except in the succession of effects; they would be produced by one set of effects, they must disappear again in producing another.

216. Amongst the general habits described as characteristic of the course of Nature, it is common to hear Principles of *Parsimony* mentioned. The conception is a very vague one, and even in the principle of least action the way in which it has been formulated is not without ambiguity. What it signifies is only clear in cases where there is some end in view which admits of being equally realised by different means, each however involving a different amount of expenditure. But the standard by which this amount is estimated is still dependent on circumstances, which make in one case the saving of Time, in another that of distance, in another that of material, the more important, or cause us to prefer an habitual method to the trouble of learning a new one. In order, therefore, to settle with any certainty the question as to the procedure which involves the least expenditure of means, a statement of the direction in which economy is most valuable must be included in the original definition of the end.

This alone is enough to show what ambiguities are likely to be involved when this conception is transferred to the operations of Nature. Assuming that Nature follows certain ends, we do not know what these are, nor can we determine what direction her parsimony must take. The one thing which we should perhaps assert would be this, that nature is not sparing in matter or in force, in Time, in distance, or in velocity, all of which cost her nothing, but that she is sparing in principles. It is this kind of parsimony which we do in fact believe to exist in Nature, especially in the organic world; by variations of a few original types, by countless modifications of a single organ the variety of organic beings, we believe, is produced, and their different wants supplied. Here Nature seems to us, if it may be permitted to our short-sighted wisdom to say so, to be wasteful of material and Time, and to reach many of her ends by long circuitous routes which it would have been possible, by departing from her habitual and typical course, to have shortened. These ideas do not hold good of mechanics, since mechanical laws apply, not to any particular type of effect, but to any and every type. We know that, within certain limits, the various elements in a mechanical effect are convertible; thus increase of velocity may make up for decrease of mass, and increase of Time for decrease of force. There cannot therefore be an economy in all elements at once for the attainment of a given end e; we must look for the least expenditure in that combination of all the different elements which amounts to less than any other combination equally possible under the circumstances.

But this gives rise to a fresh ambiguity. If we look at the matter fairly, it appears that e, which we just now described as the end or aim, is nothing more than the particular occurrence e, and it need not be said that the modes of activity which led to this result must have been exactly adequate to produce it. But, under the special circumstances in the given case, the modes of activity were at the same time the only possible ones which could give rise to e. For in order to follow a given path, it is not enough that it presents no obstacles, there must also be a positive impulse to follow it. It is therefore quite idle to excogitate different methods by which, theoretically, the end e might have been arrived at; that would require that he should analyse precisely the starting-point A from which the effect is supposed to proceed, and then, after considering all the several possibilities contained in A, that we should be able to determine that in this particular case the other methods were still equally possible. But this we shall never succeed in doing, for it involves a contradiction; it is true that the other methods may be, even in this particular case, all equally free from impediment, but there could not be positive inducements to follow them all equally; otherwise what would eventually take place would be, not e, but E, the resultant of all these different inducements. If therefore we find on comparison that the method m by which the result e is actually reached, is the shortest of many conceivable methods, what makes the possibility actual reality is not that this method has been chosen out of many others equally possible; rather we should say that m was in this case the only possible method, because any other direct method M, which might have led to the same result, lacked the conditions for carrying them into effect; in a different case, where these conditions were present, the result E would be different and the shortest way to it would be M. We must not therefore speak of parsimony in the sense of an act of choice, the exercise of which is merely a peculiar habit, not a causal necessity, of nature. The utmost that we could venture to assert is, that the Laws of Nature are so devised that the shortest way to any given result is in every case a necessary result of the laws themselves.

Yet even this statement would be no better than ambiguous. For the new truth which it seems to contain, and which makes it appear more self-evident than the preceding one, is similarly dependent on our arbitrary determination to regard as an end what is really only a result. It is true that according to the known law of reflexion a ray of light transmitted from the point a and reflected by the surface S, takes the shortest way to a point b which lies in the line of its reflexion, or again that according to the known law of refraction, if refracted by an intervening body, it takes the shortest way to a point b in the line of its exit from the refracting medium. But by whose command did the ray proceed from a precisely towards this point b and no other? That it arrives at this point is not to be wondered at, since it lies in the line of direction which the laws above mentioned prescribe to light; but for this very reason the ray is not transmitted to any of the other innumerable points c, which lie outside that direction, and which might yet deserve to be illuminated no less than b. If we conceive the attainment of the point b as a sort of end which in some way or other reacts upon the means to its attainment, the shortest way would have been for the ray at once to change its direction at a and traverse the straight line $a\,b$; this, however, was forbidden by the general laws to which it is subject, and the ray was compelled to follow a course not absolutely the shortest, but only the shortest conditionally upon the necessity of its reflexion. If, again, by an equally arbitrary assumption, we suppose a point c as that which has to be illuminated, those same laws of reflexion now appear in the light of hindrances which do not allow of the attainment of the end except by a longer way, not perhaps until the ray has been several times reflected upon many different surfaces. Hence, the only thing quite certain is this. In passing from any fully determined point A to the consequence E which flows from it, Nature makes no circuits to which she is not compelled but always takes the way which under the given conditions is the only possible but therefore also the necessary one. The parsimony of Nature consists in the fact that groundless prodigality is a mechanical impossibility.

Something more, however, remains. We can conceive laws of reflexion, e.g. which would require that each of the points on which a ray of light is to touch, though lying in the line of its projection, should yet be reached by a longer way than that by which they are reached as a matter of fact. That reflexion, once assuming its necessity, takes place according to the known law of nature in the shortest possible geometrical line, this and other like considerations may confirm the opinion above expressed, that the concrete laws of Nature are so constituted that it is a necessary characteristic of their operation to effect their results at the smallest cost. It will not, however, be doubted that the law of reflexion in question is itself a mechanically necessary consequence of the motion of light, not a codicil subsequently imposed upon that motion by Nature from free choice and preference for parsimony. All that we come to finally, therefore, is the quite general conclusion, which is also perfectly obvious, that the order of Nature does not rest on a disconnected heap of isolated ordinances. There is contained in the fundamental properties of reality, taken together with the necessary truths of Mathematics, a wonderful rationality which at countless different points gives the impression of an elaborately concerted plan and fixed aims. That even the most axiomatic principles serve a purpose, is due not to any property implanted in them, as in some strange soil, *after* they have come into being, but rather in these axiomatic principles themselves there is a deep and peculiar adaptation to purpose, which might well furnish an attractive subject for further enquiry.

CHAPTER VIII.

The forms of the Course of Nature.

217. I GAVE to this second book the name 'Cosmology,' intending to show that it would be devoted to the consideration only of those general forms and modes of behaviour, which enable us to represent to ourselves how manifold phenomena are connected together so as to form an ordered universe; it remained for the facts themselves to determine with which amongst the various possible formations the outlines thus sketched should be filled in, and these facts which are what constitute reality in the full sense, it was proposed, therefore, to leave to Natural Philosophy. Yet after all, how easy it is to invent well-founded titles for sciences of the future. If only it were as easy to discover the facts which would fill up their framework! But indeed we have not been able to establish much, even as regards those general tendencies of Nature, in spite of their seeming to be so near to the region of necessary truth. We found that they too were really dependent on the plan which is working itself out in the world. Still less shall we be able to show as long as we are in ignorance of that plan, that concrete processes and products, which can depend on nothing but it, are elements and stages in a systematic development. Such a hope was once entertained by Idealism; light and weight, magnetism and electricity, chemical processes and organic life were all made to appear as necessary phases in the evolution of the Absolute, the innermost motive of whose working was supposed to be known; not only so, but bold attempts were made to represent the varieties of plants and animals as following each other in a regular succession, and where a link was missing, to deduce it from the presupposed order of development, explaining the previous oversight of it as an accident. I see no reason for repeating the criticism that history has passed upon these attempts. It was a delusion to suppose that the forms of reality, while still inaccessible to observation, could be *deduced from* a single fundamental principle: all that could be done with such a principle was to *reduce to* it the material already given by experience, with its attendant residuum of peculiarity which cannot be explained but must be simply accepted as a fact. It did not of course follow that the interpretation of given facts which these theories had to offer were wrong throughout, and they gave rise to many fruitful suggestions which subsequent science has thankfully followed, though they had to be put in a new light before it could utilise them. At the same time, there is one direction in which even the scientific views now prevalent require to be on their guard against the continuance of a similar illusion.

The later exponents of those Idealist doctrines lived, like ourselves, under the influence of the cosmographical views which recent scientific enquiry had developed; far from participating in the fanatic notions of antiquity, according to which the earth was the centre of the Universe, and all things besides were merely subsidiary to it, they admitted the Copernican discoveries, and realised that they and all the exercise of their observation were fixed at an eccentric point in the small planetary system. Yet in spite of this they persuaded themselves that the spiritual development of their absolute was confined to the shores of the Mediterranean, and that its plastic force in the physical world was exhausted in producing the forms of plants and animals, neither of which, as they knew, could exist except upon the earth's surface. Now it is certainly an idle and profitless task to attempt really to imagine what the forms of existence and life might have been, had the circumstances been wholly different; all such attempts result in mere clumsy reduplications of the forms of existence which experience presents to us. The just general conviction that Spiritual Life, the ultimate end of Nature, does not stand or fall with the earthly means which it uses for its realisation, cannot call to its aid any creative imagination capable of actually picturing another life of which we have had no experience. But, however mistaken may be the attempts which are made in this direction, the general conviction which inspires them will always remain valuable; supposing physical science to be justified in assuming that certain physical processes prevail without variation over the whole universe, it would still be premature to assert a universal uniformity, which excluded any idea of forces peculiar in character and unexampled on the earth. So much the less ground is there for placing the concrete forms of reality, which no man can number, on the same footing with conceptions which, under the head of cosmology, we endeavoured to form of the universal rules of action to which Nature conforms. The former, therefore, I leave to be dealt with by natural philosophy, and renounce the prevailing fashion of relieving the dryness of Metaphysical discussion by picturesque illustrations selected from the experimental sciences.

218. It might, however, be truly objected, that though it may be impossible to deduce the concrete forms of nature, the reduction of them to the universal laws mentioned above is just one of the duties of metaphysic. I admit this duty, and only regret that it is one which no one can fulfil, not at least to the extent which the objection would require. The two points in which we seemed to run most counter to the ordinary view are, firstly, that of the phenomenal character of Space, secondly, that of the inner activity of Things, to which, instead of to external changes of relation between fixed elements, we ascribe the origin of events. Now, I have not neglected to insist in general terms on the necessity of starting from these inner states in order to explain even the possibility of that causative force which external circumstances appear to exercise. A more minute investigation of them, however, seemed to be forbidden, by the admitted impossibility of knowing them; and this would be the same even if more use were made than has yet been done of the hypothesis that their nature is spiritual. But this practical inapplicability does not impair the value of an idea which we found to be necessary, and to which no objection can be found either in itself or in the facts of experience. With respect to the Phenomenality of Space, I have argued at equal length and with a minuteness which has probably seemed tedious, that the appearance both of Space itself and of the changes which take place in it, is to be referred to real events which do not take place in Space, and I reserve for the Psychology what remains to be said by way of supplement to this; but, in this case also, it seems to me quite unfair to require my view to be worked out in detail. Such a requisition, if it applied to the particular perceptions of every-day life, would be as extravagant as the demand not merely to see what takes place before us, but at the same time to know the physical causes which make all that we see present itself to sight just as it does; only that here what we should ask to see through would be not physical causes but the supersensuous relations which the elements assume in the universal plan, and to which their appearance in Space is due.

Perhaps, however, no more is required than that in the case of the various main groups of natural processes, the hypotheses which had been constructed to explain them on the supposition of the reality of Space, should now give place to others equally capable of explaining the facts, on the understanding that true being does not exist in Space. If this is what is meant, I think the demand will in the future certainly be complied with, but at present this is impossible, or, if approximately possible, is not to be regarded as a slight addition to what has been already done. In order to make such a translation of physics into metaphysics possible we should require first of all to have the whole text which is to be translated, incontrovertibly fixed and settled. Nothing can be further than this is from being the case at present. As things stand now, every hypothesis which is used in explanation of the several branches of natural phenomena, is compelled, in order not to ignore any peculiarities of the object in question, to assume a plurality of original facts, which, though they may not be mutually inconsistent, exist only side by side, and are not derivable the one from the other. Still more untrustworthy is our knowledge of the border-lands in which these various spheres of natural phenomena meet. What use then would it be to show—what would be a difficult task in itself—that these hypotheses can be replaced in all points, with equally fruitful results, by a view which substituted for the supposed objects and motions in Space, determinate supersensuous relations and excitations in the inner elements of true being? We should still have no other way of determining these internal states than that by which physics discovered the corresponding external ones: we should have to assume them as primary facts, which the phenomena in question required for their explanation. But Metaphysic, if once she set herself to this task, would have to do more than this; she must be in a position to show that all these necessarily assumed individual facts are at the same time the logical consequences of those inner states, and that the nature and character of true being justifies the attribution of those states to it. As long as this, which is again in fact a kind of deduction of reality, is impossible for us, there can be little good and small hope of reward in the attempt to reduce sensible facts to supersensible ones. Leaving therefore any such attempt for another occasion, I will merely add a few general observations on the relation of speculation to the ordinary methods of experimental science.

219. Man must make the best of what he has, and not decline valuable knowledge merely because it does not at once offer him the whole truth which he wishes to know. In every science there will always be a considerable gap between the most general points of view from which we should wish to regard the given objects, and the actual knowledge which we can possibly acquire about them; and this gap proves nothing either against the rightness of those ultimate points of view or against the value of the methods by which we succeed in investigating particular facts. We must beware of that doctrinairism, which will allow no conclusion to be valid, unless it is reached by the method of a logical parade-ground, reminding us of Molière's physician, who only demanded of his patient, 'qu'il mourût dans les formes.' In respect to applied Logic it must be granted that there is some truth in the cynical remark of the Emperor Vespasian. Every method is praiseworthy which leads to a sure result; even the most monstrous hypothesis, if it really enables us to connect the facts together and to explain their mutual dependence, is better than the neatest and trimmest theory, from which nothing follows. Holding these views, I can have no sympathy with the often repeated attempts of philosophers to show that the fundamental ideas of Physical Science are inadequate, disconnected, and frequently inconsistent. Without attempting to determine how much there is of justice or injustice in this indictment, I readily admit that it is in the main true; but I am not so much struck by these defects, as filled with sincere and unmixed admiration at the manifold variety of consistent and reliable results, which, with such imperfect means at her disposal, science has established by unwearied observation and by brilliancy of invention.

I hope and believe, also, that if science continues to work with the same conscientiousness, many truths, which now appear only in necessary juxtaposition, and many others which are seemingly opposed, will enter into a nearer and better relation, as different results of one and the same original process; in fact that, as at the end of a long and complicated reckoning, a simple total will be left over, which the philosophy of the future will be able to apply to the satisfaction of its own special wants. This much to be desired result, however, can only be obtained in the first instance by means of clearly outlined hypotheses, framed so as to meet the observed facts, and modified and transformed so as to keep pace with each fresh discovery: it matters not that the expression which our suppositions assume in this intermediate stage of discovery is imperfect in form; the wished for simplicity and clearness of statement can belong only to the finished result. No other method can be substituted for this; not that of Positivism, which bids us be content with general formulæ for the observed connexion of facts without introducing ideas about the inner connexion of things, advice which at first sight commends itself, but which is entirely fruitless in practice: not a lofty philosophic intuition which only a great poetic genius could delude men into regarding as an actual means to the discovery of truth; not any speculative deduction, which hears only part of the evidence before rushing to its conclusion. These leave us where we were: Moses may stand on the mountain of speculation and pray that the laws of thought may be faithfully observed; but facts can only be brought into subjection by what Joshua is doing in the valley. After this confession, my present object can only be to analyse those conceptions by the help of which philosophy distinguishes the wealth of natural processes into groups, seeing in each group either the operation of a specific principle, or a particular application of general principles, and regarding them at the same time as contributing in different ways to the realisation of the all-embracing plan of Nature.

220. The word *mechanism*, which has so many meanings, is used by modern schools of thought to describe sometimes a particular mode of action, sometimes a class of effects produced by this action: in either case, the mechanical aspect of Nature is spoken of in terms of marked disparagement, as compared with another and different aspect, to which it is deemed inferior. What the word means is more easily learned from the customary use of language than from the conflicting definitions of the schools. All modern nations speak of the mechanism of government, of taxation, of business of any kind. Evidently, what is signified by it is, the organization of means either with a view to realising a particular end, or to being prepared for carrying out different but kindred objects. We do not, however, speak of a mechanism of politics; we expect political ends to be effected by an art of statesmanship, and this we should blame, if we saw it working by mechanical rules. This distinction in the use of the term clearly expresses the limitation that the mechanical organization of means is only calculated for general conditions, common to a number of kindred problems, and meets the requirements in question by working according to general laws.

Now, it is impossible to conform to a law in a merely general way; every application of the law must give rise to a determinate result depending on a determinate condition, whereas the law in its general expression makes the dependence only general. It seems, therefore, up to a certain point to be part of the very essence and conception of a mechanism to take account of the differences in the particular instances to which it applies. In the first place, the laws themselves which it obeys require that its effects shall be proportionate to the given circumstances; next, the circumstances themselves, their peculiar nature, resistance, and reaction, modify the action and combination of the forces which it sets in motion—also according to fixed laws—and so enable it to produce the designed effect even under unforeseen conditions. The technical industry of the present day furnishes many examples of this self-regulation of machinery; but whatever advances it may make in manysidedness and delicacy, it never escapes the limitations which popular language, as we saw, imposes upon the capabilities of mechanism. It is the ingenuity of the inventor to which alone the handiness of the machine is due; it is his calculation, his comparison of the end with the means and the hindrances to its realisation, which has enabled him so to combine the forces of Nature, that they must now lead of themselves to the desired result according to universal laws of their own which are independent of him. His penetration may have enabled him to see disturbing causes in advance and to meet them by a combination of the means at his disposal so that the disturbances themselves liberate the reacting forces which are to compensate them; even disturbing causes which he has not foreseen may by good luck be neutralised by the internal adaptation and power of self-adjustment of a machine. But all these favourable results have their limits. If they occur, they are the necessary consequences according to universal law of the joint action of the machine and its circumstances; if they fail to occur, the machine is destroyed; the power of resisting the conditions has not been given it from without, by the genius of its inventor or by a lucky chance, and it is incapable of generating such a power of itself.

Here lies the difference of statesmanship and every other practical art from what is mechanical. Every art, following as it does ends which cannot be realised of themselves, is confined to the use of means which it cannot make but can only find; it cannot compel any one of these means to produce effects which are impossible or extraneous to its nature; it can only combine together the means at its disposal in such a way that it will be compelled by the universal laws of their action to produce necessarily and inevitably the desired result. Every higher form of activity, consequently, which we are inclined to assume in Nature, even the most perfectly unrestrained freedom must, if it would be operative in the world, take just that mechanical form which is supposed at first to be inconsistent with its nature. The only privilege that distinguishes it, is the power of varying according to its aims the combination of the several mechanical elements, and of taking first one and then another part of the mechanism for its base of operations, thus making each part yield its own results. But its capabilities come to an end as soon as its object is one which cannot be produced by any combination of mechanical operations, or as soon as it can no longer bring about that particular combination which would have the result in question.

221. As regards the special meaning attached to the term 'mechanism' in their explanation of natural phenomena, philosophers undoubtedly understood by it primarily a peculiar mode of activity, the range of which was still undetermined. But it was distinctly believed, at the same time, that there was a certain special class of natural products, which was subject to the single and undisputed sway of the mechanical principle. I cannot subscribe to either of these two theories, except with essential reservations. Mechanism could only be defined in the sense in which it is employed in current language. Always determined by the given circumstances and general laws which lie behind it, never by the nature of an end which lies before it, it was contrasted (I shall return to this contrast later) as a concatenation of blind and irrevocable forces with those organic activities which seemed to follow ends with a certain freedom though they were also liable to fail in their attainment. But even within the limits of what was called the inorganic world, mechanism was opposed and deemed inferior to chemism. While in the chemical sphere, owing to the elective affinities of the elements, the specific qualities of bodies were continually destroying old forms and properties and creating new ones, thus co-operating decisively in determining the course of events, mechanical action was depreciated as a mere external process, which never gives a hearing to the distinctive nature of things, deals with them all as mere commensurable mass-values, and therefore produces no other effects but various combinations, separations, movements, and arrangements of inwardly invariable matter.

But Philosophy ought never to have believed in the reality of a mode of activity which it regarded in this light. A man or an official might be reproached for executing general laws and regulations without regard to exceptional cases, which deserve special consideration and forbearance. Such action, which we blame as mechanical, only succeeds because the combined force of human society deprives the ill-treated exceptions of the power of resisting. But things are not hindered from defending themselves by any such considerations, nor can there be anything in nature to prevent them from asserting their special peculiarities in the production of each effect, to the precise extent to which, if we may speak of them as human beings, they have an interest in so doing. It will be objected, however, that it is not meant to conceive of this mechanical agency, after the analogy of the inflexible official, as an authority of nature imposing itself autocratically upon things from without; what is meant is merely a process which is indeed developed from the interaction of things themselves, but which derives its character from the very fact that the things have no interests of their own, that they have not reached the point of letting their individuality be seen and heard, but are content to behave as samples of homogeneous mass; so far as this indifference of things extends, so far does mechanism extend. But even when stated in this improved form, the doctrine is not tenable unless either a physical process can be pointed out which takes place without being in any way influenced by the distinctive idiosyncrasies of things, or it can be shown that results in the final form of which such influences though really operative seem to have vanished, are to be considered as preconceived elements in the plan of Nature. All attempts to establish the first case are from our point of view based on a wrong foundation. After having maintained that a change of outer relations is only possible as a consequence of mutual solicitations in the inner nature of things, we can only regard a mechanism which combines things in mutual action without taking account of this inner nature and its co-operation, as an abstraction of Science, not as a reality. Science, no doubt, has need of this abstraction. Whatever distinctive differences there may be between things, at any rate the contributions which they make to the production of a single event must admit of being expressed in values of comparable action. In order to be able to estimate their effects, we must refer the laws which govern them to certain ideally simple instances, zero values or *maxima*, of their effective differences, and then, after calculating our result upon this basis, subjoin such modifications as the concomitant conditions of the given case require.

It is in this way that we arrive at the indispensable conceptions of mechanics; the conception of a rigid immutable atom, from which every qualitative change is excluded; the conception of an absolutely fixed body, from which we have eliminated any alteration of form and all other effects of composition; at the principle, lastly, which may serve to express in the shortest form what we mean by mechanism, the principle that, if several forces act together upon the same object, no one of them has any effect on the tendency to action of the rest, but each continues to operate as if the rest were not present, and it is only these several and singly calculable effects which combine to form a resultant. Now none of these conceptions expresses anything which we can regard as occurring in actual fact, not even the principle last named. But supposing that this principle were not valid—and indeed the limits within which it holds good cannot be fixed *a priori*—supposing that the tendency to act of a force were altered by its relation to other forces working simultaneously, we should still require to make use of the principle, for we could not estimate the nature of the alteration, unless we first knew what the action would be unaltered; for even though it does not occur in its unaltered form, it would still help to condition the variation which does occur. So far, however, as the principle does hold good, it merely allows us to measure results when they take place, it does not tell us how they take place: it is not the case that the forces have been indifferent and taken no account of one another: the truth rather is that they, or the inner movement of things which correspond to them, *have* taken this account of each other, only it happened that the resolution at which they arrived in this particular case was to the effect that each should maintain its former tendency to act, just as in another case it might have been that this tendency should be changed. From this it appears that these very processes which, as far as the form of their result goes, exhibit all the characteristics of mechanism, are not produced mechanically in this sense at all, and the whole conception of *mechanism* as a distinct type of action, based on the mutual indifference of things, must be banished entirely from the philosophical view of Nature.

Nor does it receive more than a semblance of support from observation. Even in cases of impact, to which most of the so-called mechanical processes are reducible, there are produced along with the imparted translatory motion permanent or elastically neutralised changes in the form of the body impinged upon, besides inner vibrations which make themselves known as Sound or Heat. The number of these secondary effects, and the completeness with which the translatory motion is imparted, depends in every case on the inner interactions which hold together the ultimate elements of the bodies, depends, i.e. on forces which have their origin in the heart of things, and which differ from each other according as things themselves differ in quality. These inner effects we are accustomed, and for purposes of science obliged, to regard as secondary, and as disturbances of the theoretically perfect instance; but in taking account of them as corrections to be added to the result which strict rules would give us, we are really correcting our own abstract conception of a pure mechanism, which, as such, has no real existence in Nature.

222. As this is the case with regard to the first of the two alternatives[1] proposed, it remains that the Philosophy of Nature can only undertake the second. Looking only at the ultimate form in which processes result, it would be possible to arrange the facts of Nature in groups according as the qualitative nature of things, which is a constant factor in each process, was more or less apparent in the results. And this is naturally the course which Idealism would have followed, had it been consistent with itself. Its object being to point out phenomena in which as a series the ends of Nature were successively realised, it might have entirely disregarded the question how all these phenomena are produced, and have considered them solely from the point of view of their significance, when once in existence. All the misunderstandings which have arisen between Idealism and the Physical Sciences, have been occasioned by this error of confounding interpretations of the ideal significance of phenomena with explanations of the causes which have led to their existence. Imposing on ourselves, then, this restriction, we might seek, in the first place, for a department of processes where there seemed to be no trace at any point of the constant silent influence of the qualitative differences of things; or where, in case the elements producing the result were homogeneous, there was no sign of the perpetual return of the process into, and its reproduction out of, the inner nature of things. It would be in such a group of activities that we should have to look for the *semblance* of a perfect mechanism.

In the small events which every day pass before us in

[1] [The treatment of ‘Mechanism’ α as a mode of Action, β as a kind of Effect, v. Sect. 220 init.]

changing succession, in the motions which partly at our instance, partly owing to causes which remained unobserved, bodies communicate to each other—we do not find this mechanical action exemplified. In these cases, though varying in distinctness, those secondary effects are never wholly absent, in which the diversity of the co-operating elements manifests itself. We find what we are looking for only in the process of gravitation, or, more properly, in the revolutions in closed curves, which result from the attraction of the heavenly bodies and an original tangential motion. Attraction itself cannot be considered as an external appendage to the constituent elements of the planets: as these elements are different, the degree of attraction would have to vary to suit the nature of each part. But the different distribution in different planets of elements varying in the degrees of their reciprocal action, determines what we call the mass of the planets; and so after having included in the conception of this unchanging mass everything which related to the qualitative nature of the elements, we find ourselves able to calculate the subsequent motions of the heavenly bodies without assuming anything beyond their original velocities and directions, and the general law of the variation of force with distance; and without being obliged to recur again to the inner nature of the elements, though it is from this that the whole result springs. It was this great spectacle of the universe maintaining itself perpetually the same, that claimed the attention of Philosophy, which saw in it the first stage of the self-development of thought in Nature, the exhibition of the universal order, which remains undisturbed by any inner movements of the particular.

Next and in contrast to Gravitation or Matter, which was strangely identified with it, was placed Light, or rather (since a name was wanted which would include not only Light but also Sound) those undulatory processes, by means of which impulses diffuse themselves on all sides, without any considerable translatory motion. It was not altogether without reason that in these phenomena of Nature an analogy was found to Mind; for it is through them, no doubt, that things convey to each other their fluctuating inner experiences, each as it were reflecting itself in the other; so that a communication between them is established, similar to that which exists between the knowing subject and its object. It was owing to a misconception that speculative Philosophy refused to allow these processes to be classed under mechanism and treated mechanically. The equal diffusion of light compels us, no doubt, to explain the force with which each particle of ether communicates motion to the adjoining particle, as due to inner experiences arising from their constant and sympathetic relationship: but as it also leads us to assume that the ether consists of none but homogeneous elements, the further progress of this occurrence of transmission admits of being treated in precisely the same way as the motions of the heavenly bodies. It is only when these undulations come into contact with material bodies, i.e. when they are reflected, refracted, dispersed, that the quality of particular bodies makes itself felt in effects, which necessitate a number of new truths derived from experience and serving as starting-points for analytical deductions. I have no intention of discussing in this place the validity of those fruitful hypotheses, on the basis of which optics has raised her imposing edifice; nor do I wish to replace them by others. I wished merely to justify to some extent the older speculation in its view, that these phenomena exhibit a new, characteristic, and important form of Nature's activity, a form in which the influences of the specific qualities of things are not indeed quite neutralised, but do not appear to dominate the whole process: the general form, in fact, of a still inoperative affinity between diverse and changing elements.

223. A different impression was produced by the

phenomena of *electricity* and *chemistry*. Philosophy here encountered the doctrine of the two electric fluids, which had already been fully developed by Physics, and was thus confirmed in regarding this as the first case in which the qualitative opposition of things appears as really determining the course of events. The further development of this branch of Physics will certainly not be able to dispense with the special presuppositions, which have been framed in consequence of this view. There seems at any rate no prospect at present of explaining that peculiar notion of absorption or neutralisation, in which forces, once in full activity, evanesce without leaving any trace of themselves, as due to a mere opposition of motions, similar to the absorption of Light by interference. Such an explanation would still leave the question, what is the principle on which these conflicting motions are distributed amongst the bodies, from which the electric appearances are elicited? And this question could hardly be answered without reinstating—though perhaps in a different form and connexion—the conception of a polar opposition of a qualitative kind. But this also does not concern us here: it is sufficient that electric phenomena, whatever may be their origin, in the form of their manifestation express precisely this idea of an opposition inherent in the nature of things.

This influence of the specific nature of agents was believed to be much more distinctly apparent in the case of *chemical* phenomena, which had likewise been already connected by Physics with electricity. The idea that in chemical as opposed to so-called mechanical action, the individual nature of things for the first time awoke, co-operated, and underwent inner transformations, was not, strictly speaking, supported by observation. Striking changes were frequently seen to take place in the sensible qualities of things, in consequence of mere changes in their composition. Hence it was possible to suppose that other changes, the origin of which was not similarly open to experimental proof, might also be due to differences not directly perceptible in the arrangement of the ultimate particles and their resulting interactions. But the chemical process, according to that view of it which was favoured by Philosophy, was that, out of a and b, a third new and simple product c resulted, in which both a and b are merged, though by reversing the process, they may again be produced out of it. This view, which obviously implies a constant and complete interpenetration of the active chemical elements, expressed the idea of which the phenomena of chemism furnished sensible illustration. As a Physical theory it remained barren, because it failed to explain how similar combinations of elements can give rise to permanently different products, as also because it left out of account the manifold analogies between combinations of essentially distinct elements.

To this view, there succeeded an exclusively atomic conception of chemistry. The elements a and b were supposed to subsist unchanged in the result c, and the properties above-mentioned were accounted for by the different positions which the various samples of a and b may assume in the product c of their combination. I do not understand why the pictures which we often see of the structure of such chemical combinations should be accompanied by the warning that they are not to be understood literally. If they are only symbols, they at once lead to a metaphysical view, according to which we should speak, not of positions in Space, but of intelligible relations of varying intensity between the actions of the absolute, which present themselves to us singly as chemical elements. If we shrink from making use of these certainly impracticable notions, of which I have spoken previously, and make up our minds to follow the ordinary view of the reality of Space, it seems to follow that either these graphic representations must be understood quite literally, or that they have no intelligible meaning at all. It is not, however, my purpose to describe the consequences which the atomic view of chemistry has had in general, and especially of late the hypothesis of Avogadro, in itself an entirely improbable one. I would only call attention to the fact that after all that can be said, our knowledge is limited on the one hand to the elements which enter into composition, on the other to the actual and probable typical forms which the composition finally assumes; the process by which the combination takes place, i.e. the true chemical process, still escapes us. Our conceptions of it cannot be made to fit with the rest of our mechanical notions, unless we admit as new data both the original difference between the elements, not reducible to physical modifications of a common matter, and the special elective affinities of these elements, which determine their general capacities of combination and the proportions in which they will permanently combine.

Even then one phenomenon, still remains dark, that which gave to chemistry its old name 'Scheidekunst' (art of division), the analysis of the combinations. Let us suppose that between all the elements, $a\ b\ c\ \ldots\ z$, the only affinity that exists is that of attraction in varying degrees of intensity. In that case if there is no new condition introduced, any reciprocal action between the two pairs $a\ b$ and $c\ d$ can only lead to their amalgamation $a\ b\ c\ d$, never to their fresh distribution into $a\ c$ and $b\ d$. And even if the affinities between a and c, b and d, be ever so much closer than those between a and b, c and d, there cannot be any separation of the elements: the most that can happen is this, that an external force, *if* it were brought to bear upon the whole combination $a\ b\ c\ d$—which would be the necessary result of mere forces of attraction—would detach a from b or c from d more easily than a from c, or b from a. Any repulsion, therefore, must come from elsewhere than the results of attraction; and as there is no evidence of direct repulsion between the single elements it can only be looked for in the circumstances which accompany the chemical process, or, as is probable, actually constitute it. These may consist in motions which disconnect the elements, or in the affinity of the elements to the different electricities, the polar antagonism of which may require them to move in these particular ways.

But however that may be, my only purpose was to show that Philosophy was right in ascribing to the qualitative differences of things a decisive influence in the sphere of chemistry, wrong in denying any such influence in that of mechanics: and that therefore though the opposition between these processes of nature is not without some reason in it, it is practically impossible to draw a sharp line of distinction between them, such as would separate their spheres, and assign to them two different principles of action.

224. But all this has now scarcely more than a historical interest; the relation of forces to *organic* activities is still the subject of conflicting opinions. In an essay on 'Life and Vital Energy,' which forms the introduction to Rudolph Wagner's Hand-Dictionary of Physiology, I defended, six-and-thirty years ago, the claim of the mechanical view to a place in the science of Physiology, a claim which was at that time still much disputed. Scientific taste has now to some extent changed; at present, not merely all the practical investigations of Physiology, but to a great extent also the formulation of its theories are dominated by the mechanical spirit; those who are opposed to it, repeat the old objections, for the most part in the old form. If, though weary of going back to these matters, I proceed now to recapitulate shortly the conclusions which were developed in the above-mentioned essay, and subsequently in the 'General Physiology of Corporeal Life' (Leipsic, 1851), it is chiefly for the sake of a remark which has been often overlooked, at the end of the essay, and which is to the effect that it necessarily contained only the *one* half of the principles which a complete biological theory implied. The other half would have touched on the question, how the mechanical treatment of vital phenomena, necessitated by the facts, harmonises with those requirements of an opposite kind, which the primary instincts of philosophy will never cease to make, as in times past. For this dispute is, in fact, an old one. I should have been able to go back to Aristotle, whose 'substantial forms' extended the dominion of the activity of Thought far beyond living things, to which in the modern controversy it is confined, while already in antiquity the Aristotelian view was elaborately opposed by the Epicurean physics, which denied the activity of thought no less unrestrictedly. The question did not, however, become one of pressing importance, until, with the development of modern science, a definite formulation had been given to the group of ideas, the application of which to explain life meets with so much opposition. Putting aside the more ethical, æsthetic, and religious grounds for this aversion, which it is not necessary here to examine, the theoretical motive which has prompted it has always been the same. The scanty knowledge which we possess of the formative influences active throughout the rest of nature, did not seem sufficient to explain the complex and yet fixed forms of organic life; their germs at any rate, it was thought, must have an independent origin, even if in their subsequent development they were subject to the Universal Laws of Nature. But further, the peculiar phenomena of growth, nutrition, and propagation, the general fact of the interdependence of continuously active functions, and that of self-preservation in presence of repeated disturbances, all this seemed to demand the continued presence and operation of that higher principle, to which had been attributed at first only the initial formation of the germ. Finally, the undefined but overpowering general impression of pervading adaptation, witnessed to the presence of an end which guided organic nature, rather than to a past which blindly compelled it. The conception of a *vital force* was the first form in which these ideas were united.

225. As long, however, as this expression was merely thrown out in a general way, it could not serve to solve the difficulty, but only to indicate its existence. It was not allowable to follow the example of Treviranus, and explain everything from the byssus to the palm, from the infusorium to the monster of the sea, as living by Vital Force: the difference between the palm and the byssus had also to be taken account of; every species of living things required its own special vital force, and every individual of the species needed its own share or its particular sample of the force. The general name Vital Force indicated, therefore, merely a formal characteristic, which could attach to many different real principles yet to be discovered. It was besides an improper use to make of the term *force*, which had been applied by Physics in quite a different sense; the appropriate word was *impulse* (Trieb). For when the general characteristic in question had to be described, the contrast was obvious. Every physical force always produces under the same conditions the same effects, under different conditions, different effects; it is always conditioned by a general law, irrespectively of the ensuing result; everything that under given circumstances the force can effect, it must necessarily effect, nor can any part of the effect be kept back, nor any addition be made to it which would not have been inevitable under the existing circumstances. To Impulse, on the other hand, we ascribe the power of changing its manner of operation, not indeed without regard to existing circumstances, but with regard at the same time to a result which does not yet exist; a power of leaving undone much that it might do, and of beginning something new instead which it is not bound by the given conditions to do at all. It had to be admitted, however, that the vital impulse never produces anything in a vacuum, but only works with the materials supplied to it by nature; and thus arose the ordinary view of vital force as a power, which, though dependent in a general sense upon material conditions, is superior to the physical and chemical laws of matter, and gives rise to phenomena which those laws will not explain.

226. I must take permission to refer to the above-mentioned essay for many details, which here I can only lightly touch on, but could not altogether omit without leaving constantly recurring fallacies only half-refuted. We are continually being told that no application of the improved means which we now have at our command will enable us to manufacture artificially a product which even remotely resembles a living organism. The fact must simply be granted. Neither cellulose nor albumen, nor any other of the tissue-forming substances of organic bodies can be produced by chemical art, although the distinction between the ternary and quaternary combinations of organic life and the binary combinations of inorganic nature, which was once so much insisted on, has long since lost its meaning: nor are we any longer under the delusion that these combinations last only so long as the vital force lasts, a delusion which any thoughtful student might have been disabused of from the first, if he had only thought of the wood of the table, at which he was writing, or of the pens and paper. Still, it is true that in none of our artificial productions is there any such connected series of chemical transformations, form-modifications and functions as could be compared with the growth, nourishment, and propagation of an organic Being: even the recently observed formation of cells out of inorganic substances, though worthy of all consideration, is not likely to prove the starting-point for new discoveries in this direction. But all that this proves is that in the present course of Nature, Life is a system of processes self-maintaining and self-propagating, and that outside its sphere there is no combination of materials, such as would make the development of such phenomena possible. Nothing is thus decided as to the conditions under which this play of forces is sustained *after* it has begun, and yet

these must first be known before it can be determined what requirements a theory as to the first origin of Life has to meet. But neither the question concerning the origin of the whole organic world, nor the consideration whether in the future it may not be possible to add to it by artificial means, must be allowed to confuse the discussion here. The only point to be considered is, whether the vital force which organic beings as a matter of fact exercise in developing themselves and resisting external injury, requires us to assume a principle of action, which is strange to the inorganic world; and whether that other vital force, which such a principle of action is assumed to be, is conceivable in itself, and adequate to explain the given facts?

227. We shall require, in the first place, for the sake of clearness, to be definitely informed as to the nature of the subject, to which the activities included under the name of vital force are supposed to belong. There has been no lack of theories which endeavoured to meet this question fairly. Some have spoken of a universal substance of Life, which they found either in a ponderable matter, or in electricity, or some other unknown member of the more refined family of ether. Others regarded the soul as the master-builder and controller of the body, assuming at the same time that plants had souls, which was, to say the least, not a fact of observation. I will only mention briefly the common defect in all these theories. It is impossible to deduce difference from a single homogeneous principle, unless we have a group of minor premisses to show why the one principle should necessarily develop a at one point, b or c at another. As has already been said, we should always have to assume as many different material bases of life as there are different kinds of living things; or else it would have to be shown to what subsequently arising causes it was due that such different forms as an oak tree and a whale could be produced out of the one substance. In the latter case the development of Life would be at once brought again under the general conception of a mechanism. For mechanism in the widest sense of the term may be said to include every case in which effects are produced by the reciprocal action of different elements, of whatever kind, working in accordance with universal Laws; and such conformity to law would have to be assumed by all these theories; they could never leave it open to doubt that, under the influence of an accessory condition a, the single principle of life would take shape in the product a rather than in b.

But metaphysic has no interest in maintaining the claims of the mechanical principle, except in this very general sense; nor, on the other hand, will physics be so narrow-minded as to insist that it is precisely from these materials and forces which we now know, and according to the exact analogy of inorganic processes, that we are to conceive of the phenomena of organic Life. 'All that physics claims, is, that whatever kinds of matter, force, or energy remain yet to be discovered, must all fall within the compass of her investigations, must all be connected together according to Universal Laws. Further, however, experience did not at all show that the choice between these accessory conditions was so unrestricted. It is not the case that every organic kind requires as the basis of its existence peculiar kinds of matter which it places at the disposal of the one vital force. The most different products of Nature are all constructed from the same storehouse of material elements, which are found on the surface of the earth. Hence, however peculiar the principle of Life may be in itself, it can never have been free from interaction with that same matter which we know to be also controlled by physical laws of its own. The principle might issue what commands it pleased, but could only carry them out (supposing the materials in question not to obey them spontaneously) by exerting those forces to which the matter is naturally amenable. We know that in all cases the contribution which is made by the several co-operating factors, to a result in the final form, may be of the most different amounts. Thus it *may* be that the form which Life is to assume in any given case is already traced by anticipation in some specific kind of substance; but the actual existence of this life is always the result of mechanical causes, in which the original substance would be only *prima inter pares*, contributing just so much to the result as can arise according to general laws from its coming into contact with the other factors. But that that is actually the case, at any rate in the sense that there are certain kinds of matter specially privileged in this respect, could not in any way be proved; the natural conclusion which the facts suggest is, that the phenomena of Life arise out of a special *combination* of material elements, no one of which has any claim to be called exclusively, or, in the degree suggested above, pre-eminently, the principle of life. The very fact which has been taken to imply a special vital principle, the fact that Life is only maintained by successive self-propagation, ought rather to lead to the conclusion that the germ of its development can only be found in a certain peculiar combination of material elements, which maintains and reproduces itself in unbroken continuity. It is, therefore, quite a matter of indifference, whether we shall ever succeed in giving a name to the general form, or in exhibiting in detail the development, of such a material combination in which life is implicit; the point is, that the supposition of a single Real principle of Life is both impossible in itself and quite barren of results, whilst on the other hand, the only thing which the mechanical view leaves unexplained is the ultimate origin of Life. I will reserve what I have to say on the Soul till later; as it neither creates the body out of nothing, nor out of itself, it can have no special dignity as regards the construction of the body (whatever other dignities it may have) except that of being *prima inter pares;* it must work jointly with the material elements which are supplied to it. The conception of mechanical action, however, is wide enough to include that of a co-operation, according to universal laws, between spiritual activities and conditions of matter.

228. It is the way of mankind to meet a theory not by direct refutation, but by expressing general dislike and pointing out the defects in the working out of it, and to magnify striking though unessential differences until they seem to be impassable gulfs. I should certainly never of my own motion speak of the living body as a machine, thus nullifying the distinction between the poverty of even our most ingenious inventions and the mighty works of Nature; but those who are so morbidly anxious to leave out of account in their consideration of life all those operations which they can stigmatise as mechanical, need to be reminded that the living body and not inorganic Nature furnishes the models of the simple machines, which our art has imitated; the pattern of pincers is to be found only in the jaws of animals; that of the lever in their limbs which are capable of movement. Nowhere else are there instances of motions produced in articular surfaces by cords such as the muscles are, and of their guidance by ligaments in definite directions: it is the living body alone which utilises the production of a vacuum and the consequent inhalation of atmospheric fluids, the pressure of containing walls[1] upon their contents, and the valves which prescribe the direction of the resulting motion. How little does all this resemble that mysterious power of immediate agency which is most eagerly claimed for the vital force!

The exaggerated pictures of the superiority of living machines to artificial ones do not rest on any better foundation. The comparison of an organism to a self-winding clock altogether ignores the drooping plant which can find no substitute for water, if water will not come to it, and the hungry animal which is indeed able to seek its own food, but yet dies of want if none is found. Irritability, or the

[1] [Of the heart and blood vessels.]

power of responding to impressions, is said to be a distinguishing characteristic of organisms; when a given stimulus is applied to them, they are supposed to react in ways which are not explicable from the nature of the stimulus; at the same time, it has been assumed that in mechanical action the cause and effect are precisely equal and similar, though not even in the simple communication of motion is this really the case, while organic life has been contrasted with it on the ground of a supposed peculiarity which is in fact the universal form of all causative activity. For it is never the case that an impression is received by an element ready made, merely to be passed on in the same form; each element always modifies by its own nature the effect of the impulse experienced. In a connected system of elements, the effects which will follow a stimulus will be more various and striking in proportion as the intermediate mechanism is more complex, which conducts the impression from point to point and changes it in the process. The same must be said of the power of recovery from injury which is supposed to belong peculiarly to organisms, and to prove clearly a continuous adaptivity superior to anything mechanical. But if it were really the case that this force of resistance raised organic Beings out of the sphere of physical and chemical necessity, why was it ever limited? If once it had become independent of mechanical influences there was no task which it need fail in accomplishing. But the numberless cases of incurable disease indicate plainly enough its limits. No doubt, when once its combinations of elements and forces have been fully matured the body is so well furnished for its purpose that even considerable changes in its environment produce reactions in it which avert or remove the disturbing influences which threaten or have begun to act upon it. But as in every mechanical product, there are limits to this power of self-preservation. There is no such power, where the body has not been blest at starting with these particular provisions, nor do we ever see the want supplied by the subsequent creation of fresh means; we much more often see the means already at its disposal forced into a reaction, which under the special conditions of the moment can only lead to further dissolution.

229. I shall not continue this polemic further, having devoted sufficient attention to it before. I simply adhere now to the decision which I then expressed. In order to explain the connexion of vital phenomena, a mechanical method of treatment is absolutely necessary; Life must be derived, not from some peculiar principle of action, but from a peculiar mode of utilising the principles which govern the whole Physical world. From this point of view, an organic body will appear as a systematic combination of elements, which, precisely because they are arranged together in this form, will be able by conforming to fixed laws in their reciprocal action, and by the help of external nature, to pass through successive stages of development, and within certain limits to preserve the regularity of its course against chance disturbances. This makes me the more sorry that Physiologists should regard this view, which embodies the necessary regulative principle of all their investigations, as being also the last word upon the subject, and should exclude every idea which is not required for their immediate purposes, from all share in the formation of their ultimate conclusions. But they will never remove from the mind of any unprejudiced person the overwhelming impression that the forms of organic life serve an end; nor will men ever be persuaded that this marvellous fact does not call for explanation by a special cause. I know full well that as a thesis it may be maintained that every result which presupposes mechanical agency presupposes nothing more than this. Nor is this new; long ago Lucretius declared that animals were not provided with knees in order to walk, but that it was because the blind course of things had formed knees, that they were able to walk. It is easy to say this, and it may be that it sounds particularly well when expressed in Latin verse; but it is impossible to believe it; there is no more tedious product of narrow caprice than such philosophy of the schools. Yet it is unfortunately true that the conviction of a higher power working for an end, and shaping life with a view to it, has too often intruded itself rashly and confusingly into the treatment of special questions; and this explains the unwillingness of conscientious enquirers to recognise what to them must seem a barren hypothesis. It cannot, however, be ignored that many of our contemporaries are animated by a profound hatred of everything that goes by the name of Spirit, and that, if a principle were submitted to them which seemed to bear traces of this, even though it was not opposed to any postulate of science, they would, none the less, turn away from it in indignation to enjoy their feast of ashes, and delighted to feel that they were products of a thoroughly blind and irrational necessity. Such self-confidence it is impossible to reason with; we can only consider the difficulties which stand in the way of the acceptance of the opposite view.

230. We must not stop short at those general accounts of the matter, which merely represent a higher power in any indefinable relation of superiority to mechanical laws without making the obedience of those laws intelligible; in speaking of this, as of all other forms of rational activity directed to an end, the first thing to do is to give a name to the subject from which the action is supposed to proceed. Now we certainly cannot speak of 'ends' with any clearness, except as existing in a living and willing mind, in the form of ideas of something to be realised in the future. Hence it was natural to look for this highest wisdom in God; and not less natural was the desire to bring again into an intelligible relation the unlimited freedom of action involved in the conception of the divine essence, and the fixed course of Nature which seems to bear no traces of that freedom. Thus arises the theory upon which sooner or later Philosophy ventures, the theory that the world was created by God and then left to itself, and that it now pursues its course simply according to the unchangeable laws originally impressed upon it. I will not urge the objection that this view provides only a limited satisfaction to our feelings; in its scientific aspect it is unintelligible to me. I do not understand what is meant by the picture of God withdrawing from the world that He has created, and leaving it to follow its own course. That is intelligible in a human artificer, who leaves his work when it is finished and trusts for its maintenance to Universal Laws of Nature, laws which he did not make himself, and which not he, but another for him, maintains in operation. But in the case of God I cannot conceive what this cunningly-contrived creation of a self-sustaining order of Nature could be; nor do I see what distinction there can be between this view and the view that God at each moment wills the same order, and preserves it by this very identity of will. The immanence of God in the course of Nature could not, therefore, be escaped from by this theory; if Nature follows mechanical laws, it is the Divine action itself, which, as we are accustomed to say, *obeys* those laws, but which really at each moment creates them. For they could not have existed prior to God as a code to which He accommodated Himself; they can only be the expression to us of the mode in which He works.

This unavoidable conclusion will not be at once nor willingly admitted: however much the world may be primarily dependent on God, the desire will be felt, that it should contain secondary centres of intelligent activity as well, not entirely determined in their effects by the mechanical system of things, but themselves supplying to that system new motives for developed activity. It was this wish which was expressed by Stahl's theory of the soul, when he spoke of it as moulding the body to its own ends. This theory was in so far correct that it conceived of the soul as a living and real Being, capable of acting and being acted upon with effect: but it missed its mark, because the formation of the body, in its most essential and irreversible features, is concluded at a time when the soul may perhaps have some dream of its future aim, but certainly cannot as yet have knowledge enough of the external world to be able to adapt the body to the conditions which life in that world imposes. Thus the advantages which the soul might seem to derive from its consciousness and power of taking thought for the proper development of the organism, are all lost; and the only power of adaptation which it remains to ascribe to it is an unconscious one. Though this conception is very frequently misapplied, it does not seem impossible to attach to it a definite meaning. All along, we have considered things as distinguished from each other by manifold differences: and although we cannot fully realise to ourselves what constitutes the essential character of any single thing, there is nothing to prevent us from assuming a certain difference of rank between them, such that when two things were subjected to the same external conditions, the one would manifest its nature in simple and uniform reactions, the other in complex and multiform ones; and these latter reactions might be such that each gave rise to some entirely new capacity in the thing, or that they all united to form a single development directed to a definite end. In that case, we shall possess in the soul a real principle at once active in the pursuit of ends and yet unconscious, such as would not be at variance with mechanical laws; for none of the possibilities that lie latent in the soul would be realised, except through stimuli acting upon it according to fixed laws, and eliciting its development step by step.

Clearly, however, in this case, the soul will no longer imply anything peculiar or characteristic; once get rid of consciousness, and it becomes a mere element of reality like other elements; and that superiority of nature, which made it so pregnant a centre of manifold forms of life, might equally well be ascribed to any other element (making allowance for differences of degree) even though it possessed none of the characteristic properties of the soul. The question as to the true origin of the soul, leads to the same conclusion. If it is conceived as eternally pre-existent and prior to the Body, it must still be confined within the limits of the course of Nature; what then is it, and where? For to suppose that it suddenly becomes a part of Nature without having previously been so, is virtually to assign it an origin. If then it is always a part of Nature, we cannot help regarding it as one among other natural elements; and as there is no reason for supposing the other elements inferior, we must ascribe to them too, and in a word to all elements whatever, the same inner capacity for organic development. And here it seems as if we were once again brought back to the unfruitful idea of a common material basis of life. For the manifold forms which these elements assume, would depend on the different modes in which they were combined by the course of Nature; hence, the form which is actually realised at any given moment, must be either the result of mere mechanical agencies—though these may be of a higher type than any with which we are familiar in Physico-Chemical processes—or else, supposing that traces of an independent activity still remain, the soul, which concentrates the different active elements upon this particular development, must come into existence afresh at the moment that they unite; and the question then arises, Whence does it come?

231. This difficulty of finding a real subject, capable of formative activity for an end, has led to attempts to dispense with a subject altogether; it was thought that the generic *Idea* or *Type* would be sufficient to account for such activity. Aristotle set the example with the unfortunate but often repeated remark, that in living things the whole precedes the parts, elsewhere, the parts precede the whole.

This saying, no doubt, gives utterance to the mysterious impression which organic life produces; unluckily, it has been regarded as a solution of the mystery. And yet what truth can be more simple than this, that Ideas are never anything else but Thoughts, in which the thinker gathers up the peculiar nature of an already existing phenomenon; or of one which he knows will necessarily exist in the future as soon as the data exist which are required to produce it? It may be allowed that Reality is so constituted, that from our point of view it is always exhibited in subordination to certain Ideas, general notions, or Types; and we may accordingly go on to say that these Ideas hold good in reality and dominate it; but their dominion is only like that of all legislative authorities, whose commands would remain unobserved if there were no executive organs to carry them out. Never, therefore, in Organic Life is the whole before the parts, in the sense that it is before *all* parts; it only has existence in so far as an already formed combination of parts guarantees that existence in the future as a necessary result of the germ here present, and not of the germ only, but also of favourable external circumstances acting upon it. Anyone who is not satisfied with this development of the whole from the parts, and desires to reverse the relation, will be required to show who the representative of the generic Idea is, who stands outside the parts and gives to the Idea, which in itself is merely potential, a real power in the real world. It must be shown where these Ideas reside, before they initiate a development, and how they find their way thence to the place where they are attracted to an exercise of their power.

Quite recently, an attempt of a different kind has been made by K. E. von Baer. We could have wished that this deservedly popular investigator had succeeded in making out his point to satisfaction; I cannot, however, persuade myself that his proposal to conceive of Nature as striving towards an end, really carries us any farther. If all that it means is, that the different forces, which are active in the construction of organisms, converge in different directions towards a common result, this fact has never been doubted; nor, considered merely as fact, is it the subject of the present controversy. The question at issue is rather this; is the cause which determines this combined action to be found merely in the course of things after they have once been set in motion? i.e. does the convergence occur when there is this motion to produce it, and not occur when there is no such motion? or is there anywhere a power not subject to this constraint of antecedent conditions, which, on its way to the attainment of an end, brings together things which but for it would exist apart? Naturally, it is this latter view which is preferred here. Yet it is not clear, how this supposed tendency to an end would differ from that which might be ascribed, e.g. to falling stones, which, while converging from all quarters of the globe towards its centre, move merely in obedience to a universal law. It is the presence of purpose alone which could constitute that difference, converting the mere end of a process into an aim, and motion to that end into an impulse. Such a purpose Baer's theory accepts, and yet by banishing consciousness, which is presupposed by it, at the same time rejects. Finally, to whom is this tendency in the direction of an end to be ascribed? It would not suit the character of the individual elements, which, varying as they do in capability, tending now to one end, now to another, need some power outside themselves to inform them upon what point they have to converge in any given case; and it is, in fact, from *Nature* that such a tendency is supposed to proceed. But, where is this Nature? It is allowable in ordinary discourse, no doubt, to use this term in such a merely general sense; but in the particular cases in which the designation of Nature as an efficient cause is intended to decide in its favour the choice between it and other agents, there should be some more accurate determination of the conception of it, as well as of the metaphysical relation in which, as a whole, it stands to its subordinate parts. We propose now to supplement the theory in this point, and thus to bring our investigations to a close.

232. The grounds which have led me to my final conclusion have been expounded at such length throughout my entire work, that what I shall now add with regard to this much debated question will be only a short corollary. Men have created for themselves a false gulf, which it has then seemed impossible to bridge over. It is not with any special reference to the opposition which has to be reconciled between living Beings and inanimate Matter, but on much farther-reaching and more general grounds that I have all along maintained the inconceivableness of a world, in which a multitude of independent elements are supposed to have been brought together subsequently to their origin, and forced into common action by Universal Laws. The very fact that laws could hold good in the same way of different elements, showed that the elements could not be what they pleased. Though not directly homogeneous, they must be members in a system, within which measurable advances in different directions lead from one member to another; on this condition only could they and their states be subsumed under the general Laws, as instances of their application. But the validity of general Laws, so established, was not enough to explain the possibility of their application in particular cases; in order that they should necessitate one event at one time and place, another at another, the changing state of the world as a whole had to be reflected at each moment in those elements, which are working together for a common result. It would be idle, however, to suppose that the elements, being originally separate, required the mediation of some 'transeunt' agency which should convey to them the general condition of the world and stimulate them to further

activity: rather, what is experienced by one element must become *immediately* a new state of another. Hence we saw that every action that takes place necessarily presupposes a permanent and universal relation of sympathy between things, which binds them together in constant union, and which itself is only conceivable on the supposition, that what seems to us at first a number of independent centres of energy, is, in essence, one throughout. It is not, therefore, to bring about any specially privileged and exalted result, that the assistance of the infinite Being M, which we have represented as the ground of all existence, is required; every effect produced by one element on another, even the most insignificant, is due to the indwelling vitality of this One Being, and equally requires its constant co-operation. If there is a class of processes in Nature, which, under the name of mechanical, we contrast as blind and purposeless with others in which the formative activity of the One Being seems to stand out clearly, the contrast is certainly not based on the fact that effects of the former kind are left to be governed by a peculiar principle of their own, whilst only in the latter does the one universal cause attempt after some incomprehensible fashion to subdue this alien force. In both cases alike the effects proceed solely from the eternal One itself; and the difference lies in *what* it enjoined in each case, in the one case, the invariable connexion of actions according to universal laws which constitute the basis of all particular conditions, in the other, their development into the variety of those particulars. But, instead of repeating this line of thought in its generality, I shall endeavour to show how it applies to the special question now before us.

233. The germ of an organic growth is not developed in empty Space, in other words, not in a world of its own which has no connexion with the whole of Things. Wherever the plastic materials are present, there the absolute One is likewise present; not as an idea that may be conceived, not as an inoperative class-type, not as a command passing between the elements of a group, or a wish without them, or an ideal above them; but as a real and potent essence present in the innermost life of each element. Nor is it, like divisible Matter, distributed among them in different proportions. It manifests itself in each one in its totality, as the unity that embraces and determines them all, and in virtue of the consistent coherence of its entire plan, assigns to each of these dependent elements those activities which ensure the convergence of their operation to a definite end. But the Absolute is no magician; it does not produce Things in appropriate places out of a sheer vacuum, merely because they correspond to the import of its plan. All particular cases of its operation are based on a system of management according to law, adapted to its operation as a whole. But I must repeat: it is not here as it is with man, who cannot do otherwise; rather this conformity with general principles is itself a part of what is designed to exist. Hence it is, that each stage in the development of organic Life seems to arise step by step out of the reactions which are made necessary for the combined elements by their persistent nature; nor is there anywhere an exception to the dependence of Life on mechanical causes.

At the same time, we are never justified in speaking of a merely mechanical development of Life, as if there were nothing behind it. There is something behind, viz. the combining movement of the absolute, the true activity that assumes this phenomenal form. We may even admit that it apparently breaks through the limits ordinarily assigned to mechanical action. I have before mentioned, and I now repeat, that the principle of mutual indifference, which Mechanics has laid down in respect to forces working concurrently, is, if strictly taken, by no means justified as a universal law. It should rather be laid down as true universally that an element a when it is acted upon by the determining circumstance p, has, by this very fact, become something different, an a which $= a^p$, and that a new force q will not exercise the same kind of effect on this modified element, which it would have exerted on it if unmodified; that the final result, therefore, will not be a^{pq}, or $a^{(p+q)}$ but, a^r. But this r could never be obtained analytically out of any mere logical or mathematical combination of p and q; it would be a synthetic accession to those two conditions, and thus not deducible except from the import of the entire course of things. This is expressed, according to ordinary views, thus—the combination of several elements in a simultaneous action may be followed by effects, which are not mere consequences of the single effects produced by the reactions between every pair of them. That which we now wrongly regard as the universal and obvious rule, viz. that effects should be summed up in a collective result without reciprocally influencing each other, would be only one special case of the general characteristic just mentioned. I shall not now enquire whether and in what direction Biological science will find itself compelled to recognise the possibility of this modification of effects; we must, however, leave a place for it in our own theory. Its admission would not in any way invalidate our conception of the mechanical order, but only extend it further. For it would be our first position even with regard to these new grounds of determination, which intrude upon the course of events, that neither did they arise without a reason, but according to rules, though rules which are more difficult for our apprehension to grasp. But at the same time we should escape from regarding Life as a mere after-effect of a Power, which having formed the mechanism, had left it to run its course. The Power would rather continue to manifest its living presence and constant activity, as operative in the phenomena of Life.

What direction our thoughts might have to take beyond this point, I am not now called on to decide. There is nothing more to be added, which could be urged with absolute certainty of conviction against those who regard the whole sum of the effects produced by this ultimate agency, not less than the inner activities whence they proceed, as still but mere facts of Nature, a tendency which the course of things has followed from all eternity; but which includes no element resembling what we understand by intention, choice, or consciousness of a purpose. Our view, it must be admitted, is no such very great advance upon the mechanical explanation of Nature, from which a refuge was sought. The development of the world would on it be no less a necessary concatenation of cause and effect; excluding all free initiation of new occurrences. Only the most extreme externalism would be avoided. The mechanism would not consist, at starting, of an unalterably fixed complement of forces, which would only suffice to effect changes of the position of existing elements. The mechanism would itself produce at certain definite points those new agencies which would be the proximate principles governing organised groups of connected phenomena. For my own part, I cherish no antipathy to the opposite view, which insists that this whole world of forces, silently arrayed against each other, is animated by the inner life of all its elements and by a consciousness which is that of an all-embracing spirit. I shall not even shrink from attempting, in the proper place, to show that there is a real Freedom which can give rise to truly new departures, such as even this latter belief does not necessarily involve. But such a demonstration would transcend the limits of Metaphysic. It would lead us to consider a mysterious problem, which our discussions down to this point have bordered upon. I have already expressed the opinion that we must not merely credit things with a persistent impulse to self-preservation; but are justified in assuming (as an hypothesis, and in order to explain the phenomena) an impulse to the improvement of their state. Now, if this hypothesis is conceivable in regard to the individual elements, it becomes almost necessary when we no longer speak of them as individuals, but conceive of them, both in their nature and in their actions, as manifestations of a single and all-embracing supreme cause whose mandates they execute. I should at the same time most unquestionably admit that this assumed tendency towards improvement, though it may be the ultimate *ratio legis* from which all special laws of action of things are derived, could never furnish us (since we cannot define this 'improvement') with anything more than the final light and colour of our view of the world; it could never serve as a principle from which those laws could be deduced. But here, the same question which we asked concerning the vital energy, suggests itself once more—If this endeavour after improvement is a fact, why does it not everywhere achieve its end? Whence come all the hurts and hindrances by which the course of Nature, as it is, so often prevents from being fully satisfied the impulses which it nevertheless excites? The conflict of forces in Nature, like the existence of evil in the moral world, is an enigma, the solution of which would require perfect knowledge of the ultimate plan of the world. Metaphysic does not pretend to know what this plan is; nor does she even assert that it is a *plan* that rules the course of events; for this would be inseparable from the idea of the purpose of a conscious being. But, if it limits itself to the belief, that existence has its cause in a single real principle, whatever its concrete nature may be, no considerations concerning these ultimate enigmas can affect the certainty of such conclusions. For, I wish here most distinctly to assert, that though I am old-fashioned enough not to be indifferent to the religious interests which are involved in these problems, the views for which I have been contending rest on a purely scientific basis, quite without reference to Religion. No course of things, whether harmonious or discordant, seems to me conceivable, except on the supposition of this unity, which alone makes possible the reciprocal action of individual existences. The disturbing effects which things exercise upon each other witness to this unity, not less clearly than the joint action of forces with a view to a common end.

234. Similarly, the limits within which metaphysical enquiry is confined compel us to exclude from its sphere the much debated question as to whether the conception of a *kind* has really that objective validity in the organic world which we ordinarily ascribe to it. It will not be supposed that we are going to fall back into thinking that the type of a kind is a real self-subsistent principle, which makes its influence felt in the world by its own inherent force. The only question is—does the disposition of things as a whole require that the forms of combination which the forces active throughout the world assume in the production of Beings capable of existence and growth, should be limited to a certain fixed number? or, on the other hand, may there not be innumerable forces intermediate between these types, and partaking in different degrees of their permanence and power of self-preservation, while the types only represent points of maximum stability? We must leave this question to be decided by the sober evidence of Natural History. Philosophy will do well to regard every attempt at an *a priori* solution of it as a baseless assumption. The bias of our minds in this case is determined by our own preconceived unverifiable opinions regarding the course of the world as a whole. Suppose, however, we assume that not merely self-conservation, but also Progress is a characteristic of the world as a whole, yet, even then, it would be conceivable that in the age of the world's history in which we now live, and of which we cannot see the limits, the forms of Life established by Nature might be incapable of addition, just as the quantities of those permanent elements which Nature uses in order to construct her products, are incapable of addition. According to this view, any forms in which things combined, owing to the influence of circumstances other than the forms determined by Nature, would have only a passing reality, and would be subsequently dissolved owing to the influence of the same circumstances which had produced them. On the other hand, nothing hinders us from introducing the alleged development within the limits of the epoch which we can observe, and regarding it as possible that new forms may come into Being and old forms pass away, and that what went before may gradually be transformed into what follows. The present aspect of the discussion on this subject forms part of a larger and more general question, the question, as to whether the world is finite or infinite.

235. It is needless to discuss at length the question as to whether the succession of events in time is finite or infinite. We cannot represent to ourselves in thought, either the origin of reality out of nothing, or its disappearance into nothing, and no one has ever attempted to take up this position without assuming, as existent in the Nothing, an originating principle or agency, and ascribing to it previous to its creative act a fixed existence of its own which has had no beginning in Time. Hence, whatever difficulties may be involved in the attempt to conceive of the course of events in Time as without beginning or end, the idea itself is inevitable. Nor need we occupy ourselves at any greater length with the question as to the limits of the world in Space. If Space is to pass for a real existence, the only difficulty is in the infinity of Space itself, which in that case is the infinity of something real. I leave this assumption, therefore, to be dealt with by those who are interested in maintaining it. On the other hand, it does not at all follow, even if Space is infinite, that the world need occupy the whole of it, as long as the content of that world admits of the predicate 'finite.' It would be quite sufficient to say with Herbart that Space sets no limits or conditions to the world, but that it occupies just so much room in Space as it requires for its movements, and that thus its boundaries are perpetually shifting. My own view of the matter is almost to the same effect. Every change in the true reactions of real elements must find room within the infinity of our Space-perception for its phenomenal manifestation as space, position, and motion. But there is nothing to compel the real existences to fill up at every moment all the empty places which our Space-perception holds in readiness for impressions that may require them.

The question therefore resolves itself into this, whether the sum of real existence in the world is limited or unlimited, a question in reference to which we follow alternately two opposite impulses. On the one hand, the idea of infinity gratifies us just because we cannot exhaust it in thought, by enabling us to marvel at the immensity of the universe, of which we then readily acknowledge that we are but a part; though, at the same time, by making it impossible for us to comprehend the world as a unity or whole, this infinity perplexes us. On the other hand, by conceiving of the world as finite, we are indeed enabled easily to grasp it as a whole; but it vexes us to think that a hindrance to its being greater than it is should have been imposed from without. This last supposition, at any rate, is plainly absurd. The world of reality is the sole source from which, in the minds that form a part of it, the notion of these countless unrealised possibilities springs. Hence arises the false idea that the Real world is limited and conditioned by what it does not produce, though it is the Real world alone that does produce this empty imagination in our minds. And this misconception has then absolutely no limits. What would be the use of assuming an infinity of real elements, if each one of them was finite? Surely it would be still better that each element should be infinite. Yet even then we should still have only an infinite number of infinite elements. Why not, in order to get rid of all limitation, assume the existence of an infinite number of worlds, both of infinite magnitude themselves, and composed of elements whose magnitude was infinite? There is therefore *prima facie* no objection to the finite character of real existence—whereas, the character of infinity is opposed by Physics, not merely as inexhaustible by thought, but also as involving certain special mechanical difficulties. The unlimited distribution of matter would make impossible a common centre of gravity. No one point would have any better claim to be regarded as such than the rest. But what is our motive in looking for a centre of gravity? and what exactly do we mean by it? The supposition could not be entertained, unless it were regarded as self-evident that the same laws of reciprocal action which obtain between the particles of matter in our planet, and which we call Laws of Gravitation, obtain also throughout the whole range of existence. I well know how little precedent there is for doubting this fact. It is, indeed, ordinarily taken for granted without the slightest misgiving. And yet, in the absence of positive proof derived from observation, it can only be a bold argument from analogy. It seems to me by no means a self-evident fact, that all the real elements which are contained in the infinity of space, including even those which are stationed at the furthest points, are held together according to a single law by the uniting force of gravity, just as if they were mere samples of the mass to which it applies, and without individuality of their own. The Law of Gravitation is only known to apply to the bodies of our own planetary system. Besides this, there is only the conjecture, which may be a true one, that certain of the binary stars are kept in their courses by a similar mutual attraction, the law of which we do not as yet know. But that the same influence by which one system of material elements is made to cohere, extends as a matter of course to every other coherent system in the Universe of Space; this is by no means such an established and irrefutable truth as is, e. g. the uniform diffusion of the undulations of light through all Space.

For a reason which has already been several times touched upon, I am forced to proceed at this point by a different path from that which is ordinarily followed in the physical Sciences. If I really thought that the number of the real elements, or of the systems which are formed from such elements, was infinite, then, though I should certainly not regard them as having no connexion with each other, I should just as certainly not imagine that the relation subsisting between them was so monotonously uniform that they should be treated as mere samples of homogeneous mass endowed everywhere with the same force, so as to raise the question of their common centre of gravity. In each of these several systems the inner relation of the parts might be essentially peculiar, depending on the plan which governed its structure. Similarly, the several systems might be united by different kinds of relations into the one universal plan. Not that, in insisting on this point, I have any wish to maintain that Real existence *is* infinite, any more than I wish to maintain that it is finite. I have no sympathy with the point of view from which this question thus conceived seems to be one of real importance. I have more than once expressed my conviction that everything is subject to mechanical Laws; but I have at the same time asserted the essentially subordinate character of these Laws, when considered with reference to the Universe as a whole. I do not know if my expressions have been understood in the sense in which they were intended. Certainly they were not meant to imply that previous to the creation of the world there existed a fixed sum of real elements, along with a code of absolute mechanical Laws, and that an organizing power then entered on the scene, and had to make the best of these resources. I have throughout taken as my starting-point the living

nature of the real existence, that unity whose ess
can only be expressed, if we are to attempt to real
to our intelligence, as the import of a thought. Out o
import there arose (what was not prior to it) the fundam
system of most general laws, as a condition which Re
imposes on itself and its whole action. But just beca
dependent on this import, the system possessed a wealth
meaning and power of accommodation, adequate to provide
not merely for the uniformity of processes which never
vary, but also for the manifold variety of activities which are
required by the animating idea of the Whole. I should
be the last to deny the necessity and value of the other
point of view which, as represented by modern mechanics,
conducts calculations based on the abstract conceptions
of Mass and its constancy: Force, and the conservation
of Force, the inertia and invariability of the elements.
Not only do we owe to this method the greater part of
our present knowledge of Nature, but we may also safely
assume it as a guide throughout the whole range of our
possible observation. At the same time, I should be the
last to ascribe to these notions, being as they are abstractions out of the fraction of the world's course which is
accessible to us, that metaphysical certainty which would
fit them to serve as a key to the solution of questions
which are such as to transcend all experience of this.
kind.

What I have now to say in regard to the question of
infinity has been already indicated in several passages
of my work. If the reality of the world is to be found in a
thought which fulfils itself in every moment, the question as
to the finite or infinite character of this thought is as
meaningless as the question as to whether a motion is sweet
or sour. As regards, however, the different and everchanging related points, by means of which the thought
realises itself, we would remark, in the first place, that their
number is not absolutely finite or infinite. It is not, indeed,

xed quantity at all. It is, at each moment, precisely the realisation of the thought demands and its living ity produces. This heterodox assertion I have already ured on, thereby placing myself in opposition to the ma of the constancy of Mass. Supposing we fancied that had a standard in terms of which the sum of real existence at any given moment of its history $= m$, it might very well at the next moment be found to $= \mu$. In the same way as the world might take up just so much space as t should require at any given moment, so the Idea which animates it would create for itself just so many elements as are needed in order to accomplish its development. Not as if there had been some material substance present from all eternity, which was afterwards merely differently distributed according as the Idea might require, nor yet as f the Idea created new elements out of nothing. These new creations would spring from the Idea itself, which is the cause of all things. Enough, however, has been said on this point. It would be hopeless to attempt to bring these thoughts home to anyone who was convinced that a fixed quantity of matter had been ordained to exist from all eternity. Whether, at any given moment, the number of the real and active elements is unlimited, or whether there are certain fixed limits within which the numbers vary, I confess myself unable to say. The question itself involves confusion, until we have fixed on the unit the number of whose recurrences is sought. It could have absolutely no meaning for those who have admitted the infinite divisibility of matter. It would be intelligible only, if it were held to apply to individual atoms or to separate and distinct groups of elements, as, e. g. the number of the stars. Here I will only say quite shortly that I am content to assume that the number of material existences s limited, provided it is understood that this number must suffice to enable them to carry out the behests of the Idea, and that if this same condition is fulfilled, I am equally content to conceive of their number as infinite. In this latter case, the impossibility of reckoning their number would be due merely to a defect in us. It would not be a fault on their side, or inconsistent with their reality.

236. The progress of observation has led us to the conviction that the formation of the earth's crust took place gradually, and that organic life could not have existed throughout the stages of this process in its present state. This imposes on us the necessity of attempting to show how the forms of life at present existing were developed out of earlier and simpler ones. In the heat of the controversy on this subject, care should have been taken not to confuse two questions which ought to be separated. Only one of them belongs to Metaphysic, that, viz. as to the determining principles which have been active throughout the course of this development. I feel all the less inducement to make any addition to the rapidly increasing literature which the discussion of this question has called forth, inasmuch as, before this controversy had begun to rage, I endeavoured to bring together whatever seemed to admit of being said, with any claim to respect, in favour of explaining all cases of adaptation as due to a fortuitous concourse of accidents, a view which has a recognised place in the History of Philosophy. In the second chapter of the fourth book of the Microcosmus, I treated expressly of this derivation of the Cosmos from Chaos, and I cannot convince myself that the more recent arguments from the same point of view add anything of importance to those well-known ones of former times which are there mentioned. I content myself with referring to what I then said in regard to the details of the question. My conviction on the matter as a whole needs not again to be stated here. The controversy will become milder with time; at least this will be so, in so far as it is conducted in the interests of Science and not from a feeling of invincible repugnance to every

Idea which is suspected of favouring the cause of Religion. An improvement in this respect is already to some extent visible. Those who pray too much are destined, says the proverb, to pray themselves through heaven and to keep geese on the other side. A better fate has befallen those who, out of a conscientious regard for the interests of Science, have felt themselves compelled to derive Organic Life from blind chance and purposeless matter. They have invested their original principles with so much reason and power of internal development, that nothing but the caprice of their terminology which keeps to the names of Matter, Mechanism, and Accident, for what other people call Spirit, Life, and Providence, seems to prevent them from relapsing into notions which they have before strenuously opposed.

237. On the other hand, as regards the second question to be distinguished, that, viz. as to the actual development of Organic Life, this is purely a matter of Natural History. Philosophy is not concerned to dispute or to deny any results of observation on this subject, which are based on sufficient evidence. Not even Religion should presume to prescribe to God the course which the world's development must have followed subsequently to its creation. However strange the path may have been, we might be sure that its strangeness could not remove it from His control. Considering that the human body requires to be kept alive each day by absorbing into itself nourishment derived from common natural substances, there can be no reason in claiming for it a manner of origin so exceedingly distinguished. And with regard to the whole matter we would say that man esteems himself according to *what* he is, and not according to that *whence* he arose. It is enough for us to feel that we are now not apes. It is of no consequence to us that our remote and unremembered ancestors should have belonged to this inferior grade of life. The only painful conclusion would be that we were destined to turn into apes again, and it was likely to happen soon. It seems to me, therefore, that from the point of view of Philosophy these scientific movements may be regarded with the most perfect indifference. Each result, so soon as it had ceased to be a favourite conjecture and had been established by convincing proof, would be welcomed as a real addition to knowledge. The very remarkable facts of Natural History accumulated by the unwearied research of Darwin, might be provisionally welcomed by Philosophy with the warmest satisfaction, whilst, on the other hand, the pretentious and mistaken theories based on those facts might be not less completely disregarded. All that Philosophy herself can contribute towards the solution of these questions is, to warn us against making unfounded assumptions, which, whilst they are themselves to some extent of philosophical origin, rob Science of its fairness. Whatever may have been the state of the earth's surface, which first occasioned the production of organic life, it cannot but be improbable that the required conditions should only have been present at a single point; equally improbable, considering the diversity of the terrestrial elements which were subjected on the whole to uniform influences, that organic germs of the same kind only should have been generated at all points; and finally, it is extremely improbable that this productive period should have lasted only long enough for the occurrence of an instantaneous creative act, instead of being so protracted that the conditions, slowly altering while it still lasted, might superadd fresh creations to the earlier ones instead of merely developing their further phases. Nor is there any difficulty in imagining that these various organic beings, though produced at different times and on different spots of the earth, would still present numberless analogies of structure. The equation which contained the conditions of the union of elements so as to be capable of life would restrict all possible solutions within determinate limits. Hence, according to what is at any rate the most probable supposition, Organic

Life is derived from an original multiplicity of simple types having a capacity for development.

Here we break off. We cannot pursue further the attempts which are now being made to arrive at an explanation of the first beginnings and the final destiny of things. Our knowledge of the present state of the globe and of the forces that act upon it, does enable us to form an idea, imperfect indeed, but not contemptible, with regard to its fate in the future; and it is of importance for Science to consider to what end the processes which we now see in operation would lead, supposing them to continue unchecked and to follow the same laws. From this point of view, we are able to appreciate those ingenious calculations which draw conclusions as to the final state of the world from our experimental knowledge of the economy of heat. They are, however, nothing more than the indispensable computations which draw out this portion of our physical knowledge into its results. For this purpose we are obliged to assume the continuance of the conditions which are operative at present. Whether this hypothesis will be verified, or whether the end towards which things now seem to point, will not sooner or later be shown by fresh discoveries in a new light, no one can decide. At the same time, however, the fate which most attempts to forecast the future by means of statistics have hitherto met, has been of the latter kind. Hence, we must be on our guard against crediting as a prophetic announcement with regard to the future, conclusions which follow, no doubt, necessarily on the arbitrary assumption that the given conditions are the only ones to be taken into account. Still less do we intend to busy ourselves with the fancies of those who relate to us, just as if they had been themselves present, how things were first produced; how, e. g. the inorganic elements of the earth's crust found themselves united in the form of crystals capable of imbibition, and in systems endowed with life and growth; or, again, how the atmosphere of the primitive world settled upon the earth in the shape of protoplasm, and there struck roots of the most various kinds. This insatiable desire to get beyond the general principles which still admit of being applied to the investigation of these problems, and actually to conjecture those special circumstances which are simply inaccessible to our knowledge, may, by way of palliation, be considered to be characteristic of that historical sense by which the present age is distinguished, thus contrasting favourably with former ages, when, owing to their speculative bias, men sought for truth not in matters of fact but in ideas that had no reality in Space and Time. Yet I do not know in what the worth of history would consist, if facts were in truth only described as having occurred in this or that place, without any attempt being made to pass beyond the facts and their succession, and to lay bare the nerves which govern the connected order of things always and everywhere. But for this purpose history must above all things be *true*. Every fact of the Past which can be demonstrated by certain proof we shall esteem as a real and valuable addition to our knowledge. On the other hand, those rash anticipations of knowledge, entertaining at first, but wearisome in their recurrence, have nothing to do with this laudable 'historical sense,' but spring from the dangerous inclination to anecdote simply for its own sake. It is thus that our own generation, maintaining its opposition to Philosophy, endeavours to console itself for its want of clearness in respect to general principles by a vivid exercise of the sensuous imagination. If we come upon pile-dwellings in some forgotten swamp, we piously gather together the insignificant remains of a dreary Past, supposing that by contemplating them we shall grow wiser and learn that which a glance into the affairs of everyday life would teach us with less trouble. Compared with such objects as these how small a chance of notice have the Philosophical ideas, which represent the efforts of long ages to obtain a clearer insight into eternal truth. If only these ideas could be stuffed! Then it might be possible that beside a fine specimen of the Platonic idea and a well-preserved Aristotelian entelechy even the more modest fancies which in these pages I have devoted to speedy oblivion, might attract the attention of a holiday sight-seer.

BOOK III.

ON MENTAL EXISTENCE (PSYCHOLOGY).

CHAPTER I.

The Metaphysical Conception of the Soul.

THE old Metaphysic of the Schools reckoned among its problems the construction of a Rational Psychology. This name was not meant to imply that the science in question could dispense with such a knowledge of its object as should agree with experience; the design was merely to bring the general modes of procedure which were observed in that object into connexion with metaphysical convictions as to the possibility of all being and happening. I will not ask here how much or how little the science accomplished; but I accept the end it set before itself as a limit for my own discussions. There is at present a strong inclination towards the empirical investigation of psychical phenomena, in all their manifold complexity, and I am not opposing this inclination when I confess some want of confidence in the trustworthiness of its results. Speaking generally no great doubt can be felt as to the nature of those associations of impressions, by means of which the whole of our sensuous view of things as well as the riches of our mental culture are in the last resort acquired; but the ingenious attempts which have been made to demonstrate the way in which particular portions of this total sum actually came into our possession, have not the same certainty. Often, instead of being founded on empirical evidence, they are merely descriptions of the modes in which we can without any great difficulty imagine the material in question to have originated; sometimes they are accounts of processes of the possibility of which we persuade ourselves only because we use as self-evident means of explanation mental habits which it is really our first business to explain. It is not my purpose, however, to lessen the deserved sympathy which these valuable efforts have won; but this book must come to an end somewhere, and therefore they are excluded from it; and my wish here is simply to overcome, for a moment at least, the disfavour which any metaphysical treatment of these subjects is apt to encounter.

When we say that we adopt an empirical stand-point we must mean more than that we wish to stand still at this point; we really intend it to be no more than the starting-place from which we may appropriate the field of experience around us. Now, considered as such a point of departure, the knowledge of those facts which are furnished by experience is indispensable to every psychology alike; and even those attempts which have been especially stigmatised as transcendent, are in the end simply interpretations of the material supplied by observation. The divergence of opinion does not really begin till we ask by what method we are to appropriate in the form of theory that which, from the empirical position, we all see with the same eyes. In speaking of the physical investigation of nature I pointed out how slight and how arduous its progress would be if it confined itself to bare observation and refused to connect the given facts by framing hypotheses respecting that nature of things which cannot be observed. And I may now appeal for confirmation to the excellent attempts which have been made in psychology to reach, at least at one point, the beginnings of an exact science—the point I refer to is the question how the strength of a sensation is related to that of its external stimulus. For these attempts have at once become involved in a mass of theoretical and speculative problems, to the settlement of which a future experience may perhaps contribute much but which it will certainly never completely solve. If then we are compelled to use as a basis *some* hypothesis respecting the connexion of physical and psychical phenomena, why are we to take the first hypothesis that comes to hand? Why not go back to the most general ideas that we necessarily form respecting all being and action, and so attempt to define the limits within which we can frame suppositions, sometimes trustworthy and at other times at all events probable? But, further, even supposing it were possible, in the investigation of this special subject, to find a point of departure which should be productive of results and yet should imply no fixed pre-judgment as to the nature of the subject, a difficulty would still remain: for though this freedom from pre-suppositions would be possible for this particular investigation, it would still be unacceptable to us as men. We may be warned to abstain from discussing questions which do not seem to be soluble by the special methods of a particular science; but the warning will never deter the human race from returning to these riddles; for a consistent opinion about them is not less important and indispensable to it than are those explanations of observed facts which in this field can never be more than fragmentary. I shall therefore attempt to extend these metaphysical considerations to the sphere of Psychology, and so to bring them to a conclusion. For the elaboration of many particular points I may refer to the corresponding sections of the *Mikrokosmus;* here I wish to bring together the essential points treated in the *Medicinische Psychologie*, (Leipzig, 1852), which I shall not reissue, and to show the metaphysical connexion which in those two works could not be sufficiently brought out.

238. Let us leave out of sight, to begin with, anything

which the earlier part of this enquiry might offer by way of foundation for what is to follow. If we do this, we shall have to confess that mental life is given us, as a fact of observation, only in constant connexion with bodily life. Accordingly the supposition at once suggests itself that this mental life is nothing but a product of the physical organization, the growth of which it is observed to accompany. Yet such a view has never been more than a doctrine of scientific schools. We meet with the word 'soul' in the languages of all civilised peoples; and this proves that the imagination of man must have had reasons of weight for its supposition that there is an existence of some special nature underlying the phenomena of the inner life as their subject or cause. It is, I think, possible to reduce these reasons to three, of very different value. The first I will refer to, the appeal to the *freedom* which is said to characterise mental life, and is distinguished from the necessity of nature, has no weight. It is a conviction with which we begin our enquiry and to which we hold, that all events in external nature form an uninterrupted series of causal connexion according to universal laws; but this necessity is not a fact of observation. There remain always vast tracts of nature, the inner connexion of which is simply unknown to us and which can therefore furnish no empirical verification of that presupposition. But, when we come to mental life, not even those for whom freedom is in itself a possible conception can regard it as the *universal* characteristic of that life. They can demand it only at one definite point, viz. the resolutions of the will. Everything else, the whole course of ideas, emotions, and efforts, is not only, in the souls of animals and men alike, manifestly subject to a connexion according to universal laws, but the denial of that connexion would at once destroy the possibility of any psychological enquiry; since it, like every other enquiry, can be directed to nothing but the discovery of conditions universally valid.

239. The second reason which led to the conception of

the soul was the entire *incomparability* of all inner processes—sensations, ideas, emotions, and desires—with spatial motion, figure, position, and energy; that is, with those states which we believe we observe in matter, or which we can suppose it to experience if we see in it only what the physical view of nature gives it out to be. It is a very long time since philosophy recognised this incomparability, and it needed no new discovery or confirmation. It has escaped no one except those who, out of their prejudice in favour of a desired conclusion, have not been afraid of the logical error by which two different things are held to be of the same kind simply because as a matter of fact they are connected with one another. We may imagine a quantity of movements of material elements, and we may attribute to them whatever degree of complexity we choose; but we shall never reach a given moment at which we can say, Now it is obvious that this sum of movements can remain movements no longer but must pass into sweetness, brightness, or sound. The only obvious change we could ever anticipate from them would be into a fresh set of movements. We shall never succeed in analytically deducing the feeling from the nature of its physical excitant; we can only connect the two synthetically; and the physical event does not become a condition of the rise of the feeling until the sum of motions in which it consists meets with a subject which in its own nature has the peculiar capacity of producing feeling from itself. In this fact a limit is at once placed to all physiological and psychological enquiry. It is utterly fruitless to attempt to show how a physical nervous process gradually transforms itself (as we are told) into sensation or any other mental occurrence. There remains only the different but extremely important task of discovering *what* psychical event a and *what* physical stimulus a are as a matter of fact universally connected in the order of nature, and of finding the law by which a undergoes a definite change and becomes β, when a by a change equally definite (but definable only by a physical standard and not a psychical one) becomes *b*. This is a point at which the professedly empirical method and the metaphysical change their *rôles*. The former, in pursuing the dream of an identity of physical and psychical processes, leaves the field of experience far behind it and does battle with our most immediate certainty that they are not identical: the latter, when it refrains from describing an event which cannot occur at all, is not denying the connexion between the two series of events; but it limits itself to a more useful enquiry, it investigates the laws according to which the results of that connexion change, and it forbears to ask questions, which to begin with at any rate cannot be answered, regarding the mode in which that connexion is in all cases brought about.

240. On the other hand we must beware of drawing conclusions too definite from this incomparability of physical and psychical processes. All that follows unavoidably from it is that we should reserve for each of these two groups its own special ground of explanation; but it would be going too far to assert that the two principles, which we must thus separate, necessarily belong to two different sorts of substances. There is nothing to be said at starting against the other supposition, according to which every element of reality unites in itself the two primitive qualities, from one of which mental life may arise, while the other contains the condition of a phenomenal appearance as matter. On this view, instead of having, on the one side, souls destitute of all physical activity and, on the other, absolutely self-less elements of matter, we might suppose that the latter, like the former, possess in various grades an inner life, though a life which we cannot observe nor even guess at, so long as it has no forms of expression intelligible to us. And with regard to the cause which would unite these two attributes in what exists, this theory would be as much within its right in refusing to discuss it as ours was in simply appealing to the fact of a connexion between two series of incomparable processes. It seems to me that every mode of thought, which calls itself Materialism, ultimately rests on this supposition, or on a little reflexion must be led to it; the matter from which such modes of thought would deduce mental phenomena, is privately conceived by them as something much better than it looks from outside. So it comes about that it can be held a fair problem, to deduce the mental life of an organism from the reactions of the psychical movements of the corporeal elements in the same sense in which its bodily life arises as a resultant from the confluence of the physical forces of those elements. And if we were confined to the external observation of a psychical life not our own, I do not know of anything perfectly decisive that could be alleged against this supposition. But, according to it, every psychical manifestation would be merely the final outcome of a number of components destitute of any centre: whereas our inner experience offers us the fact of a *unity of consciousness*. Here then is the third and the unassailable ground, on which the conviction of the independence of the soul can securely rest. The nature of this position I proceed to explain.

241. It has been required of any theory which starts without pre-suppositions and from the basis of experience, that in the beginning it should speak only of sensations or ideas, without mentioning the soul to which, it is said, we hasten without justification to ascribe them. I should maintain, on the contrary, that such a mode of setting out involves a wilful departure from that which is actually given in experience. A mere sensation without a subject is nowhere to be met with as a fact. It is impossible to speak of a bare movement without thinking of the mass whose movement it is; and it is just as impossible to conceive a sensation existing without the accompanying idea of that which has it,—or, rather, of that which feels it; for this also is included in the given fact of experience, that the relation of the feeling subject to its feeling, whatever its other characteristics may be, is in any case something different from the relation of the moved element to its movement. It is thus, and thus only, that the sensation is a given fact; and we have no right to abstract from its relation to its subject because this relation is puzzling, and because we wish to obtain a starting-point which looks more convenient but is utterly unwarranted by experience. In saying this I do not intend to repeat the frequent but exaggerated assertion, that in every single act of feeling or thinking there is an express consciousness which regards the sensation or idea simply as states of a self; on the contrary, everyone is familiar with that absorption in the content of a sensuous perception, which often makes us entirely forget our personality in view of it. But then the very fact that we can become aware that this *was* the case, presupposes that we afterwards retrieve what we omitted at first, viz. the recognition that the perception was in us, as our state. But, further, there are other facts which place in a clearer light what in the case of single sensations might remain doubtful. Any comparison of two ideas, which ends by our finding their contents like or unlike, presupposes the absolutely indivisible unity of that which compares them: it must be one and the same thing which first forms the idea of a, then that of b, and which at the same time is conscious of the nature and extent of the difference between them. Then again the various acts of comparing ideas and referring them to one another are themselves in turn reciprocally related; and this relation brings a new activity of comparison to consciousness. And so our whole inner world of thoughts is built up; not as a mere collection of manifold ideas existing with or after one another, but as a world in which these individual members are held together and arranged by the relating activity of this single pervading principle. This then is what we mean by the unity of consciousness; and it is this that we regard as the sufficient ground for assuming an indivisible soul. As compared with the thousand activities of this unity involved in every act by which two ideas are referred to each other, it is a matter of indifference whether at every moment that particular act of relation is explicitly performed by which these inner states are apprehended in their true character, as states of this active unity. Although this reflexion is possible, we can think of many conditions which frequently prevent it taking place. But that it can take place at all proves to us the unity of the active subject which performs it.

242. Further discussion is, however, needed, in order to show the necessity of our conclusion and to explain its meaning. First, as to its necessity: even if we admit the unity of consciousness, why are we bound to trace it back to a particular indivisible subject? why should it not resemble a motion which results from the co-operation of many components; seeing that this resultant, like the unity of consciousness, appears perfectly simple and gives no indication of the multiplicity of elements from which it arose? I answer: such an idea seems possible only because we state the mechanical law, to which we appeal, in slovenly short-hand. We must not say, 'From two motions there comes a third simple motion:' the full formula is, When two different impulses act simultaneously on one and the same material point, they coalesce at this point into a third simple motion *of this point;* they would not do so if they met with different elements, nor would the resultant have any significance if it were not a motion of that very same element in which they met. If we wish then to make an analogous construction of consciousness, it is indispensable that we should mention the subject whose states we have to combine. Thus if $a, b, c, \ldots z$ are the elements of a living organism, each of them may have at once a physical and a psychical nature and each of them may be capable of acting in accordance with its two natures; but the fact still remains that these actions cannot stream out into the void and be states of nobody, but must always consist of states which one element produces in other elements. Supposing this reciprocal action took place equally among them all, then the impressions received and imparted would be equalised, and the end of the process would be that each one of the elements would reach the same final state Z, the resultant of all the single impulses. If then Z were a consciousness, this consciousness would be present as many times as there were homogeneous elements: but it would never happen that outside, side by side with, or between these elements a new subject could be formed, privileged to be the personified common spirit of the society of interacting units. Doubtless, however, the homogeneity we have assumed will not be found to exist; the constituents of the organism will differ from one another; they will be conjoined in accordance with their nature, and will have different positions, more or less favourable to the spread of their interactions; and at whatever moment we suppose the course of these interactions to be finished, the result will probably be that the different elements will have reached different final states $A, B, \ldots Z$, depending on the degree of liveliness with which each element has received the influences of the others, and on the measure in which it has succeeded or failed in concentrating those influences in itself. In this case it becomes still more impossible than before to say which of all this array of resultant consciousnesses is the object of our search, the soul of the organism: but in this case as in the former, it is certain that there cannot arise, outside of and beyond all these elements, a new subject which in its own consciousness should bring together and compare their states, as we who are investigating can compare them in the unity of *our* consciousness.

Our only remaining resource would be to fall back on the idea of Leibnitz and to say that although the countless monads which compose the living creature are essentially homogeneous, there is nevertheless among them a *prima inter pares*, a central monad, which in virtue partly of its superiority in quality and partly of its favourable position between the rest, is capable of the intensest mental life and able to over-master all the others. This central monad would be what we call our soul, the subject of our one consciousness; the others, though they too have psychical movements of their own, would be for our direct inward experience as inaccessible as the inner life of one person in a human society is for that of any other. Thus the end at which this attempted construction would arrive would not be that it set out to reach. It too would have to recognise the absolutely indivisible unity of that which is to support our inward life: and, instead of the hope of showing this unity to be the resultant of many co-operating elements, there would remain the more moderate assumption that these many elements stand to the one being in manifold relations of interaction. Such a view has no longer any special peculiarity, beyond, first, the idea that all elements of the body have a soul-life, although this soul-life has not much significance for ours; and secondly, (though this applies only to the hypothesis I am describing, and not to Leibnitz) the doubtful advantage of being able to attribute to the one element which is the soul not only psychical predicates but the predicates of an element which is operative after the fashion of matter.

243. I said that the *meaning* of the unity of consciousness, as well as the necessity of assuming it, needed some further explanation. My remarks on this meaning ought to be saved by their connexion with the rest of a metaphysical work like the present from the misunderstanding with which my previous accounts of the subject have met. The conclusion we have now reached is usually expressed by saying that the soul is an indivisible and simple substance; and I have used this formula in all innocence, as an intelligible name. How it can be misunderstood I have learned from the way in which my esteemed friend Fechner in his *Atomenlehre* characterises my view in opposition to his own. It was natural to him as an investigator of Nature, and probably his intimacy with the most eminent representatives of the Herbartian philosophy made it still more natural, to understand by substance a physical atom or one of the simple real 'existences' of that school. But I had given no special occasion for this misunderstanding: on the contrary I had put forward the proposition which was censured and therefore could not have escaped notice; 'It is not through a substance that things have being, but they have being when they are able to produce the appearance of a substance present in them.' I have discussed this point at sufficient length in the Ontology, and have now only to show its consequences for our present question. When from the given fact of the unity of consciousness I passed on to call the subject of this knowledge existence or substance, I could not possibly intend by doing so to draw a conclusion which should deduce from its premisses something not contained in them but really new. For my only definition of the idea of substance was this,—that it signifies everything which possesses the power of producing and experiencing effects, in so far as it possesses that power. Accordingly this expression was simply a title given to a thing in virtue of its having performed something; it was not and could not be meant to signify the ground, the means or the cause which would render that performance intelligible. Was substance to be one or many? It would have been too absurd to suppose this power of producing and experiencing effects in general to have its ground in *one* universal substance, and then to expect that a grain of this substance, buried in each individual thing, would quicken this general capacity into the particular ways of producing and experiencing effects which distinguish that thing from all other things. On the other hand the supposition that each thing, instead of being carved out of the matter of the universal substance, is a substance on its own account would have at once led us back to our starting-point, and we should have recognised the name substance to be, what it really is, simply the general formal designation of every way of producing and experiencing effects, but not the real condition on which in each particular case the possibility of doing so and the particular way of doing so depends. I was therefore very far from sharing the view of those who place the soul in the mid-current of events as one hard and indissoluble atom by the side of others or as an indestructible real existence, and who fancied that its substantiality, so understood, offered a foundation from which the rest of its phenomena could be deduced. The fact of the unity of consciousness is *eo ipso* at once the fact of the existence of a substance: we do not need by a process of reasoning to conclude from the former to the latter as the condition of its existence,—a fallacious process of reasoning which seeks in an extraneous and superior substance supposed to be known beforehand, the source from which the soul and each particular thing would acquire the capacity of figuring as the unity and centre of manifold actions and affections.

The reason why, in spite of this, I thought it worth while to designate the soul as substance or real existence, I shall mention hereafter when I come to oppose the pluralistic view suggested by Fechner: my point was not so much the substantiality as the unity of the soul, and I wished to emphasize the idea that it is only an indivisible unity which can produce or experience effects at all, and that these words cannot be applied in strictness to any multiplicity,—an idea which I attempted to bring out more clearly in the *Mikrokosmus*, (i. p. 178[1]). But, relying on the fact that the imagination is accustomed to connect this idea of unity with the name 'substance'

[1] [E. Tr. i. 159.]

or 'real existence,' I considered that these two expressions, even in that meaning of them which I have described and repudiated, might still, when once the true account of the matter had been given, be used as serviceable abbreviations of it.

244. It is natural at this point to think of Kant's treatment of that Paralogism of the pure Reason which seeks to establish the substantiality of the soul. We may sum up his criticism thus: It is a fact that we appear in our thoughts as the constant subject of our states, but it does not follow from this fact that the soul is a constant substance; for even the former unity is in the end only our subjective way of looking at things, and there are many things which in themselves may be quite different from what they must needs seem to us to be. This last idea is certainly incontrovertible, but it does not affect the point which constitutes the nerve of our argument. I repeat once more, we do not believe in the unity of the soul because it appears as unity, but simply because it is able to appear or manifest itself in *some* way, whatever that may be. The mere fact that, conceiving itself as a subject, it connects itself with *any* predicate, proves to us the unity of that which asserts this connexion; and, supposing the soul appeared to itself as a multiplicity, we should on the same grounds conclude that it was certainly mistaken if it took itself really to be what it appeared. Every judgment, whatever it may assert, testifies by the mere fact that it is pronounced at all, to the indivisible unity of the subject which utters it.

But, I am well aware, I shall still be reproached with having neglected the fine and subtle distinction which Kant draws between the subject of our inward experience and the unity of the Soul considered as a thing in itself; he admits the unity of the former, but prohibits any conclusion to that of the latter. It is a difficult task, and one in which I have no interest, to dissect Kant's final ideas in this section of the Critique of Reason[1]; I shall content myself with explaining clearly the difference between my view and that which I conjecture to be his. Kant is without doubt right when he is opposing that traditional argument for the substantiality of the soul, the object of which was to make that quality, when it had been inferred, a *medius terminus* for fresh consequences, as, for instance, that of immortality; but he was mistaken when he looked on this inference as a further goal which it is our misfortune that we are unable to attain. In the very prohibition he utters against a conclusion from the unity of the subject to that of the substance, he admits that this conclusion would have an important bearing, if only it could be drawn; and all that seems to him to be wanting is the links of argument which might justify us in bringing the soul under this fruitful conception of substance and all the consequences it legitimately involves. That Kant cannot free himself from this idea, is shown by a foot-note[1] which in the first edition of the Critique is appended to the doctrine of the Paralogisms. It runs as follows: 'An elastic sphere which collides with another in a direct line, communicates to it its whole motion and, therefore, (if we regard nothing but their positions in space) its whole state. Now if, on the analogy of such bodies, we suppose substances, one of which imparted to the other ideas together with the consciousness of them, we can imagine a whole series of these substances, of which the first would impart its state, together with the consciousness of that state, to the second, the second would impart its own state, together with that of the preceding substance, to the third, and this again would communicate to another, not only its own state with the consciousness of it, but also the states of all its predecessors and the consciousness of them. Thus the states of all the substances which had undergone changes, together with the consciousness of these states, would be transferred to the last substance: and in consequence this last

[1] [Kritik d. r. V. p. 290-2, Rosenkranz' ed.]

substance would be conscious of all these states as its own, and yet, in spite of this, it would not have been the same person in all these states.' In this way, according to Kant, the identity of the consciousness of ourselves in different times would be possible even without the numerical unity of the soul.

The various assumptions, which are made at starting in this note, are so strange that a criticism of their admissibility would be unbearably prolix: one can only say of them, Certainly, if it were so, it would be so. But if the communication of a completed state together with the consciousness of it is possible, why should we not go further and make an approach to the actual state of affairs by assuming that, over and above this, the fact of this communication will be an object of consciousness for the soul receiving it? In that case the process would resemble the propagation of culture by tradition and instruction. It is in this way, at least, that the busy soul collects by industry the thoughts of its predecessors; but then it is at the same time conscious that the thoughts it receives are not its own, but what it has received. And fortunately there is another point at which the comparison fails; for the original possessor does not lose his thoughts by communicating them. All this, however, matters nothing: but what is the meaning of the conclusion, 'and yet there has not been the same person in all these states'? The fact is the very reverse; it was not the same sphere that served an abode for the personality; but the person is one, in the same sense in which it is possible for any substance capable of development to be one, although at the beginning of its history it is naturally poorer in recollected experiences than it afterwards becomes: and what Kant maintains is nothing but a strange transmigration of the soul, in which the personality, while it grows in content, passes from one substratum to another. I will not dwell longer on the oddities of this unfortunate comparison; but it shows—and this is its only serious interest—that there seemed to Kant to be some meaning in the idea, that beneath the concrete nature or content of anything there lies in the intelligible world a thing in itself, destitute of content, but serving as a means of consolidating the reality of the concrete thing, or useful to it in some other way, I know not what; and that it makes some difference to the unity of consciousness, whether its substratum consists of the first, or second, or third of these things in themselves, whether it is always the same one, or whether it is many of them in succession; and this although there were even less difference between them than there is between those elastic spheres, the positions of which in space at least gives a reason for supposing that there is more than one of them. Nor was this at all the object which the Paralogism criticised sought to reach. No one who wished the doctrine of immortality to be assured, could concern himself with anything but that continuity of his consciousness which he desired not to lose; he would be heartily indifferent to the question whether the thing in itself which was to be the substratum of that continuance occupied in the series the position n or $(n + 1)$.

I come back then to the point, that the identity of the subject of inward experience is all that we require. So far as, and so long as, the soul knows itself as this identical subject, it is, and is named, simply for that reason, substance. But the attempt to find its capacity of thus knowing itself in the numerical unity of another underlying substance is not a process of reasoning which merely fails to reach an admissible aim; it has no aim at all. That which is not only conceived by others as unity in multiplicity, but knows and makes itself good as such, is, simply on that account, the truest and most indivisible unity there can be. But in Kant's mind, so at least it seems to me, the prejudice is constantly recurring, that a thing may in a certain peculiar sense *be* unity, and that this is metaphysically a much prouder achievement than merely to make itself good as unity, since this last capacity may perhaps also belong to that which is not really or numerically one.

245. A further question now becomes inevitable. On what does this living unity of self-consciousness rest? Or, to put the problem in its customary and shorter form, what is the soul, and how are we to decide respecting its destiny, if our decision can no longer be drawn from the claims which might be advanced in favour of every substance as such, according to its traditional conception? Here again I need only answer by recalling the preliminary convictions to which our ontology has led us. We know that when we ask 'what' anything is, we commonly mean by this word two different things; firstly, that which distinguishes it from other things, and, secondly, that which makes it a thing, like other things. The error which it was our object to avoid lay in the belief that, corresponding to these two constituents of our conception, there exist in reality two elements capable of entering into an actual relation to each other. But we found our most serious obstacle in the habit of adding to these two constituents of our idea a third, which though foreign to them is supposed to guarantee their connexion: this third constituent is that empty 'matter' of existence on which the content of things is supposed to depend. To anyone who is disposed to agree with me in these ontological conclusions, it must seem utterly inconceivable that we should ask for the 'what' of a thing, and yet look for the answer in anything except that which this thing is and does; for that we should enquire as to its 'being,' and yet seek this anywhere except in its activity. And in the same way here it must seem equally unintelligible that we should suppose we do not know the soul, because, although we know all its acts, we are unluckily ignorant of the elastic sphere to which, according to Kant's comparison, the nature manifested in these acts is attached; or that instead of seeking the living reality of the soul in its production of ideas, emotions, and efforts, we should look for it in a nameless 'being,' from which these concrete forms of action could not flow, but in which, after some manner never to be explained, they are supposed to participate. But I have already disposed of these generalities, and will not return to them. Every soul is what it shows itself to be, unity whose life is in definite ideas, feelings, and efforts. This is its real nature: and if it were alone in the world, it would be idle to ask how this reality is possible, since we have long ago decided that the question how things are made is not admissible. It is only the fact that the soul is involved in a larger world, and meets with various fortunes there, that makes it necessary to seek within this whole the conditions on which its existence, and the origin or preservation of that existence, depends. Within this sphere the soul shows itself to be to a certain extent an independent centre of actions and re-actions; and in so far as it does so, and so long as it does so, it has a claim to the title of substance: but we can never draw from the empty idea of substance a necessary conclusion to the position which the soul occupies in the world, as though its modes of action had their ground and justification in that idea.

It will be obvious against what view this remark is directed. A pluralism which considers the order of the world derivable from a number of elements, perfectly independent of one another, and subject only to a supplementary connexion through laws, naturally includes in its idea of the original nature of these elements indestructibility and immutability. Unless then the soul is to be connected with the juxtapositions of these stable atoms as a perishable side-effect, the only resource of this view is to include it among the number of such eternal existences. Thus the soul can rely upon its rights as a pre-mundane substance, and rest assured that in no changes of the world, whatever they may be, can either an origin or an end be ascribed to it.

The fact that this reasoning leads to a double result

is, on the face of it, inconvenient. We might be glad to accept its guarantee for immortality, although no great satisfaction is given to our desires by a mere continuity the nature of which remains undecided; but the other conclusion which is forced on us at the same time, the infinite pre-existence of the soul before the earthly life we know, remains, like the immortality of the souls of all animals, strange and improbable. Our monistic view has long since renounced all these ideas. The order of the world, the existence of all things and their capacity for action, it has placed wholly and without reserve in the hands of the one infinite existence, on which alone the possibility of all interactions was found to rest; and it has nowhere recognised a prior world of ideal necessity, from which things might derive a claim to any other lot than that which the meaning of the whole has given them in order that they may serve it. Our first and foremost result is therefore this: the question of the immortality of the soul does not belong to Metaphysic. We have no other principle for deciding it beyond this general idealistic conviction; that every created thing will continue, if and so long as its continuance belongs to the meaning of the world; that everything will pass away which had its authorised place only in a transitory phase of the world's course. That this principle admits of no further application in human hands hardly needs to be mentioned. We certainly do not know the merits which may give to one existence a claim to eternity, nor the defects which deny it to others.

246. We cannot pass quite so quickly over the question of the *origin* or genesis of the soul. How it can be brought about, or how the creative power of the absolute begins to bring it about, that an existence is produced which not only in accordance with universal laws produces and experiences effects and alterations in its connexion with others, but also in its ideas, emotions, and efforts, separates itself from the common foundation of all things, and becomes to a certain extent an independent centre,—this question we shall no more attempt to answer than we have others like it. Our business is not to make the world, but to understand the inner connexion of the world that is realised already; and it was this problem that forced us to lay down our limiting idea of the absolute and its inner creation of countless finite beings. This idea we found it necessary to regard as the conception of an ultimate fact; and we cannot explain the possibility of the fact by using the images of processes which themselves spring from it in a way we cannot explain. But when the life of the soul does arise, it arises before our eyes in constant conjunction with the physical development of the organism: and thus questions are suggested as to the reciprocal relations of two series of events which, as we have already remarked, cannot be compared, and which therefore might seem inaccessible to one another. Where, we may be asked, does the soul arise, and in what way does it come into this body which is just beginning to be, and which was destined for it; since we are forbidden to regard it as a collateral effect of the physical forces, and as having its natural birthplace in this very body? The question may seem natural, and yet it is only an imagination accustomed to strange images which can ask it. We are not to picture the absolute placed in some remote region of extended space, and separated from the world of its creations, so that its influence has to retraverse a distance and make a journey in order to reach things; for its indivisible unity, omnipresent at every point, would fill this space as well as others. Still less ought we, who hold this space to be a mere phenomenon, to imagine a cleft between finite beings and the common foundation of all things, a cleft which would need to be bridged by miraculous wanderings. Wherever in apparent space an organic germ has been formed, at that very spot, and not removed from it, the absolute is also present. Nor, I must once more repeat, is it simply this class of facts which compels us to assume such an action of the absolute. We may regard the process by which things that possess a life and soul are formed as something unusual and superior; but the presence of the absolute which makes this process possible is no less the basis necessarily implied in the most insignificant interaction of any two atoms. Nor again do we think of its presence as a mere uniform breath which penetrates all places and this particular spot among them, like that subtle, formless, and homogeneous ether from which many strange theories expect the vivification of matter into the most various forms: but the absolute is *indivisibly* present with the whole inner wealth of its nature in this particular spot, and, in obedience to those laws of its action which it has itself laid down, necessarily makes additions to the simple conjunctions of those elements which are themselves only its own continuous actions, simple additions where the conjunctions are simple, additions of greater magnitude and value where they are more complicated. Everywhere it draws only the consequences, which at every point of the whole belong to the premisses it has previously realised at that point. It is thus that it gives to every organism its fitting soul; and it is therefore needless to devise a way or make provision for the correct choice which should ensure to every animal germ the soul which answers to its kind. Again, so long as the soul was regarded as indivisible substance, it could only be supposed to enter the body at a single instant and in its entirety: whereas, if we renounce these ideas of an external conjunction, we need no longer wish to fix the moment at which the soul enters into a development which at first is supposed to produce only physical actions.

We have all along regarded the interaction of the absolute with all the elements of the world as eternal and incessant. It is present just as continuously in the first development of the germ; and in the same way there is nothing to prevent us from looking at the formation of the soul as an extended process in time, a process in which the absolute gradually gives a further form to its creation. Doubtless we shall never be able to picture this process to ourselves; but at any rate there is no force in the possible objection that such a gradual development contradicts the unity of the soul. For we are speaking, not of a composition of pieces already present in separation, but of the successive transformations of something established at the beginning of the process. And if this again should seem to contradict the idea of one unchangeable substance, I recur to my previous assertion; it is not because the soul is substance and unity that it asserts itself as such, but it is substance and unity, as soon as, and in so far as, it asserts itself as such; and if it does this gradually in a greater degree, and with a growing significance, I should not hesitate to distinguish in its substantiality, and in the intensity of its unity, countless different grades which it traverses by degrees when first it is being formed, and the last and highest of which it may perhaps be incapable of reaching during the whole of its terrestrial and super-terrestrial existence.

And now, after our picture has been thus altered, collecting its various traits, I may return to an earlier statement: if anyone were in a position to observe the first development of the soul, just as with the microscope we can observe the physical development of the germ, the result would infallibly be that everything would look to him exactly as materialism believes it actually to take place. As the structure progressively differentiated itself, he would see appearing, not all at once, but by degrees, the faint and gradually multiplying traces of psychical activity; but nowhere would he meet with the sudden irruption of a power, which seemed foreign to the play of the elements active before his eyes: he would see the whole condition of things which has been thought to justify the view that all psychical life is a side-effect of the physical process of formation. This condition of things we admit; and the view based on it we reject. All the single manifestations which could thus be observed might no doubt be regarded as products of the interaction of the physical elements; but the unity of consciousness, to which at a later time our inward experience testifies, cannot, in the absence of a subject, be the mere result of the activities of a number of elements, and just as little can this subject be created by those activities. Nor again is it out of nothing that the soul is made or created by the absolute; but to satisfy the imagination we may say it is from itself, from its own real nature that the absolute projects the soul, and so adds to its one activity, the course of nature, that other which, in the ruling plan of the absolute, is its natural completion.

247. I know well that our metaphysical enquiries are constantly and jealously watched by certain side-thoughts of our own; and here they raise the question whether we are not in the interests of the intellect laying down positions which will afterwards prove fatal to the requirements of the emotional side of our nature. In subjecting the origin of psychical life to the dominion of law, are we not once more reducing the whole course of the world to that necessary evolution of a mere nature in which no place remains for any free beginning and, therefore, none for any guiding providence? I admit that there is ground for such doubts, but not that it is my duty to meet them here. If the need that is expressed in them is a justifiable one, still it is only where its justification is successful that we can attempt to satisfy it without cancelling what we have previously found to be necessary for the theoretic intelligibility of the world. So long then as psychical life is realised in countless instances after the same universal patterns, and so long as the same processes are repeated countless times in every single soul, we cannot refuse to admit a connexion which follows universal laws and which here, as elsewhere, shows like results following on like conditions, and the same changes in the former following on the same changes in the latter. We may put aside the question whether this connexion is all that the reality of things conceals or includes: whatever may be necessary to complete it, it cannot itself be denied.

There are two directions, therefore, in which a mechanical point of view may extend its claim over these subjects. It has been attempted long since in the case of the inward life of the soul, and the conception of a psychical mechanism is no longer unfamiliar to us: I have met with less sympathy for that other idea of a physico-psychical mechanism, the object of which was to base the commerce between soul and body on a series of thoughts similar to those which we apply to the interaction of physical elements. Accepting with gratitude the pleasanter name 'psycho-physical mechanism,' which by Fechner's ingenious attempts has been introduced into science, I will once more attempt to defend those outlines of my theory which I sketched in the *Medicinische Psychologie* (1852). According to some views my proposal is impossible; and according to others it is superfluous. The essence of it lay in the attempt to regard the soul as an existence possessing unity, and the body as a number of other inter-connected existences, and to regard the two as the two sides, neither identical nor disconnected, from the interaction of which mental life proceeds, that life being *in posse* based on the proper nature of the soul, but stirred to actual existence by the influences of the external world.

248. I need not be prolix in opposing those who adduce the incomparability of things psychical and material as an objection against the possibility of any interaction between them. Admitting this incomparability, it would still be an unfounded prejudice to suppose that only like can act on like, and a mistake to imagine that the case of an interaction of soul and body is an exceptional one, and that we are here to find inexplicable what in any action of matter upon matter we understand. It is only the false idea that an action or effect[1] is a complete state, transferable from

---

[1] [Cf. § 57, *supra*.]

one substrate to the other, which misleads us into demanding that any two things which are to influence one another should be homogeneous: for, if that idea were correct, it would of course follow that b, to which the effect passes, and a, from which it issues, must be sufficiently similar to give it admittance in the same way. But, as a matter of fact, the form of any effect proceeds from the nature of that on which the external cause acts, and is not determined exclusively by the latter; and no species of conditions can be adduced, the presence of which is indispensable to enable one thing a to excite another thing b so to manifest its own nature. To our sensuous imagination, it is true, no interaction but that of similar elements (similar at least in their external appearance) presents itself as a connected image; but it is only our sensuous imagination that seeks to retain for every case of action the homogeneous character which it fancies it understands to be an essential condition in this particular case. And this is just where it deceives itself. I have frequently pointed out how often we suppose ourselves to understand something, when our senses are simply occupied with a variegated and unbroken series of phenomena. So long as we are merely looking at the outside of a machine we do not imagine that we comprehend it: but when it is opened and we see how all its parts fit into one another, and how at last it brings out a result utterly unlike the impulse first imparted, we think that we understand its action perfectly. And it really is clear to us, in so far as the explanation of a complicated process means its reduction to a concatenation of very simple actions which we have made up our minds to consider intelligible; but the action which takes place between each pair of the simplest links of the chain remains just as incomprehensible as before, and equally incomprehensible whether those links are like one another or not. The working of every machine yet known rests on the fact that certain parts of it are solid and that these parts communicate their motions; but how the elements manage to bind one another into an unchanging shape, and how they can transmit motions—and this is what is essential in the process of the action of matter upon matter—remains invisible, and the similarity of the parts concerned in the action adds nothing to its intelligibility. When then we speak of an action taking place between the soul and material elements, all that we miss is the perception of that external scenery which may make the influence of matter on matter more familiar to us, but cannot explain it. We shall never see the last atom of the nerve impinging on the soul, or the soul upon it; but equally in the case of two visible spheres the impact is not the intelligible cause of the communication of motion; it is nothing but the form in which we can perceive something happening which we do not comprehend.

The mistake is to desire to discover indispensable conditions of all action; and we are only repeating this mistake in another form when we declare the immaterial soul, as devoid of mass, incapable of acting mechanically on a dense material mass, or conceive it as an invulnerable shadow, inaccessible to the attacks of the corporeal world. We might without hesitation take an opposite point of view, and speak of the soul as a definite mass at every moment when it produces an effect measurable by the movement of a corporeal mass. And in doing so we should be taking none of its immateriality from it; for with bodies also it is not the case that they are first masses and then and therefore produce effects or act; but according to the degree of their effects they are called masses of a certain magnitude. The soul again is no less capable of *receiving* effects through the stimulus of material elements than they are from one another, although it does not stand face to face with them in an equally perceptible shape; for as between those elements themselves shape and movement, impact and pressure, determine nothing but the external appearance behind which, and the scene on which, the imperceptible process of action goes on.

And, lastly, in our present metaphysical discussion we need not have entered on these objections at all. We have given up that simple and thorough division of reality, which places matter on one side and the mind on the other, confident and full of faith in regard to the former, timid and doubtful about the latter. Everything we supposed ourselves to know of matter as an obvious and independent existence, has long since been dissolved in the conviction that matter itself, together with the space, by filling which it seemed most convincingly to prove its peculiar nature, is nothing but an appearance for our perception, and that this appearance arises from the reciprocal effects which existences, in themselves super-sensuous, produce on one another and, consequently, also upon the soul. There may, therefore, be some other way in which the soul is separated from these existences; but it is not parted from them by the gulf of that incomparability which is supposed to be a bar to all interaction.

249. So long as we believe this gulf to exist, we naturally try to bridge it, and therefore raise the pointless question respecting the bond which holds body and soul together. What is the use of a bond except to hold together things which, being perfectly indifferent to each other and destitute of all interaction, threaten to fall asunder? And how is a bond to do its work except through the connexion of its own parts, a connexion which one cannot suppose to be in its turn effected by new bonds between these parts, but which must rest in the end on their own interactions? And if in this instance it is clear that the binding force of the bond consists simply in the interactions which flow from the inner relations of its parts to one another, why should the case be different between the body and soul? Their union consists in the fact that they can and must act on one another, and no external bond which embraced them both could supply the place of this capacity and necessity, unless its inclusion of them were already based on their own natures. Besides, how poverty-stricken is the idea of this single bond, which in our parsimony we fancy will suffice us! Even supposing it to exist, where are we to find the positive ground of the nature and form of those actions or effects which, as a matter of fact, take place? The reason for their existence cannot be found by another appeal to the indifferent bond; it would have to be sought in the peculiar natures of the things connected. Whatever number of different interactions body and soul can effect in virtue of the relation of their natures, so many bonds are there which unite them and hold them together: but to look for the one nameless bond which should take the place of all these, is vain, absurd, and wearisome. Even if we understand it to be merely a *conditio sine qua non* for the exercise of capacities based on something else, we still must refuse to admit it; for the body and soul were never separated from one another like two bodies which cannot act on one another chemically until they are brought together. One word, lastly, on the sarcasm which reproaches us with forming the personality of man by adding two ingredients together. It is just this addition that is made by the one external bond; and what we want is not it but the multiplicity of a complex double and united life. But in spite of this unity we do not look for man's personality in body and soul alike, but in the soul alone. We seek in the body only the echo or appearance of its action; for the body is and remains for the soul a part of the external world, though that part which it can most directly rule and to whose influence it is most immediately susceptible.

250. There is another question on which I wish to touch, and these remarks at once suggest it. If the interaction of body and soul is an easy matter, why not go a step further, instead of still maintaining a separation into two interacting sides? At how many points have we come close to an opposite view! We did not regard the soul as something steadfast in itself from eternity, something which enters as an indissoluble substance into the machinery of the body's formation; we admitted that they arise together. Even the supposition that the soul arises gradually according as the bodily organization approaches its completion, did not seem to us impossible. What is there now to hinder the confession that it is simply a consequence of this physical concatenation of atoms? And if on the other side it is conceded that, so long as we abide by the customary physical ideas, we cannot deduce the origin of a psychical process from the co-operation of material atoms, why need we hold to those ideas? Why not adopt that wider view, which holds that if a number of elements meet together, then, according as the number of the connected parts and the multiplicity of their relations increase, perfectly new effects or actions may be connected with those meeting elements, effects which do not follow on the interaction of two atoms alone, and which therefore we never can discover, so long as we try to find the conclusions of such complicated premisses by merely adding together the interactions of each pair of them?

In answering this question I must first go back to an earlier statement. Even supposing we could unreservedly approve of these ideas, still the only purpose we could put them to would be to deduce from them what is given us in experience; that must not be put aside as a matter for doubt, on the ground that our presuppositions are not found to lead to it. Now what is connected with these associations of many elements is not merely psychical states, phenomena, events, or whatever we like to call them. For each of these results inexorably demands a subject, whose state or stimulation it is; and psychical life, so far as it is a given object of inward experience, includes for us the fact of a *unity* of this subject, to which the events we have spoken of are or can be referred as something that befalls it. I will not repeat my demonstration that the analogy of the formation of physical resultants can never lead us to this unity, unless we take beforehand as a fixed point the unity of the subject in which a variety of elements is to combine: I will only add that the ideas I have been mentioning offer no new expedient which could lead us beyond that deduction of resultants. Since so much that is new has to arise from the combination of the atoms, it seems to me that we should have to make up our minds to the final step, and maintain that from a certain definite form of this combination there also arises, as a new existence, that one subject, that very soul which collects in itself the states previously scattered among the subjects of the individual atoms. But the mere admission that psychical unity springs from physical multiplicity is no merit in the theory; it simply states the supposed fact, and so gives expression to a very familiar problem, but it offers us no further explanation of it. On the other hand, the expression employed is scarcely peculiar to the view in question; for the psychical unity of which it speaks is simply what we mean by the word substance. It is under this title then, as substance, that the soul would become the foundation on which our account of the rest of its life would be based; for by nothing short of this should we have complied with the postulates which experience imposes on our attempts at explanation. And at this point I should take leave to pursue the same point of view still further. According to it, it is possible that a certain state of things may be the real ground of a consequence which we cannot analytically deduce from it but can only conjoin to it as something new; but if this is so, it is possible that the soul, once arisen, may go its own way and unfold activities which have their sufficient ground in it alone (when once it has come into being), and not in the least in those other facts which led to its creation. There would remain therefore not a shadow of necessity for the proposal to connect with every activity of the soul as its producing condition a corresponding activity of the body, and we should simply come back to that psycho-physical mechanism which allows each side a sphere of interaction, but at the same time accords to each a field for an activity of its own in which the other has no constant share.

251. I have still something to add to our hypothesis. 'When the elements $p, q, r \ldots$, are combined in the form F an effect or action Z is conjoined with them, which does not follow from the single effects of the elements when taken in pairs:' this is a pleasing expression, and one that satisfies the imagination. But who has conjoined the effect with them? Or, not to insist unfairly on the words, how are we to conceive the fact that a law holds good for the various elements $p, q, r \ldots$, which determines the effect Z for their form of combination F? How are we to conceive this other fact, that those elements take notice that at a given moment this F is present, i.e. that a case has arisen for the application of the law which was not present the moment before? Or lastly, if we recollect that that form of combination signifies nothing but an affection of those elements already present in them, in consequence of which they are no longer $p, q, r \ldots$, but $\pi, \kappa, \rho \ldots$, still the question would remain, how did this change in the state of each become noticeable by every other, so that they could all conspire to produce the further action Z? I have already raised these questions more than once, and the necessary answer to them has seemed to be that the course of the world is not comprehensible by a pluralism which starts with an original multiplicity of elements reciprocally indifferent, and hopes afterwards through the mere behest of laws to force them to take notice of each other. Apart from the unity of the encompassing Reality which is all things at once and which determines their being and nature, it is impossible to conceive the arising of any action at a given place and time, whether that action be one of those the content of which we believe to be deducible from the given circumstances, or one of those which can only be regarded as a new addition to them. I repeat this here in order to defend the hypothesis of the preceding paragraph. For I should certainly never set anyone the task, out of ten elements to make an eleventh arise equally real with them. It is not from them that, on this hypothesis, the substance of the soul would spring; nor would it arise above them, between them, or by the side of them, out of nothing. It would be a new creation, produced by the one encompassing being from its own nature as the supplement of its physical activity there and then operating.

252. To a certain extent no doubt I should be merely disputing about words, if I insisted on these statements still further in opposition to Fechner, considering that his works testify so fully to his enthusiasm for a unity of all things which should be at once ideal and effective. Yet it would not be altogether a verbal quarrel; I am anxious to take this opportunity of declaring against a point of view which may be at any rate surmised from the expressions he has chosen. After what I have said I need not repeat that, in my eyes, nothing is gained in the way of clearness by the invention of the name 'psycho-physical occurrence,' or 'psycho-physical process.' I admit that the expression may have a meaning when applied to a single element, in which, as I said before, we conceive physical and psychical stimulations to exist together. But when it is used to explain that life of the soul, which is supposed to develope itself from the co-operation of a system of elements, it seems to me to be attractive only because of its indistinctness. Where we find it difficult to define the connexion between two members of a relation which must be kept apart and distinct, we all feel some weakness for ideas which represent the two as an original unity and thereby dismiss the object of our enquiry from the world. In the present case I can find no clear account of the definite single subject to which each single instance of this process is ascribed, and no statement of the manner in which these actions or effects work into each other and form a composite whole. What is more important, however, to me is the difference between the lights in which we view what is perhaps the same set of ideas. I allude to the general remarks at the end of the second volume of Fechner's *Elemente der Psychophysik* (p. 515). In this passage I find that he observes upon and supplies though in a peculiar form, what I looked for in vain in other statements of the pluralistic hypothesis. I do not doubt at all that, for those who are accustomed to the terminology, the waves and principal waves of the psychophysical activity, like its sinking or its rising over certain thresholds, are something more than short and pictorial designations of actual facts in the life of the soul; that they are signs which, through their capacity of taking a mathematical form, may lead to more definite formulations of reciprocal relations of those facts. But I cannot help feeling that in these descriptions of what happens the real condition of its happening is also looked for; or, if this is a misunderstanding, that at any rate there is much provocation for it. For if no idea of this kind had had a hand in the matter, many of the explanations that are given would be in reality nothing but elegant transcriptions of familiar thoughts into this sign-language, transcriptions which do not directly advance the enquiry: and the reader will not suppose that he has gained anything by them unless he is allowed to take these images for the discovery of something hitherto unknown, of the instrumentation, so to speak, on which the realisation of the psychical processes rests.

One of the last sentences of this celebrated book (p. 546) may explain what it is I object to. The substrate of what is psychical, we are told, is something diffused through the whole world and connected into a system by universal forces; the quantity of consciousness depends simply on the quantity, and not on the quality of the psycho-physical motion; and this quality should rather be connected only with the quality of the phenomena of consciousness. Thus every motion, whatever its form and whatever its substrate, would, on reaching a certain specified value, contribute something to consciousness, whether that consciousness be our own or that of another person or a general consciousness; and every particular form of motion—i.e. every particular collocation and series of velocity-components—would carry with it its appropriate psychical phenomenon of the appropriate form, so soon as the components entering into that form all exceed a certain quantitative value.

'In this way we dispense with the magical charm, the *qualitas occulta*, which is supposed to qualify for psychical effects only this or that exceptional form of motion.' 'What is unconscious and what is conscious in the world will represent merely two cases of the same formula, which is the standard at once of their relation and of their transition into one another.'

I maintain nothing respecting the meaning intended in these words: I maintain only that they may easily be understood, or misunderstood, to recommend a view, the admissibility of which I certainly contest. However much we may bring the phenomena of two different series of events under one and the same formula—and I do not deny that it is possible to do so—still all that the formula in any case does is to describe the phenomena after they are actually there; it is not the reason why they are actually there. If all the hopes here expressed of the psycho-physical calculus were fulfilled, we should nevertheless still be unable to dispense with that *qualitas occulta*, which brings, not to an exceptional kind of motion, but to *every* motion the capacity for an activity which does not lie in the motion itself. I may be told that what I miss is already included in the character of the motion as *psycho-physical*; and indeed it is not so much the meaning of these sentences that I wish to object to as the manner in which it is expressed. Still there appears everywhere as something first and foremost a universal mechanism, which of itself is supposed to produce this result, that, in relation to certain forms of motion, there arises, as their natural and necessary consequence and as the consequence of nothing beside them, a mental activity; for even the general formula which is to include conscious and unconscious as two cases, must obviously, as the common element *of* which they are cases, mean not the mere abstract formula, but always in the last resort that which is itself unconscious, namely, motion. The beautiful thoughts in which Fechner contradicts this interpretation will be put aside by most of his readers as excusable day-dreams; but there are many who will make use of his expressions in order to shelter under a great name their favourite doctrine of the *generatio aequivoca* of everything rational from that which is devoid of reason.

CHAPTER II.

Sensations and the Course of Ideas.

253. OUR mental life is aroused anew at every moment by sensations which the external world excites. But the things without us become the cause of our sensation not through their mere existence, but only through effects which they produce in us; through motions, in which either they themselves approach the surface of our body until they touch it, or which they from their own fixed position communicate to some medium, and which this medium in turn propagates from atom to atom up to that surface. And therefore, though language describes things as objects which we see and hear, we must not allow these transitive expressions to suggest the idea that our senses, or our soul by means of them, exercise some activity which goes out to seek for the external objects and brings them to perception. Our attitude is at first one of simple waiting; and although when we strain our eyes and ears in listening or watching we may seem to feel in those organs something of such an outgoing activity, what we really feel is not this but a different activity,—one by which we place them in a state of the utmost sensitiveness for the impressions we expect.

Now it is self-evident that sensations, which we have at one time and not at another, can only arise from the alteration of a previous state, and therefore only through some motion which brings about this alteration. The old idea therefore that the mere assumption of a specific substance or caloric was sufficient to account for our feeling of heat was, apart from all other objections, intrinsically false: for this caloric, even if it were present, could not, in the absence of any motion, produce either the sensation of heat or those other effects which would prove that it itself was present. But that is one objection which I fear will be raised against the doctrine that all our sensations and perceptions depend on motions of the things which are to be their objects. From an ontological point of view I regarded a certain sympathetic *rapport* as the ultimate ground of every possible interaction. But, I may be asked, if this idea is sound, why should not things exist for one another apart from any physical intermediation; and why should not we perceive things immediately, without having to wait for the impact of their propagated motion on us? That sympathy, I answer, the name of which was borrowed from a dubious quarter, was not such a community of all things as is destitute of order and degree. On the contrary, we found that the elements of the whole stood to one another in relations varying widely in their closeness or distance; and it was to these elements we ascribed an immediate sympathy which needs no artificial means for its production. The degree of this closeness or distance determines for any two elements the number of intermediates necessary for their interaction; necessary, not because the laws of a premundane system of mechanics would render the interaction impossible in the absence of these intermediates, but because, in their absence, it would be in contradiction with the degree and nature of the relation on which it is founded, and with that meaning of the whole which again is the foundation of whatever mechanical laws hold good in the world. Thus in our view, the motions in question, the physical *stimuli* of the senses, are not the instrumental conditions, which place all things for the first time in relations to one another and to us, but *expressions* of that existing and irremovable network of conditions which the meaning of the world has established between the states of those things. We know that in any chain, along which an action or effect is propagated, there is necessarily pre-supposed in the last resort a wholly immediate action between each link and that which lies next to it. The fantastic idea which extends this direct reciprocal influence to anything and everything, and would accordingly place the soul in a communion, free from all physical intermediation, with distant objects, cannot therefore be theoretically proved impossible. But inability to controvert a point of view lies a long way from belief in its validity. Considering that the whole of the known and waking life of the soul is based throughout upon that physical intermediation, we can only answer asserted experiences of an interruption of this connexion by the most decided disbelief, and these experiences could call for attention only if occasioning causes could be assigned, adequate to produce such remarkable exceptions in the course of nature.

254. On their arrival in the body the external stimuli meet with the system of nerve-fibres prepared for their reception. The change which they set up in these nerve-fibres becomes the internal sense-stimulus, which is the more immediate cause of our sensation. We leave it to physiology to ascertain exactly what takes place in this nervous process. The answer to that question could have a value for psychology only if it were so complete as to enable us to deduce from the various modifications of the process the corresponding modifications of the sensation and to express the relation in a universal law: whereas the mere subordination of the nervous process under a specific conception is only of importance for the question whether we have to consider it as a mere physical process or whether it is itself something psychical. The latter view is frequently met with. The sensation is said to be formed already in the nerve, and to be transferred by it to consciousness. If this assumption is to have any clearness it must name the definite subject to which it ascribes the act of sensation; for sensations which nobody has cannot be realities. Now this subject of sensation could not be found in the whole nerve, as such, which is an aggregate of unnumbered parts: it is only each single atom, however many of them we suppose to be strung together in the whole nerve, that could be, by itself, a feeling thing. But to this difficulty must be added a familiar fact. The external sense-stimulus does not become the cause of a sensation in us, unless the nerve remains uninterrupted throughout its whole course, from its peripheral point of stimulus up to the central portions of the nervous system. If its continuity is broken by a cut, the influence of the external stimulus on consciousness is removed. Whether the idea, to which this fact naturally gives rise, is correct or not,—the idea that the soul has its seat in a particular spot to which the incoming impression must be directed,—or in what other way we are to explain the truth that this integrity of the nerve-fibre is an indispensable condition of our sensation, we need not here discuss. In any case there is a propagation of the stimulation in the nerve itself, and all its parts cannot be at once in the state of sensation pre-supposed. But it is impossible that one and the same sample of sensation can be handed on from one atom of the nerve to another like a packet; all that can happen is that each single element of the nerve becomes, in virtue of its own state, a stimulus to the next to produce the same state in itself. Now that this excitation is not produced by a direct sympathy, is proved by that interruption to its propagation which results from any mechanical breach of continuity. Such a sympathy would pass undisturbed across the point of section, and would feel no effects from changes in physical relations of which it would be from its very nature independent.

We are therefore compelled to introduce a physical connecting link for the effect we have presupposed. Through the external sense-stimulus there is produced in the first nerve-element the physical state *r* and, in consequence, in the same element the state of sensation *s*. By this change the first element is compelled to awake in the second, its neighbour, the same state *r* and, in consequence, the sensation *s*. Thus, through the physical impact of one element on another there would be propagated at the same time the creation of the corresponding sensation. But where would this end? Wherever and however this chain of atoms with their internal excitations may at last connect itself with the soul, the sensation of the soul, *our* sensation, would arise out of the soul itself simply through the influence of the last *r* with which the last nerve-atom stimulates it, in precisely the same way in which this sensation was produced in link after link of the chain. Whatever service then can be rendered by the nerve in aid of the production of our sensation, it can render just as well by transmitting a merely physical change, as if each of its atoms experienced the same psychical state which is to arise in us at the end of the whole process. A piece of news which passes in the form of a letter from hand to hand along a series of messengers, reaches the recipient no more securely and is no better understood by him if each of the intermediates knows and feels it. Doubtless we shall never be able to portray the action of that final *r* on the nature of the soul; but we cannot do so any the more by adding to the physical process *r* the sensation *s*. This *s* in its turn could only occasion the production of our sensation S in some perfectly indemonstrable way; it could not itself pass over into us. On the other hand the propagation in the nerve of a physical process *r* up to this mysterious moment, is something which the fact of experience alluded to compels us to assume. It is sufficient, therefore, to regard the nervous process as a propagation of something, taking place in space and time in a definite direction and with a definite velocity; the precise nature of that which is propagated concerns us but little, and, since these are the only forms of its propagation which are of importance, it may be described as merely physical.

255. The conscious sensation itself, the red or blue that we see, the sound that we hear, is the third and last link in this series of occurrences, and it is familiar to us. We know that this content of sensation admits of no comparison either with the external sense-stimulus or with the nervous processes. There is nothing in the redness of red, the blueness of blue, or the sound of the heard tone, which suggests a larger or smaller number of vibrations of a medium; yet science has indirectly discovered such vibrations to be the occasion of these sensations. In the same way they give us no information respecting that which *directly* occasions them, the process which goes on in the optic or auditory nerve at the moment when these sensations are produced in us; they are consequences, not copies, of their stimuli. Thus they are internal phenomena in the soul, and in this sense of the words the doctrine of the subjectivity of all sensations has long been the property of philosophy and required no acquaintance with the functions of the nerves.

There is another sense of the words, according to which the sensations are held to be *merely* internal phenomena, and the external world to be neither resonant nor silent, neither bright nor dark, but to possess only mathematical predicates of number and magnitude, of motions and their complications; and in this sense of the words the doctrine was in antiquity an insufficiently proved inference, and it remains so for the physiology of the present day. None of the proofs which are commonly appealed to in support of it, can close every way of escape to the opposite view. Anyone who wishes to maintain that things themselves remain red or sweet, will affirm, as we do, that it is not through their *being* that they can appear to us as they are, but only through effects which, in accordance with their nature, they produce on us. These effects or actions, which proceed from them and are sense-stimuli to us, are no doubt only motions and themselves neither red nor sweet; but what is there to prevent our supposing that, by acting through our nerves, they make that same redness or sweetness arise, as our sensation, in our souls, which also attaches as a quality to the things themselves? Such a process would be no more wonderful than the performances of the telephone, which receives waves of sound, propagates them in a form of motion quite different, and in the end conducts them to the ear retransformed into waves of sound. Anything which deprives things of the medium through which their excitations could reach us; anything again which has beforehand imparted to the medium motions which prevent the passage of those excitations, would of course either hinder things from appearing to us at all or would make them appear with other qualities, and so would lead us to suppose that none of these qualities belong to things themselves at all.

There are no individual proofs by which these assertions could be controverted; and yet the doctrine of the mere subjectivity of the qualities of sensation is certainly sound. Their own nature makes it impossible for us really so to represent them to ourselves as qualities of things, as we profess to do. There is no meaning in speaking of a brightness seen by nobody at all, of the sound of a tone which no one hears, of a sweetness which no one tastes: they are all as impossible as a toothache which nobody has got. There is only one place in which what is meant by these words can possibly exist, the consciousness of a feeling being: and there is only one way in which it can exist, the way of being felt by that being. Without doubt then, things are red only so far as they appear to us; *in* itself a thing could only have a particular look if it could look *at* itself.

256. According to a theorem of the doctrine of specific energies, every nerve, by whatever stimulus excited, invariably calls forth sensations of one and the same kind, the special sensations of its own sense; and it makes no difference whether the stimulus is one appropriate to the nerve or not. If this were a fact, its physical reason would not be hard to imagine. Let us take a composite system of parts. External stimuli, so long as they are not so violent as to destroy the internal connexions of this system, will cause a motion followed by an effort to return to equilibrium; and these will take place in forms which essentially depend on the structure of the system, which in that case remains unchanged. So with the nerve; disturbances of a certain magnitude would injure it; but to less violent stimuli it would always respond with the same reactions, and these reactions would depend on its peculiar structure. But then, if these reactions are to be different in the case of every single nerve, the structure of the various nerves must be different; and this variety of structure we do not find in the nerves themselves, though we may perhaps look for it in the central portions to which they lead.

But in any case the facts themselves are generalised in this theorem to an extent which actual observation does not justify. We know nothing of waves of sound which produce in the eye a sensation of light, nor of waves of light which produce tones in the ear. The main support of the hypothesis lies in the sensations of light which frequently arise in the eye from impact or pressure, as well as from electrical stimulation. But there are other considerations which compel us to assume in the media of the eye the presence of the same ether which serves for the diffusion of the light outside; and accordingly, when in consequence of impact the ponderable elements of the tense eyeball fall into oscillation, we can scarcely help supposing that they impart this oscillation at the same time to the ether. Thus the same objective motion of light which commonly, as an adequate stimulus, comes from without, may be excited in the eye by this oscillation of the eyeball, and a similar motion might be excited by electric currents; such motion not being sufficient to cast any observable rays outwards, but strong enough to stimulate the nerve to produce a sensation of light. Again, in the case of the inadequate stimuli which actually do create a sensation of *sound*, the question is prudently avoided whether they may not do so by accidentally exciting such vibrations as form the natural stimulus of the auditory nerves. The excitation of *taste* by electricity certainly depends on the adequate stimulus, the chemical processes which are here set up; the notion that it can also be produced by laceration of the tongue seems to have been an illusion, and it will be useless for insipid dishes to look for help in this quarter: and as to the remaining sensations, we do not know at all what the adequate form of the stimuli is which actually must reach the nerves in order to produce them.

We may leave it therefore to physiology to decide whether the real meaning of the present widely-spread doctrine of the division of labour is not rather this;—that every nerve is excited to its function only by its own adequate stimulus, and that other stimuli either leave it unaffected or else interfere with it, but that at the same time there are stimuli of various kinds which, along with their own effects, frequently produce the adequate stimuli as side-results. The only interest psychology has in the question lies in opposing the fondness for a mysterious psychical activity which, on the authority of the facts I have mentioned, is attributed to the nerves and not to the soul, to which it really belongs. To speak of a substance of the sense of sight, and to say that this substance converts every possible motion that reaches it into a sensation of light, is not to describe facts but to use a piece of physiological metaphysic; of which I am not sure that it is at all more elegant than the metaphysic of philosophy.

257. However complete the separation may be between sensations and the stimuli which occasion them, these two series of occurrences are, as a matter of fact, connected, and we shall not suppose that this connexion of fact is destitute of any principle. We shall always find ourselves presupposing that like groups of sensations correspond to like groups of stimuli, and different groups of the one to different groups of the other; that the difference of these classes of sensation is proportional to the difference which exists between the classes of stimuli; that wherever the stimuli of a given group are arranged in a progressive series or, in their progress, reach marked points of eminence, the corresponding sensations are arranged in a similar series and accordingly reproduce both the progress and the points of eminence; that, lastly, in the unity of the soul its various kinds of sensation not only *are* together as a fact, but in their meaning are coherent according to some rule, though that rule may not be expressible in mathematical terms.

But of an empirical confirmation of this presupposition we find but faint traces. Not only is it impossible to say why waves of ether must necessarily be felt as light; but, even if this fact were given as a starting-point, no theory, however much it emphasized the unity of the soul, could prove that this same soul must in consistency perceive waves of sound as tones, and other affections as taste or smell. So far as we can see, that unity produces, from a nature of its own which is quite unknown to us, the various classes of sensation, each for itself and apart from the others; and, even after we have come to know them, all that we can connect with their impressions are vague and fantastic ideas respecting the organization of a universal realm of sensations. Again, when we come to the individual groups, the only one which confirms our supposition is the group of sounds. Here the increase in the height of a tone corresponds to an increase in the number of waves within a given unit of time. The ascending scale, which is just as clearly an ascent as is the increase in the number of waves and yet is quite unlike that increase, repeats in its own specific form the progress in the series of stimuli. Wherever this series attains, through the doubling of a previous number of waves, a marked import, there the sensation follows with the marked impression of the octave of the key-note, and thus again in its own particular way represents sensuously the likeness and difference of the two series. On the other hand the colours, though their prismatic order rests on a similar increase in the number of waves, give no one who is unprejudiced the impression of a similar progress; and the reason of this possibly lies in the peculiar nature of the nervous process which intervenes between the stimulus and sensation, and which we cannot take into consideration because we do not know it. In the cases of the remaining senses we have no exact knowledge of the nature of their stimuli, nor have we succeeded in discerning any fixed relations between their individual sensations. We do not possess even names for the various smells, except such as describe them by their origin or their incidental effects; and among the multitude of tastes the only ones that can be distinguished as well-defined are the four forms of acid, alkaline, sweet, and bitter. Hypothetical theories carry us no further. In the case of sight and hearing alone we know that each sensation rests on the total effect of a very large number of successive impulses, and changes with the alterations of this number within the given unit of time; whether the single impact of a wave of light or sound would be observable by our senses, and if so in what way, is utterly unknown to us. Still we can generalise this fact with some probability. Perhaps it is true of all our sensations that they rest not on a constant and indiscriminate stream of excitation, but on the number of alternations of excitation and non-excitation included in a certain time; the nature of the process, which thus in the form of oscillation stimulates the soul, might be a matter of less importance, and the same perhaps for all the nerves. But then again this supposition makes it no easier to connect the various kinds of sensation with one another in a progressive series; and we have further to admit the possibility that our human senses do not include the whole range of sensible existence, and that other living beings may have other forms of sensation unknown to us and answering to processes which entirely escape our perception.

258. There is at any rate one point at which the modern psycho-physical investigations have resulted in the beginnings of an exact knowledge regarding the relation between sensation and stimulus. The commonest observation of a brightening light or a rising sound shows us that our senses can detect very slight alterations in the strength of an impression. But we never reach a moment at which, judging merely by the direct impression, we could say that one brightness was twice or thrice as strong, or one sound half as strong, as another. In consequence of this inability to reduce to numerical equivalents the more and less which we perceive, it is impossible for us to place a series of values of stimuli side by side with the values of the corresponding sensations, and so to formulate a universal law according to which the intensity of the latter would depend on the strength of the former. There is however one judgment we can pronounce, if not with absolute yet with sufficient certainty, viz. that there is or is not an observable difference between two sensations. To this point accordingly were directed those experiments, the object of which was to discover, first of all, what amount of increase a stimulus requires in order that the sensation which belongs to it as increased may begin to distinguish itself from the sensation of its previous strength; or, again, to discover the limit of slightness down to which the difference between two strengths of the stimulus can be diminished without removing the possibility of the sensations being distinguished. With regard to the moderate stimuli which are strong enough to excite a distinct sensation, and yet do not approach the point at which their intensity disturbs the function of the nerve, Fechner and many others since, following E. H. Weber's example, have made a very large number of experiments; and these experiments lead with sufficient unanimity to the result that that difference between any two stimuli which makes it possible to distinguish the corresponding sensations from one another, is not a constant quantity, but, in the case of each class of sensations, amounts to a definite fraction of the intensity already possessed by that one of the two stimuli from which we start. We are not interested in following the various mathematical formulations of Weber's Law, or the corrections which its application has appeared to render necessary; we may ascribe the latter to the influence of the particular circumstances which, as in the case of most natural laws, prevent the phenomena from answering precisely to a law which in itself is valid.

The experiments themselves give no further result than that described above; they do not tell us in what way the difference between the stimuli makes it possible for us to distinguish the resulting sensations—whether it is by producing a difference of *strength* between these sensations, or whether we are aided by qualitative changes set up in the content of the sensation and dependent on the difference of the stimuli. Nothing but our direct impression can decide this point, and it certainly does not seem to me that this impression speaks quite clearly in favour of the first alternative. A concentrated solution of an acid does not simply give us the same taste in a stronger form which a more diluted one gives us in a weaker form; it also tastes *different*. Two degrees of heat, though they rest on differences of intensity in the same stimulus, are felt as different sensations and not merely as different degrees of strength in the same sensation. If this is not so clear in the case of slight differences, the fact is all the clearer that our direct impression makes us speak of heat and cold as two positive opposites, and does not lead us to recognise in them mere differences of degree. Lastly, no one who experiments on degrees of brightness by means of shadows compared with the ground on which they are thrown, feels sure that he is merely comparing differences of intensity in the same sensation; the shadow is not only a less degree of illumination, but it looks *different* from the brighter ground—black if it is on a white ground.

I do not wish to lay any great stress on these doubts; still they would have to be removed before we could follow with entire security the theory which deduces from the experiments I have alluded to a law respecting the strength belonging to the sensation, and its dependence on the strength of the stimuli. Supposing them removed, we should then regard the transition from the point at which two sensations are indistinguishable to that at which their difference is just observable, as an increase, the same in amount in all cases, in the strength of the first of the two,— and so the law in question would take this form: Where the intensity of a sensation increases *by equal differences*, that is, in arithmetical progression, it implies in the strength of the stimulus an increase in geometrical progression. Thus the activity of sensation would be one of those activities which it becomes increasingly difficult to heighten as the degree of liveliness already attained increases.

259. Our present result, according to which the sensation does not follow the growing strength of the stimulus at an equal speed, would not, if taken by itself, present any extraordinary problem. But none of the theories which have been formed on this point explain why the continuous curve of growth in the strength of the stimulus is not *continuously* followed by the slower augmentation in the strength of the sensation,—why, on the contrary, there remains an interval throughout which the stimulus strengthens without showing any result, until at last, on its reaching a final degree of strength, it produces an observable difference in the sensation. This difficulty, I think, is most easily met by the physiological view which attempts to explain it by reference to the mode in which the nerves are excited. It is a problem soluble in mechanics, so to construct a system of material parts that a force which impels continuously is nevertheless prevented by internal hindrances from exerting its influence except intermittently at certain moments. Following this analogy we should have to suppose a structure of the nerve of such a kind that, given a certain attained degree of excitation, a definite concentration and heightening of that excitation is necessary before such a motion of the nerve can be produced as will afford a stimulus to the rise of a new sensation; thus the sensation would increase in intensity proportionally to these intermittent excitations. On the other hand, we do not in the least know how and where such an arrangement is to be presumed in the nervous system. There is less probability to my mind in the *second* hypothesis, according to which the nervous excitation increases proportionally to the stimulus and continuously. This hypothesis has to look to the nature of sensation itself for the reason both of the slower rate and of the want of continuity in its increase; there is nothing in the mere idea of sensation which could with any probability be supposed to take the place of the machinery which must, *ex hypothesi*, be absent. Nor is the solution offered by the *third* view more convincing. The sensation, it tells us, increases in strength proportionally to the stimulus and the nervous process, but perception brings the actually increased intensity of the sensation to consciousness in a different relation and discontinuously. The separation of these two processes, the sensation and the perception of what is felt, we shall be able to justify later on; but we certainly shall not be able to find in the nature of a perceiving activity, as such, any reason for its *not* perceiving something. If the idea could be made plausible, that the act of distinguishing two impressions—an act which is always at the same time an act of comparison—is guided not by single differences between them, but by their geometrical relation, still the only deduction we could draw from this idea would be that, given two pairs of impressions, this act would find an equally great difference between the members of each pair, supposing that in both cases these members stood to one another in the same ratio. But I do not know why that act should fail to distinguish *at all* those which did *not* stand in that ratio.

260. No method has yet been discovered of experimentally determining the consequences which result from simultaneous impressions on different senses; it is even doubtful what goes on when the same sense is excited in several ways at once. We are accustomed to the notion of a mechanism of ideas; but the attempt to go further and to oppose to it the notion of a chemistry of ideas, can be met only with the utmost distrust. As long as two external stimuli a and b are producing effects in the same nerve-element, there must ensue, in this physical sphere, the formation of that resultant c which the conjunction of all the mechanical conditions renders possible and therefore necessary. To this resultant c, which alone reaches the soul as an exciting motive, corresponds the simple sensation γ; and this γ is not the resultant of the two sensations a and β which the two stimuli, if taken separately, would have produced, but appears *instead of* them, since they are unable to arise. If, on the other hand, we suppose that a and b, either because they are transmitted in different nerve-elements, or because they do not form one indistinguishable resultant within the nerve, have actually produced the two sensations a and β, the result will be that the contents of the two sensations do not blend in consciousness into a third simple sensation, but remain apart and form the necessary pre-requisite of every higher activity of mind in the way of comparison and judgment.

At the same time I must allow that there are objections to this last view. For though the theoretical assertion that the soul is compelled by its own oneness to attempt to fuse all its internal states into an intensive unity, could decide nothing so long as our inward experience offered no example of such a result, it is on the other hand indubitable that the simultaneous assault of a variety of different stimuli on different senses, or even on the same sense, puts us into a state of confused general feeling in which we are certainly not conscious of clearly distinguishing the different impressions. Still it does not follow that in such a case we have a positive perception of an actual unity of the contents of our ideas, arising from their mixture; our state of mind seems to me rather to consist in (1) the consciousness of our inability to separate what has really remained diverse, and (2) in the general feeling of the disturbance produced in the economy of our body by the simultaneous assault of the stimuli. As to the *first* point, I recur to that distinction of sensation and perception, to which we found the psycho-physical theory obliged to appeal. The act of distinguishing two sensations is never a simple sensation; it is an act of referring and comparing, which may supervene on those sensations, but need not always do so. Where it is prevented, the result is not that the sensations melt into one another, but simply that the act of distinguishing them is absent; and this again certainly not so far that the fact of the difference remains entirely unperceived, but only so far as to prevent us from determining the amount of the difference, and from apprehending other relations between the different impressions. Anyone who is annoyed at one and the same time by glowing heat, dazzling light, deafening noise, and an offensive smell, will certainly not fuse these disparate sensations into a single one with a single content which could be sensuously perceived; they remain for him in separation, and he merely finds it impossible to be conscious of one of them apart from the others. But, further, he will have a feeling of discomfort—what I mentioned above as the *second* constituent of his whole state. For every stimulus which produces in consciousness a definite content of sensation, is also a definite degree of disturbance and therefore makes a call upon the forces of the nerves;

and the sum of these little changes, which in their character as disturbances are not so diverse as the contents of consciousness they give rise to, produce the general feeling which, added to the inability to distinguish, deludes us into the belief in an actual absence of diversity in our sensations. It is only in some such way as this, again, that I can imagine that state which is sometimes described as the beginning of our whole education, a state which in itself is supposed to be simple, and to be afterwards divided into different sensations by an activity of separation. No activity of separation in the world could establish differences where no real diversity existed; for it would have nothing to guide it to the places where it was to establish them, or to indicate the width it was to give them. A separation can only proceed from a mixture of impressions which continue to be diverse, and then only if, owing to favourable circumstances, the single constituents of the mixture are, one after the other, raised above the rest by an access of strength, so as to facilitate comparison and the apprehension of the width of the individual differences: if ideas of the single impressions have once been acquired, it may then be possible to dissociate them even in the unfavourable case of such a mixture as that described above. In this way it might perhaps happen that many apparently simple sensations may be dissociated into several sensations of the same kind; for example, in a colour we might separate the other colours which formed its constituents, or in a tone the partial tones of which we were unconscious at first, or in tastes and smells the elementary sensations which were combined in a variety of different ways and of which at present we have no knowledge. Thus within these narrow limits a real chemistry of sensations, combining different elements into a new quality of sensation, is not inconceivable. But after all our experience up to the present time it remains uncertain whether this intermingling into new resultants has not in all cases already taken place among the physical excitations in the nerve or in the central portions of the nervous system.

From these premises again, a conclusion might be drawn respecting those sensations which attach to others in the way of contrast, and do not need a particular external stimulus. I do not think they can be considered reactions of the soul unoccasioned by anything physical. It might be possible to take that view of the false estimates of magnitude which make a sudden silence ensuing on deafening noise, or a darkness ensuing on dazzling light, appear extraordinarily deep; for these are not sensations, but comparisons. And yet even in these cases the probable cause of the judgment is the distance between the degrees of excitation in the nerve, a distance just as great as that between the sensations. But a colour β cannot attach to another a by way of contrast or complement through a mere reaction of the soul. Even if we imagine in the soul a disturbance which seeks a compensating adjustment, the aim of that search can be no more than an opposite *Non-a*, the whereabouts of which is unknown. That it is β and nothing but β which gives the desired satisfaction we know only from experience; to seek the reason of the fact in a comparison of the two impressions a and β, is to seek it in something far from self-evident; it must lie in the way in which the nerve acts, and this activity of the nerve must attach the excitation which leads to β to the excitation which produces a, in the character of an effort to attain equilibrium.

261. Neither observation nor theory have so far thrown any light upon the interval which intervenes between the occurrence of a sensation and its disappearance from consciousness. If we say that it gradually diminishes in strength until at last it reaches zero or disappears below the threshold of consciousness, we merely describe what we think we can imagine to be going on; no one can *observe* the process, since the attention necessary for observing it makes it impossible. Whether this hypothetical view has a sufficient theoretical justification, is doubtful. Beside the presupposition that a diminution of the activity of representation, from its strength at a given moment down to its disappearance, must be continuous, the physical law of persistence is called in, in order to make the undiminished continuance of the sensation appear as the natural course of events, and its disappearance from consciousness as the problem to be explained. This last idea is not free from difficulty. A material atom undergoes no internal change during its motion,—at least according to the ordinary view of that motion,—and its state in any new place q is exactly what it was in its former place p; it follows therefore that it itself contains nothing which would at any point resist a further motion, and that the cause of the change or the checking of this motion must come from outside. The soul, on the other hand, when it feels a, falls into an internal state differing from its state when it feels β: if we consider it capable of reacting against stimuli at all, we must admit that there may lie in its own nature the permanent motive which stirs it to oppose every one-sided manifestation of its capacity that may be forced on it, and therefore stirs it also to eliminate the state of sensation forced on it by the external stimulus. If indeed it were able *completely* to annul what has occurred, it would be wholly impassive and therefore incapable of interaction; but might not its opposing effort be strong enough to repress the sensation into a condition of permanent unconsciousness?

If we leave this question, which cannot be decided, we may seek the causes of hindrance or checking partly in the new impressions which arrive from outside, partly in those far less familiar ones which are constantly being brought to the soul by the changing states of the body. The first of these, the struggle of ideas with one another, served as the foundation of Herbart's theory of the internal mechanism of the soul-life. I put aside at present the doubts which are suggested by the metaphysical basis of this theory; the unchangeability of a soul which yet experiences changing internal states; its effort to fuse them all into a unity, and the shipwreck of this effort on the differences of the ideas; the assumption, lastly, that the soul finds a satisfaction in at least lessening the strength of the parties whose opposition it has to tolerate. We accept simply as a hypothesis what Herbart offers us as the foundation of his theory, the hypothesis that ideas check one another according to the degree of their strength and of their opposition; and we utilise his just rejection of figurative modes of speech. Consciousness, as he tells us, is not a space in which ideas appear side by side. Even if it were a space, still the ideas are not extended things which require a definite place to exist in, rigid bodies which are incapable of condensation, and therefore push one another from this narrow stage. Nor, lastly, is there any original repulsion of ideas against ideas; it is only the unity of the soul in which they attempt to exist at the same time, that turns their mere difference into a struggle. The question now is, Does our internal observation confirm these hypotheses?

262. We have in thought to separate two things which never appear apart in the real world; the content to which the activity of representation or sensation is directed, and this activity itself which makes the content something represented or felt: to both of these we might attempt to apply the conceptions (*a*) of opposition and (*b*) of variable strength. (*a*) Now I cannot find anything given in internal observation which testifies to a checking of ideas according to the degree in which their *contents* are opposed. Doubtless we hold a simultaneous sensation of opposite contents through the same nerve-element to be impossible; but I do not know that the idea of the positive and of affirmation exercises any special repulsion against the idea of the negative and of negation; on the contrary, every possible comparison of opposites implies that the two members of the comparison do *not* check one another. If, on the other hand, we apply the opposition to the representing *activity*, it is doubtless self-evident that two of its acts which are opposed in respect of their action will cancel one another; but this proposition, if self-evident, is also fruitless, for we have no right whatever to presuppose that the ideas of two opposite contents rest on an opposition of the representing activities in respect of their mode of action. Thus we do not know where in such action we are to find oppositions which are to have a mechanical value.

(*b*) The conception of a variable strength of ideas suggests similar doubts. In the case of the sensations of an actually operating sense-stimulus, it did not seem worth while to draw the distinction I have just used; the hearing of a louder noise, or the seeing of a brighter light, is always at the same time a greater activity, excitation, or affection; and it is not possible to hear loud thunder as loud and yet to hear it weakly, or to feel a brighter light to be brighter and yet to feel it less strongly than a dimmer light. But the case may well be different with our ideas; by which name I understand, in accordance with usage, the image in memory of an absent impression, as opposed to the sensation of the present impression. The difference between the two is clear enough. The remembered light does not shine as the seen light does; the remembered tones do not sound as heard tones do, although they reproduce in their succession the most delicate relations of a melody; the idea of the intensest pain does not hurt, and is nothing compared to the least real injury. I will not enquire whether this difference is due to the fact that an idea, as a remembrance having its origin in the soul only, is not accompanied by any bodily excitation, whereas such an excitation accompanies every sensation and is the cause of its beginning and continuance; or whether that view is correct which, in spite of its not receiving much support from the direct impression of internal experience, assumes that in sensation and idea alike there is always a physical nervous excitation, and that the difference in the two cases is only one of degree.

Now whatever we remember we can certainly represent in idea in all the degrees of which its content is capable; but it is not so clear that the representing activity directed to this content can itself experience the same changes in magnitude. We cannot represent more or represent less to ourselves one tone of a given height and strength, or one shade of a colour; the attempt to do so really introduces a change in the *content*, and we are representing a stronger or weaker tone, a brighter or duller colour, instead of merely representing more or representing less the same tone and the same colour. Nor does internal observation give us any more justification for regarding this activity of representation, like the activity of sensation, as *proportional* to the content to which it is directed. The idea of the stronger does not call for or cause any stronger excitation or greater effort than the idea of the weaker. The images of memory resemble shadows, which do not differ in weight like the bodies that cast them. Thus it appears so far as if the conception of a variable strength, when applied to our ideas, may hold good of their content, but not of the psychical activity, to which the mechanical theory at starting certainly intended it also to apply.

263. To this it may be objected that the capacity of being heightened, possessed by the representing activity, cannot be disclosed by a trial made on purpose. Such an experiment, it may be said, naturally brings before us the maximum attainable by that activity in reference to the content chosen, and does not bring to our notice the lower degrees to which it sinks, and through which it passes on its way to extinction. It cannot be denied, we may be told, that the distinction of clearer and dimmer ideas signifies something which really exists in consciousness and which confirms our belief that the activity has various grades although we cannot directly observe them. To this objection I should give the following answer. I cannot convince myself that internal observation testifies without more ado to the reality of dim ideas in this sense of the word. If the image of a composite object in our memory is dim, the reason is not that the image is present, with all its parts in their order, and that consciousness sheds only a weak light over the whole. The reason is that there are gaps in the image; some of its parts are entirely absent; and, above all, the exact way in which those parts that are present are connected, is usually not before the mind, and is replaced by the mere thought that there was some connexion or other between them; and the wideness of the limits within which we find this or that connexion equally probable, without being able to come to a decision, determines the degree of dimness we ascribe to the image. Let us take as an example the taste of a rare fruit. We either have a complete idea of this taste, or we have none at all: and the only reason why we suppose that we really have a dim idea of it is this;—we know from other sources that fruits have a taste, and the other characters which are present to our memory and which tell us the species of the fruit, move us to think only of that particular class of tastes which belongs to this species; the number of the tastes which lie between these limits and between which we hesitate, determines again the degree of the obscurity of the idea, which we suppose ourselves to possess though we are really only looking for it.

To take another example; we try for a long time to remember a name, and then, when one is suggested to us, we at once recognise it to be the right one. But this does not prove that we had an obscure idea of the right one, and now recognise it as the right one by comparing it with the name that is uttered. For on what is this recognition to rest? The name that is uttered might be wrong; so that, before we could proceed, we should have to show that the obscure idea with which that name was found to be identical, is the same idea we are trying to find. Now this idea we are trying to find is distinguished from others for which we are not looking, by its connexions with remembrances of some qualities or other in the object whose name it is or whose content it signifies; for we cannot try to find the name of something, unless this something can be distinguished from other things which we do *not* mean. When, then, the right name is uttered, the sound of it fits these other remembrances of the object without trouble or resistance, and in its turn calls them up anew or extends them; and this is the reason why it seems to us the right one; whereas any wrong one that is uttered would be foreign to the other ideas that come to meet it. And supposing that the word we wanted to remember were one we did not understand, still there must be some memory or other even of it remaining behind, with which the uttered word must agree; whether it be the number of syllables, or the quality of the vowels, or some prominent consonant, or merely the circumstances in which we heard it, or the momentary general feeling with which its sound was once connected. In none of these cases therefore have we an obscure idea; we are merely looking for the idea which we have not got at all, and helping ourselves in the way I have mentioned. But no idea that we really have, whether simple or complex, can be heightened in the strength with which it is represented; and the complex idea only seems to be so, so long as it is imperfect. No one who thinks of all those ideas of parts which together form the idea of the Triangle, and also of the way in which they are really connected, can further strengthen his activity of representing this complete content. If the geometrician seems superior to the beginner in this point, it is not because he represents this content more, but because he represents more than this content, viz. the innumerable relations which are conjoined with this figure in connected knowledge.

264. I am not rejecting what we all regard as a correct interpretation of the facts, the assumption, I mean, that ideas push one another out of consciousness, and change one another into permanent unconscious states of the soul. For these states we retain a name which is really self-contradictory, unconscious ideas, in order to indicate that they arose from ideas and are capable, under certain circumstances, of being re-transformed into ideas. But all that this assumption actually says is that the ideas have exercised a certain power against one another, and that some of them have come off victorious over the rest; it does not follow as something self-evident, though we naturally infer it, that they must have owed their power to a degree of strength which belongs to them as such. In fact we had no means of measuring this strength of theirs at all before the struggle took place; we only attribute it to them by reasoning backwards after we have seen the issue of the struggle. And further, the victory does not always fall to that side which in itself is the stronger; favourable circumstances may give it to the weaker. Since then this assumption of a variable strength is found to apply not to the activity of representing but only to the content of the ideas represented: and since on the other hand, if we follow experience, we cannot maintain that the idea of the stronger *content* always overcomes that of the weaker, but meet with numberless cases of the opposite event, the result is that we must look for the source of the power exerted in something that *attaches* to the representing activity and is in its nature capable of degrees of intensity.

I may say at once that this power rests neither on any strength in the activity itself nor on that of the content represented, but on the amount of our *interest* in the latter. If we could observe the first stirrings of a soul still destitute of experience, we should certainly find that that sensation[1] which, in its total effect, is the greater agitation of the soul

---

[1] ['Sinnliche Empfindung' translated merely 'sensation,' to avoid the use of 'sensation of sense,' and 'feeling' which has been reserved for 'Gefühl.']

and therefore the stronger in respect of its content, overcomes the others which, measured by the same standard, are the weaker. But in the developed life, which alone we can observe, the strength of the sensation is of far less moment than that which, in the connexion of our memories, intentions, and expectations, it means, indicates, or foretells. Many external stimuli, therefore, are unregarded by us, if the strong sensations which they would naturally produce have no relation to the momentary course of our thoughts. Very slight stimuli attract our attention if they are intimately connected with these thoughts. And this is still more the case with our mere remembrances which are unsupported by any present bodily excitation.

This interest of our ideas, which constitutes their power, has a constant element and a variable one. I cannot suppose that any sensuous impression could be originally entirely indifferent to us. Each, it seems to me, as being an alteration of our existing state, must create an element of pleasure or pain; the former, if it occasions an exercise of possible functions within the limits in which this exercise answers to the conditions of the well-being and continuance of the whole; the latter, if it sets up changes which in their form or magnitude contradict those conditions. The general economy of the vital functions may be assumed to be nearly constant; and therefore, when the impression is repeated at later periods, the same element of emotion will always attach to it, just as the same kind of light-waves, repeated thousands of times in succession, always calls forth the same sensation of colour. But this fixed component of the interest is far outweighed by the variable one which an impression acquires in the course of our life through its various connexions with others, connexions which enable it to recall these others in memory. One impression, which in itself is accompanied by an insignificant constant element of emotion, may, if it is connected with a second, the accompanying emotion of which is strong, excite a more lively interest than a third impression, the feeling of pleasure or pain attached to which comes between the two. But this interest of an impression changes not only with the number of those with which it is connected and with the constant emotion attaching to them, but also with our momentary state of feeling at the time when it occurs. And for this state of feeling the total content of the impression has more or less value, according to the closeness or distance of its relationship to that which is moving our feeling at the moment. If in the case of the representing activity as such it was difficult to point out different degrees of strength, it seems not less self-evident that all *emotions*, on the other hand, have various degrees of intensity. The force of ideas therefore seems to me to rest on their concatenation with emotions; and if I spoke of their strength I should use the word merely to express the fact that they are victorious over others, and the understanding that their victory occurs in this way and in no other.

265. Respecting the connexion of ideas, a point to which these remarks have already led us, we have little to recall. We know that, on the renewal of an idea a, another idea b which we have had before may return to consciousness without requiring any separate external reason for its reappearance. This fact, which alone can be directly observed, we interpret as a *reproduction* of the idea b by the idea a, without meaning by our use of the word to give any account of the process through which a succeeds in recalling b. But then from this fact we infer that, even in the time during which both a and b had vanished from consciousness, there must have been a closer connexion between them than is given alike to them and to all other ideas by the fact that they belong to one and the same soul. This specific connexion we call the *association* of the ideas a and b, a name again which denotes a necessary presupposition but gives no explanation of the exact nature of this connexion, i.e. of that which distinguishes it from the more remote connexion obtaining between all the states of one subject. Any attempt to find such an explanation would be fruitless: but there is another question, which ought to be answered, viz. What are the universal rules according to which this inexplicable junction of ideas takes place? It is customary to distinguish four kinds of association. Two of them I hold to be fictions of the brain, and the other two I reduce to one. The former consist in the assertions that similar or like ideas on the one hand, and on the other hand opposite ideas are preeminently associated; and to these assertions I find nothing in internal observation to correspond. I do not know, at least, that the idea of one tone usually recalls all other tones to memory, or the idea of one colour all other colours; or again, that the idea of brightness suggests that of darkness, or the sensation of heat the remembrance of cold. Where anything of this kind seems to occur, it is plainly due to different causes from the simple association of these ideas as such. If we are calculating, and at a given moment are engaged in comparing quantities and referring them to one another, there is a special reason why the idea of the *plus* we affirm should make us think of the *minus* we reject. In the night we who are busied with plans for the future have abundance of reasons for thinking of the day we long for: and so on in many cases not worth counting up. The third and fourth classes are composed of the associations of those impressions which are perceived either at the same time as parts of a simultaneous whole, or one directly after another as parts of a successive whole; and their existence is testified to in a variety of ways at every moment of our daily life, the connected guidance of which rests wholly on them. But the separation of these processes into two classes seems to me needless. Not because the apprehension even of a spatial whole takes place, as is supposed, through a successive movement of the glance which traverses its outlines: I shall have later on to mention the reason why this movement is necessary in order to make reproduction secure; but it is none the less indubitable that the momentary illumination of an electric spark makes it possible to perceive objects and gives us images of them in memory. What is of more importance is that in temporal and spatial apprehension it is just the absence of observable connecting links between a and b which joins these two together so closely and in so pre-eminent a degree, that we give the name of association to their conjunction alone, although there must be some conjunction between a and c, b and d, as well. I shall return to this point immediately; but, before going further, I will merely point out how superfluous it is to distinguish from the *indirect* reproduction of one idea b by another a—the case so far considered—the *direct* recalling of the same a by a. We should know nothing whatever of this fact, the reproduction of a former a by the present a, if the two were simply present, with no distinction between them, at the same time. To know the present a as repetition of the former a, we must be able to distinguish the two; and we do this because not only does the repeated a bring with it the former one which is its precise counterpart, but this former one also brings with it the ideas $c\ d$ which are associated with it but not with the present a, and thereby testifies that it has been an object of our perception on some former occasion but under different circumstances.

266. Respecting the great ease with which a successive series of ideas is reproduced in the order of their succession, a fact which it would be superfluous to illustrate, an attractive theory has been developed by Herbart. Let us suppose that the external impressions $A\ B\ C\ldots$ follow one another in time, and that the first of them awakens the idea A; on its appearance in consciousness, which is never empty, this idea A will at once sustain a check from the contents already present in consciousness; and, owing to this check, its strength will have been reduced to a at the moment when the new idea B is aroused. The only association formed therefore will be between a and B—the association $a\,B$—and there will be no association $A\,B$ in consciousness at all. The combination $a\,B$, again, sustains the same check, and will be weakened to the degree $a\,b$ at the moment when C makes its impression C: the association that arises will be $a\,b\,C$, and no other will arise. Again, when D acts, it finds $a\,b\,C$ checked into $a\,\beta\,c$: it is this therefore, and only this, that connects itself with D. If now the series of external impressions, or that of their ideas, is repeated, A will not call up all the rest forthwith, nor will it call them up with the same degree of liveliness, for it never was in actual fact connected with them: not until it itself has sunk to the strength a, will it reawaken B with which alone it was associated; nor until $a\,B$ in its turn has sunk to $a\,b$, will it reproduce C; and in this way the series is repeated in memory in its original order.

The advantages of this view are not indissolubly connected with the conception, which we were unable to accept, of a variable strength of our ideas. Associations are not formed between those impressions alone which we hold apart as separate *ideas*, each having its distinct content; but every idea connects itself also with the momentary tone G which characterizes our universal vital *feeling*, or the general feeling of our whole state, at the instant when the idea appears; and, as many experiences testify, the recurrence of the general feeling G reproduces with no less liveliness the ideas which were formerly connected with it. But, again, the arrival of a new idea A changes this feeling G into g_1: then the second idea B connects itself with this association $A\,g_1$, and in its turn changes g_1 into g_2: with this new association, and with it alone, is connected C; and in this way the succession of these $g_1 g_2 g_3$ becomes the clue by help of which the reproduction of the ideas, in their turn, arranges itself; G must be changed again into g before B can be again produced by the association gB.

In the next chapter I shall mention other considerations which recommend this point of view to us; I content myself here with the remark that it promises to be of use when we come to consider the reproduction of the component parts of a spatial image by one another. If we assume that the perception of the spatial image $ABCD$ is brought about by the eye traversing this whole successively and repeatedly in various directions $ABCD$, $ACDB$, $ADCB$, ..., the question will still remain, how does it come about that a later consciousness understands the various series, arising from these voluntarily chosen directions, to be merely various subjective apprehensions of the single objective order $ABCD$? If this understanding is to be attained, it will be necessary that, at every step we choose to take within $A \ldots D$, the position of each element relatively to its neighbour should be indicated by a definite general feeling g arising in the course of this movement; and this feeling must be of such a kind that the various g's, which arise in the different directions of the movement from part to part, when compared and adjusted, give as their result these fixed actual positions of the single ideas in the total order $ABCD$. How we are to conceive this process more in detail, I shall show later on.

I close here these brief remarks on the forces which are active in the course of our ideas. I have not noticed the more general share taken in it by the body. Highly significant as that share is, I should seek it in a different direction from the present one. There are no physical analogies either for associations or for reproductions; and although it is asserted that they too are merely products of co-operating nervous currents, those who make this assertion have not yet been able to show, even in a general way, what we should require to have shown,—how these processes can be mechanically construed at all. But this again is a point to which we shall have to return at a later time.

CHAPTER III.

On the Mental Act of 'Relation[1].'

267. IF we glance at a number of coins laid side by side in no particular order, each of them produces its image in the eye, and each image produces the corresponding idea. And yet it often happens that, when we look away, we cannot tell how many coins we have seen. That, nevertheless, we have seen each and all of them, and, therefore, that their images have been conscious ideas, we know from the fact that *sometimes* we succeed in counting them over in memory, without needing to have the external impression repeated. This and countless similar experiences convince us that we have some ground for distinguishing between feeling and the perception of what is felt[2]; but at the same time they show that we must not press this distinction further than the statement that the consciousness of the relations existing between various single sensations (among which relations we reckon here the sum formed by the sensations when united) is not given simply by the *existence* of these relations considered as a fact. So far we have considered only single ideas, and the ways in which they either exist simultaneously in consciousness and act on each other, or else successively replace one another; but there exists in us not only this variety of ideas, and this change of

---

[1] ['*Von dem beziehenden Vorstellen.*' Cp. sect. 80, end. There is no English verb for 'to put in relation;' to 'refer' has been used where a verb seemed indispensable.]

[2] [In this sentence *Empfindung*, elsewhere translated 'sensation' to distinguish it from *Gefühl*, which is translated 'feeling,' 'emotion' (see § 266), is rendered 'feeling,' because we have no verb in English corresponding to the substantive 'sensation.']

ideas, but also an idea of this variety and of this change. Nor is it merely in thought that we have to distinguish that apprehension of existing relations which arises from an act of reference and comparison from the mere sensation of the individual members of the relation; experience shows us that the two are separable in reality, and justifies us in subordinating the conscious sensation and representation of individual contents to the *referring or relating act of representation*, and in considering the latter to be a higher activity,—higher in that definite sense of the word according to which the higher necessarily presupposes the lower but does not in its own nature necessarily proceed from the lower. Just as the external sense-stimuli serve to excite the soul to produce simple sensations, so the relations which have arisen between the many ideas, whether simultaneous or successive, thus produced, serve the soul as a new internal stimulus stirring it to exercise this new reacting activity.

268. The possibility of all reference and comparison rests on the continuance in an unchanged form both of the members which are to be referred to one another, and of the difference between them. When once two impressions a and b have arisen, as the ideas 'red' and 'blue,' they do not mix with one another, disappear, and so form the third idea c, the idea 'violet.' If they did so, we should have a change of simple ideas without the possibility of a comparison between them. This comparison is itself possible only if one and the same activity at once holds a and b together and holds them apart, but yet, in passing from a to b or from b to a, is conscious of the change caused in its state by these transitions: and it is in this way that the new third idea γ arises, the idea of a definite degree of *qualitative* likeness[1] and unlikeness in a and b.

Again: if we see at the same time a stronger light a and a weaker light b of the same colour, what happens is not

---

[1] [Aehnlichkeit.]

that there arises, in place of both, the idea c of a light whose strength is the sum of the intensities of the two. If that idea did arise, it would mean that the material to which the comparison has to be directed had disappeared. The comparison is made only because one and the same activity, passing between a and b, is conscious of the alteration in its state sustained in the passage; and it is in this way that the idea γ arises, the idea of a definite *quantitative* difference.

Lastly: given the impressions a and a, that which arises from them is not a third impression $= 2\,a$; but the activity, passing as before between the still separated impressions, is conscious of having sustained no alteration in the passage: and in this way would arise the new idea γ, the idea of *identity*[1].

We are justified in regarding all these different instances of γ as ideas of a higher or second order. They are not to be put on a line with the ideas from the comparison of which they arose. The simple idea of red or blue, as it hovers before us, does not suggest to us any activity of our own which has contributed to its existence; but, in return for this loss, it gives us a directly perceptible content. The ideas γ, on the contrary, have no content at all of their own which can be perceived by itself. They are therefore never *represented* in the strict sense of the word, as the simple idea is; never represented, that is, so that they stand before us now as resting perceptible images. They can be represented only through the simultaneous reproduction of some examples or other of a and b, and through the repetition of the mental movement from which they arose.

269. I may look for the objection that this description of the way in which the relating activity proceeds is strange and incapable of being clearly construed. I admit the objection, but I see no reproach in it. It is possible that

[1] [Gleichheit.]

better expressions may be found, to signify what I mean: my immediate object is to indicate what happens at least with such clearness that every one may verify its reality in his own internal observation. It is quite true that, to those who start from the circle of ideas common in physical mechanics, there must be something strange in the conception of an activity, or (it is the same thing) of an active being, which not only experiences two states a and b at the same time without fusing them into a resultant, but which passes from one to the other and so acquires the idea of a third state γ, produced by this very transition. Still this process is a fact; and the reproach of failure in the attempt to imagine how it arises after the analogies of physical mechanics, falls only upon the mistaken desire of construing the perfectly unique sphere of mental life after a pattern foreign to it. That desire I hold to be the most mischievous of the prejudices which threaten the progress of psychology; and at this point, which seems to me one of the greatest importance, I once more expressly separate myself from views which are meeting now with wide-spread assent: first (a), from the attempts to construe the life of the soul materialistically, psycho-physically, or physiologically, without regard to its specific peculiarities; and, secondly (β), from a view which must always be mentioned with respect, that view of the psychical mechanism, by which Herbart rendered, up to a certain critical point, great services to science.

As to the first point (a), these attempts either persistently pass over the problem whence that unity of consciousness comes, which is testified to by the most trivial exercise of the activity of representation in comparison; or they deceive us by the apparent ease with which single formulas, believed to have been discovered for single psychical events, gives rise in their combination to new formulas, in which even the desired unity is supposed to be attained. But this whole superstructure of oscillations upon oscillations, of embracing waves upon partial waves, this discovery of unities in the shape of points of intersection for different curves,—all this leads to pleasing wood-cuts, but not to an understanding of the processes they illustrate. Mathematical formulas in themselves determine nothing but quantitative relations, between the related points which have been brought into those formulas by means of universal designations. Such formulas, therefore, subsume the definite real elements or processes, to which they are applied, under a universal rule; and no doubt these elements or processes may really fall under the rule in respect of those properties in virtue of which they were subsumed under it. But the universal rule in its formal expression no longer reminds us of the special nature of the object to which it is applied; and thus, partly owing to the different values given to the quantities contained in it, partly through its combination with other formulas, a number of consequences can be drawn from it, respecting which it remains entirely doubtful whether they mean anything whatever when they are applied to the definite object in question; or, if they do mean anything, what the actual processes and agencies are which in the real thing lead to an occurrence corresponding to the result of the calculation. The first of these two cases I will not discuss further, though examples of it might be adduced. If we have begun by calling the conditions under which an effect appears, a threshold, we must, of course, have something that either passes over it or fails to reach it; and then these portraits of the deductions drawn from a metaphor easily pass for self-evident facts. If in a calculation, in which x signifies the liveliness of a sensation, we come to a negative x, we consider ourselves justified in speaking of negative sensations too. There are various ways of making mythology: at present the mathematical turn of imagination seems to take the lead. Respecting the second case I shall meet with a readier assent. Formulas do not produce events; they copy them after real causes have created them, and they copy only individual aspects of them. No coincidence of formulas, therefore, can ever prove that the events which meet or fuse in them, also fuse as a matter of course in the real thing without the help of any particular cause to bring about this union. If this cause, without which the event is metaphysically unintelligible, could be included in the calculation, and that in such a way that every peculiarity of its procedure found a precise mathematical expression,—then, and only then, would these quantities be rightly denominated, and only then could the calculus securely predict from their universal relations the further consequences which may be drawn.

270. In opposition to Herbart, again (β), I must repeat the doubts I expressed long ago in my *Streitschriften* (I, Leipzig, 1857). When Herbart calls that which goes on in the simple real being when it is together with others, its self-preservation, he raises hopes that in his general view the specific conception of activity will get its rights; a conception which we shall always believe to signify something special and something really to be found in the world, although we find it quite impossible to define what we mean by it, when we oppose it to a mere occurrence, in any way approaching to a mechanical construction. Did we deceive ourselves in this view of Herbart's intention? Ought we to have taken self-preservation for an active form of speech describing a mere occurrence, which, without anything being done by anybody, simply ends, as a matter of fact, with the result that something continues in preservation, the non-preservation of which we should rather have looked for as the probable end of the occurrence?

The further course of the Herbartian psychology would confirm this interpretation. For, according to this psychology, if the soul was ever active at all, it never was active but once It asserted itself against the stimuli which came from without, by producing the simple sensations: but from that point it became passive, and allows its internal states to dominate its whole life without interference. Everything further that happens in it, the formation of its conceptions, the development of its various faculties, the settlement of the principles on which it acts, are all mechanical results which, when once these primary self-preservations have been aroused, follow from their reactions; and the soul, the arena on which all this takes place, never shows itself volcanic and irritable enough to interfere by new reactions with the play of its states and to give them such new directions as do not follow analytically from them according to the universal laws of their reciprocal actions.

But the limitation of the soul's activity to these scanty beginnings was neither theoretically necessary at starting, nor is it recommended by its results. It was due to Herbart's quarrel with an earlier psychology, with the assumption of a number of original faculties which, doubtless to the detriment of science, were then considered to contain everything necessary to the production of results, whose causes are in reality formed only by degrees and ought to have been made the object of explanation. Here lie Herbart's unquestionable merits, and I need not repeat that I fully recognise them. But they lie side by side with that which I regret to have to call his error. The mere plurality of these faculties, even the view of them as mere adjacent facts the real connexion of which remained unintelligible, could not, taken alone, justify Herbart in going so far the other way as to base the development of the mind upon a single kind of process and the consequences flowing from it. For he himself both knew and said that the simple sensations from which he started are just as independent of one another as were the faculties he rejected; that we cannot conceive any reason why a soul that feels ether-waves as colours must, in consistency, perceive air-waves as sounds; that therefore the soul has just the same number of primal faculties irreducible to one another as of single sensations different from one another. He did not on that account surrender the unity of the soul, or doubt that in it this multiplicity is bound together by some connexion, albeit that connexion entirely escapes us. Now if this one nature of the soul can produce simultaneously, or, so to speak, on the same level of its action, such manifold expressions of its essence, why should it not in the same way produce manifold expressions successively at different periods of its development? Why should not its own internal states, through their increasing multiplicity, win from it new reactions, for which in their simpler forms they gave no occasion? There is certainly nothing impossible in the idea of a constantly renewed reaction, in which that whole essence of the soul that is always present casts new germs of development into the machinery of its internal states; and a view that rejects this source of aid could have proved it to be superfluous only by its own complete success. That I do not find this view everywhere thus successful, I shall have to mention again; here I will refer to three points.

First, the deduction of the perception of Space. I have already spoken of its impossibility and will not refer to it again at length. We must content ourselves with regarding this perception as a new and peculiar form of apprehension, which, proceeding from the essence of the soul, attaches, as a reaction of the kind just described, to a definite manifold of impressions, but does not of itself issue from that manifold. The second point is attention: I shall have to mention it directly in the course of the present discussion. Thirdly, in the case of any act of reference or comparison, Herbart's psychology seems to me to take no account of the eye which perceives the relations obtaining between the single ideas; the consciousness of the investigator which has performed this task of perception everywhere takes the place of the consciousness investigated, which is required to perform it. It is of no avail to answer that it is implied in the very notion of the soul as something that represents, that it perceives everything that exists and occurs in it, and therefore that it perceives the relations in which its single ideas stand to one another: the need of a deduction of the perception of space is by itself sufficient to disarm this rejoinder. For Herbart agrees that the impressions which muster in the simple essence of the soul, are together in the soul in a non-spatial way. A consciousness which as a matter of course perceived their reciprocal relations, could only apprehend them as they are, as non-spatial. But this is not what happens: consciousness changes them and reproduces in perceptions of something side by side in space what in themselves are only together with one another in a non-spatial way. Here then the perception is at the same time a new creation of the form in which it takes place: but even in those cases where there is nothing novel in the reaction to surprise us, the perception of relations is no mere mirroring of their existence, but at the least the new creation of the very idea of them.

271. Expressed in Herbart's terminology, my view would take the following form. The soul is stimulated by the external sense-stimuli s_1, as stimuli of the first order: and in consequence it forms the simple[1] sensations which we know, and to which perhaps the simplest feelings of sensuous pleasure and pain ought to be added as creations which arise with equal readiness. But the various relations (whether of simultaneous multiplicity or of temporal succession) which exists between the sensations or the images they have left in the memory, do not simply exist, they form for the soul new stimuli s_2, stimuli of a second order, and the soul responds to them by new reactions. These reactions differ according to the difference of their stimuli, and cannot be explained from these secondary stimuli themselves, but only from the still unexhausted nature of the soul,

---

[1] ['Einfachen sinnlichen Empfindungen,' v. note on p. 224.]

which they stir to an expression of itself for which there was previously no motive. Among these reactions we count the perception of Space, which holds a certain simultaneous manifold together; the time-ideas of a change, which are not given by the mere fact of temporal change; lastly, not only these ideas[1] of the kind γ, which measure theoretically the existing relations between different contents, but also among other things, the feelings of pleasure and pain which are connected with these relations. Obviously, on this view, any condition of feeling or any series of referring activities, directed in the way of comparison or judgment to different contents of given ideas, may become in its turn a new stimulus to the soul, an object of a still higher reflexion; but it would be mere trifling to reckon up reactions of a third and fourth order, unless a detailed psychology, for which this is no place, had succeeded in pointing out distinctly in internal observation the processes which would justify us in assuming this ascending scale of orders. And for the purposes of metaphysic such a course would bring us no further than we are brought already by the recognition, once for all, that the soul is in no case a mere arena for the contentions of its internal states, but the living soil, which, in each instantaneous creation that it brings into being, has produced at the same time new conditions for the generation of still higher forms.

272. There is only one point, therefore, with regard to which I will continue these remarks. Those ideas[1] γ, the origin of which I touched on above, were, so far as they were then considered, in themselves no more than definite single ideas of a quantitative or qualitative difference, or of a single case of identity. It is only when we suppose this same referring activity of knowledge to be applied to many repeated cases of a similar kind, that we understand how the *general* ideas of quantity and quality arise in the same way. As to the origin of universal conceptions generally,

[1] [v. § 268.]

we are sometimes told that they arise from our uniting many single examples: those parts of the examples which are like one another are accumulated, those which are opposed cancel one another, those which are dissimilar dim one another. But this mechanical mode of origination presupposes that the individual ideas, in balancing one another so as to produce the universal, have disappeared and been lost; and the contrary is the fact. They continue to exist; and it is not out of them that the universal is produced, but side by side with them: it could not be felt at all *as* universal, as something that is true of them among others, if they had vanished and simply left it behind as their production. The structure of the different kinds of universal conception is very complex, and it is the business of Logic to analyse it. Psychology can do no more than base their origin on a more or less intricate exercise of the referring activity through which we apprehend the different relations of the constituents which have to be united in them. The idea produced by this group of activities is not of the same kind as those *ideas*, which, as the direct result of external impressions, represent a perceptible fixed content; it is a *conception*, and the apparently simple name which language gives to it is never more than the expression of a rule which we require ourselves to follow in connecting with each other points of relation which are themselves conceived as universal. We can fulfil this requirement[1] only if we allow our imagination to represent some individual example or other, which answers to this rule, while at the same time we join to our perception of this individual the consideration that many other examples, and not this one only or exclusively, can with equal justice be used as the perceptible symbol of that which cannot in itself be perceived.

273. The fact of *attention* still remains to be mentioned. It was depicted by psychologies of an earlier date as a moveable light which the mind directs on to the impressions

---

[1] [On the nature of Universal Ideas, cp. Logic, sect. 339.]

it receives, either with the view of bringing them for the first time to consciousness, or else in order to draw the impressions already present in consciousness from their obscurity. The first of these alternatives is impossible; for the supposed light could not search in consciousness for something which is not there: the second at least leaves the obscurity in which the ideas are supposed (without any reason being given for it) to find themselves, very obscure. The necessary complement of this view would lie in the perception that the direction of this moveable light cannot be accidental, but must depend on fixed conditions, and that therefore it must naturally be the ideas themselves that attract attention to themselves. But I think the view I am speaking of was right in regarding attention as an activity exercised by the soul and having the ideas for its objects, and not as a property of which the ideas are the subjects. The latter notion was the one preferred by Herbart. According to him, when we say that we have directed our attention to the idea b, what has really happened is merely that b, through an increase in its own strength, has raised itself in consciousness above the rest of the ideas. But, even were the conception of a variable strength free from difficulty in its application to ideas, the task which we expect attention to perform would still remain inexplicable. What we seek to attain by means of it is not an equally increasing intensity of the represented content, just as it is, but a growth in its *clearness*; and this rests in all cases on the perception of the relations which obtain between its individual constituents. Even when attention is directed to a perfectly simple impression, the sole use of exerting it lies in the discovery of relations; it could achieve nothing, and a mere gazing at the object, even if it were heightened to infinity, would be utterly fruitless, if there were nothing in the object or around it to compare and bring into relation. If we wish to tune a string exactly, we compare its sound with the sound of another which serves as a pattern, and try to make sure whether the two agree or differ; or else we take the sound of the string by itself and compare it at different moments of its duration, so as to see that it remains the same and does not waver between different pitches. We shall assuredly find no case in which attention consists in anything but this referring activity; and, on the other hand, there are moments when we cannot collect ourselves, when we are wholly occupied by a strong impression, which yet does not become distinct because the excessive force of the stimulation hinders the exercise of this constructive act of comparison. So closely is the distinctness of a content connected with this activity that, even after the eye has repeatedly traversed the outlines of a sensuous image, we use a new expedient to secure the image in our memory: we translate its impression into a description, in which, through the aid of the developed forms of language, the internal relations of the image are subsumed under the conceptions of position, direction, connexion, and movement (all of them conceptions of relation), and which prescribes a rule enabling us to re-create the content of the impression through successive acts of representation or thought.

274. The interest which the idea *a* possesses at a given moment, has two factors,—the stable value of the idea for emotion, and the variable significance which this value possesses for our total state at the particular time. And this interest is the condition which on the one hand awakes attention and enchains it, and on the other hand diverts and distracts it. The latter case occurs when the associated ideas *b*, *c*, which *a* reproduces, exceed *a* in momentary interest; then it is that the course of our thoughts moves in those strange leaps, which we know so well, which we understand in their general conditions, but the direction of which we can seldom follow in any particular instance. It is however in this fact, that the idea *a* is, to a greater or less extent, able through its associations to attract and bring back our attention to itself, that the greater or smaller force consists which it exerts on the course of our ideas; and further, it is in this that there lies the measure of strength which we are accustomed to ascribe to the idea as an inherent quality. If a has merely served as a point of transition to the more rapid awakening of other ideas $b, c,$ neither of which reconduct us to a, we regard a as an idea that was weak, or that only raised itself slightly above the threshold of consciousness; and alas! by this figure of speech we too often suppose ourselves to have described the real condition on which the slight influence of the idea depends. But it is not at the moment when a is passing through consciousness that we rate it as clear or obscure, strong or weak; it is only at a later time, and when other occasions reproduce it and convince us that it must have been in consciousness at a former moment, that it appears to us as an idea that was weak; and it appears so, because we do not remember any referring act of attention which at that time, by analysing its content, made it strong, or which, by pursuing its relations to other ideas, assigned it a determinate position in the connexion of our inner life. Lastly it is obvious, according to our general view, not only that every activity of attention that has been put forth may become an object to a higher consciousness, but also that there need not be any such reflexion on what has been done. The oftener we have made like relations between a number of points of reference the object of acts of comparison and reference, the more is there connected with the new example, in the manner of a fixed association, the idea of the universal relation under which its relations are to be subsumed. When impressions first occur, we are often unable to connect and judge them without consciously considering how we are to use our ideas in order to do so; but, when the impressions are repeated, these acts of connexion and judgment frequently take place without any such considerations being necessary: and so we are easily deceived into thinking that in these cases there was really no operation to be performed, and that the mere existence of the relations between the single impressions makes the perception of those relations a matter of course.

My object in devoting this chapter entirely to the referring activity was to emphasize its decisive importance. I may remind the reader that it is really this activity whose delicacy is directly measured by the psycho-physical experiments respecting our capacity for distinguishing impressions, and that all assertions as to the strength of sensations, are, in so far as they rest on these experiments, theoretical deductions drawn from this immediate result of observation.

CHAPTER IV.

The Formation of our Ideas of Space.

275. THE concluding remarks of the last chapter may serve to introduce the discussion which is to follow on the psychological genesis of our ideas of space and the localisation of the impressions of sense. In this discussion I must use the freedom claimed by every one who holds, as I do, that our perception of space is merely subjective. In consistency no doubt we should have to consider our own body, as well as the organs of sense by means of which it takes possession of the external world, to be nothing but appearances in ourselves; to be, that is, the ordered expression of a different non-spatial order, obtaining between those supersensuous real elements, which the all-embracing meaning of the world has made into a system of direct immediate links of connexion between our soul and the other constituents of the world. It is not impossible to make this point of view clear to oneself in a general way, and to see that the questions, now to be dealt with, respecting our sensuous commerce with the outer world, might be expressed in the language of that view; but to carry it out in detail would lead to a prolixity as intolerable as it would be needless. Needless, for this reason, that, if the perception of space is once for all fixed by the nature of our mind as our mode of apprehension, this perception has a rightful existence for us, and we can hardly propose to look down upon that which has the power of shedding clearness and vividness upon relations which can be perceived by us only in this way and not in the form they actually possess. It is enough to have assured ourselves at a single point in metaphysic that spatiality is only our form of apprehension, perhaps also a form belonging to every being that has a mind. After it has been shown in a general way how the true intelligible relations of things admit of an ordered manifestation within this form, we may again merely in a general way, subsume this special instance of those relations, the structure of our own body, under that general demonstration; but in the further course of our enquiry we shall everywhere substitute for the conception of the system of intelligible links of connexion between ourselves and the world that spatial image of our body which, unlike the conception, can be perceived. Accordingly, we presuppose here the ordinary view; for us, as for it, the world is extended around us in space; we and the things in it have determinate places in it; the actions or effects of those things on us are propagated in determinate directions up to the surface of our body, and, passing somehow to the soul, produce in its perception a spatial image; the component parts of which have the same reciprocal positions—either exactly the same or within definite limits the same—as the external things by which they, as sensations, were produced.

276. Owing to the directness of the impression we receive from the external world, it seems as though the spatial perception of that world came to us without any trouble on our part, as though we need only open our eyes to take possession of the whole glory of the world as it is. Yet, as we know, and as many experiences at once remind us, it is not by merely existing that things are objects of our perception, but solely through their effects upon us. Their spatial relations, no less than others, come to our knowledge not by the mere fact of their existence, but only through a co-ordination of their effects upon us, a co-ordination which corresponds to the relative position of the points from which those effects proceeded. And, conversely, the possibility of correctly concluding from the impression these effects produce on us to the spatial relations of their causes, depends on the extent to which those effects preserve their original co-ordination in being propagated up to the point at which they impress us.

But here begin the misunderstandings which obscure the way before us. Our bodily organs offer an extended surface, on the various points of which these impressions may be grouped in positions similar to those held by the points in the outer world, from which they came. It is therefore possible for an image to be produced which has the same aspect as the object whose image it is; and this possibility has often seemed enough to make all further questions superfluous. But in fact it has only doubled the problem. If it was not clear how we perceived the object itself, it is no more clear how we perceive its image; and the fact that one resembles the other makes matters no plainer. So long as this image consists simply in a number of excitations of nervous points arranged in a figure corresponding to the figure of an external object, it is no more than a copy, brought nearer to us or diminished, of that which *may* be the object of a future perception, but it does not give us any better rationale of the process through which that thing *becomes* the object of perception.

The question how this fact of nerve-excitation becomes an object of knowledge for the soul at once gives rise to divergent views. We may imagine the soul to be immediately present in the eye: there, as though it were a touching hand, with its thousand nerve-points it apprehends the individual coloured points exactly in the position they actually have in the eye; and to many this view seems to make everything clear. They forget that it would be just as difficult to show how the feelings of touch which the hand receives justify us in referring the various points apprehended to definite positions in space: before they could do so we should have to presuppose that each position of the hand in space was already an object of that perception which was precisely what we were trying to explain; then, no doubt, it would be certain that every point of colour lies at that spot in space where the hand apprehends it. Others appeal to the physiological fact that stimulations of the nerves are conducted to the brain by isolated fibres, which may be supposed to lie (where they end in the central portions) in the same order in which they begin in the organ of sense. Thus, it is said, each impression will be conducted by itself and free from intermixture with others, and all the impressions will retain, in being conducted, the same geometrical relations of position which they possessed in that organ. All that this idea accomplishes, again, is to bring the copy, which has taken the place of the distant external thing, rather nearer to the spot where we suppose the mysterious transition of the physical excitation into a knowledge of that excitation to take place.

But how does this come about? How does the soul come to know that at this moment there is a stimulation of three central nervous points, which lie in a straight line or at the corners of a triangle? It is not enough that that which happens in these points should have differences in its quality, and produce on the soul an effect corresponding to those differences: but it would also be necessary that the spatial relation of the stimulating points should not only exist, but should also produce an effect on the soul and so be observed by it. Perhaps at this point we might conceive of the soul itself, or of its consciousness, as an extended space, into which the excitations of the nerves might be continued in their original order and direction: and then the whole solution of the riddle would consist in a mere transition. But, even if we supposed the many impressions to have thus really appeared in the soul in exactly that shape in which they came from the external objects, still this fact would not be the perception of this fact. Even if we regarded each of these excitations not simply as the condition of a future sensation, but as a present state of the soul, a conscious sensation, yet, in spite of this, the perception of the relations between them would remain to be accomplished by a referring consciousness, which in the unity of its activity excludes the spatial distinctions holding between its objects. When we perceive the points *a*, *b*, *c*, in this order side by side, our consciousness sets *a* to the left and *c* to the right of *b*: but the *idea* of *a*, through which we thus represent *a*, does not lie to the left, nor the idea of *c* to the right, of the idea of *b*; the idea itself has not these predicates, it only gives them to the points of which it is the idea. And, conversely, if we still suppose consciousness to be a space, and further that the idea of *a* lies in it to the left of the idea of *b*, this fact would still not be the same thing with the knowledge of it; the question would always repeat itself, How does the extended soul succeed in distinguishing these two points of its own essence, which at a given moment are the places where that essence is stimulated; and by what means does it obtain a view of the spatial line or distance which separates the two from one another? The connecting, referring, and comparing consciousness, which could perform this task, could never be anything but an activity which is unextended, intensive and a unity—even if the substantive being to which we ascribed this activity were extended. In the end the impressions would have to pass into this non-spatial consciousness; and therefore we gain nothing for the explanation of the perception of space by interposing this supposition,—a supposition which in any case is impossible for us to accept.

277. Let us return then to the other idea, that of a supersensuous being, characterised only by the nature of its activity. Now it is doubtless incorrect to think of the soul under the image of a point, for, if a thing is non-spatial, its negation of extension ought not to be expressed in terms of space; still the comparison may be admitted here where we only wish to draw conclusions from that negation. This premised, it is obvious that all those geometrical relations which exist among the sense-stimuli and among the nervous excitations they occasion must completely disappear in the moment when they pass over into the soul: for in its point of unity there is no room for their expansion. Up to this point the single impressions may be conducted by isolated nerve-fibres which preserve the special nature of each impression; even in the central portions of the nervous system similar separations may still exist, although we do not know that they do so; but in the end, at the transition to consciousness, all walls of partition must disappear. In the unity of consciousness these spatial divisions no more exist than the rays of light which fall from various points on a converging lens continue to exist side by side in the focal points at which they intersect. In the case of the rays indeed the motion with which they came together makes it possible for them to diverge again, beyond the focal points, in a similar geometrical relation; in the present case, on the other hand, the required continuation of the process consists not in a re-expansion of the impressions into a real space, but in the production of an idea—the idea of a space and of the position of the impressions in that space. This perception cannot be delivered to us ready-made. The single impressions exist together in the soul in a completely non-spatial way and are distinguished simply by their qualitative content, just as the simultaneous notes of a chord are heard apart from one another, and yet not side by side with one another, in space. From this non-spatial material the soul has to re-create entirely afresh the spatial image that has disappeared; and in order to do this it must be able to assign to each single impression the position it is to take up in this image relatively to the rest and side by side with them. Presupposing then, what we do not think need be further explained, that for unknown reasons the soul can and must apprehend in spatial forms what comes to it as a number of non-spatial impressions, some clue will be needed, by the help of which it may find for each impression the place it must take, in order that the image that is to arise in idea may be like the spatial figure that has disappeared.

278. We may illustrate this requirement in a very simple way. Let us suppose that a collection has to be arranged in some new place in exactly the same order that it has at present. There is no need to keep this order intact during the transport; we do whatever is most convenient for the purposes of transport, and when it is finished we arrange the several pieces of the collection by following the numbers pasted on them. Just such a token of its former spatial position must be possessed by each impression, and retained throughout the time when that impression, together with all the rest, was present in a non-spatial way in the unity of the soul. Where then does this token come from? It cannot be the point in external space from which the sense-stimulus starts, that gives to it this witness of its origin. A blue ray of light may come from above or from below, from the right or from the left, but it tells us nothing of all this; it itself is the same in all cases. It is not until these similar stimuli come in contact with our bodies that they are distinguished, and then they are distinguished according to the different points at which they meet the extended surface of our organs of sense. This accordingly may be the spot at which the token I am describing has its origin, a token which is given along with the stimulus in consequence of the effects produced by it at this spot, and which in the case of each single stimulus is distinct and different from that given along with any other stimulus.

And now that fact regains its importance, which we could not admit as a short-hand solution of these problems; the isolation of the conducting nerve-fibres. I cannot help remarking in passing that physiology is mistaken when it finds the exclusive object of the structure of the nervous system in the unmixed conduction of individual excitations. In the optic nerve we find this structure devoted to that purpose; but the olfactory nerve, which possesses it no less, shows very little capacity for arousing such a multiplicity of separate sensations as would correspond with the number of its individual fibres. Nor is it only in the nerves that we meet with these elongated unramified fibres; we find them in the muscles also, and yet the isolated excitation of a single fibre certainly cannot be the object here, where the simultaneous and like stimulation of many fibres is required for the attainment of any useful result. Thus we must suppose, I think, that the wide diffusion of this structure of the fibres has a more general explanation. Perhaps their forms were the only ones possible to the forces which shape an organic form, and a foundation for greater effects may have been producible only through adding together such elementary organs. Perhaps again the physical processes, on which the activities of life rest, are necessarily connected, within narrow limits, with the fineness of the fibre, and could not take place in masses of a thickness discernible to the naked eye. But however this may be,—however this structure came into being,—when once it is present, it can without doubt be used for the purpose of separating the impressions of sense. Each single fibre, at the spot where it receives the stimulus, can attach to it the extra-impression described, and can transmit it to consciousness, stamped with this character, and preserved by the isolation of the fibre from mixture with other physical excitations.

279. A further assumption is necessary before we can make use of this process to explain the localization of impressions. We must suppose that similar stimuli give rise in each nerve-fibre to a special extra-impression, an extra-impression which is different in the case of every single fibre, and which connects itself, in the manner of an association, with that main impression which depends on the *quality* of the stimulus,—connects itself, therefore, in such a way that neither of the two impressions, the main one and the extra one, interferes with the peculiar nature and tone of the other. It must be confessed that we have no anatomical knowledge of a diversity in the single nerve-fibres so manifold as this assumption requires. But this diversity may consist not only in properties which escape all the expedients our external observation can employ, but in the very spatial position of the fibre; we might suppose, that is, firstly, that in a number of fibres lying side by side interactions take place which produce different states of susceptibility in the fibres lying at different spots in this system; and, secondly, it is no less possible that the excitations of each fibre may acquire a particular tone from the effect produced on it by occurrences in the surrounding tissues. But this question of detail, again, we must leave undiscussed; what is certain is that no other view of the matter can dispense with an assumption similar to that for which we have suggested an explanation. In order to know whether a push we felt when our eyes were shut came against our hand or our foot, it is necessary that, the two pushes being in other respects of equal measurement, the total impression should be different in the two cases. In such a case it is of no use to appeal to associations, and to say that on a former occasion the impression of the push was connected with a simultaneous visual perception of the place that received it, and that now when the push is repeated it reproduces this perception. For in the course of life we unfortunately so often receive pushes on all parts of the body, that the impression in question will have associated itself almost indiscriminately with the images of all of them: it will be impossible, therefore, in the case of a repetition to decide to which of these parts the impression is to be referred, unless in this new case the impression itself once more tells us to which of them we are to refer it: it is necessary, in other words, that the impression now recurring should be provided with a clear token of its present origin. Let $A B C$, then, stand for three diverse stimuli, $p\,q\,r$ for three different spots in an organ of sense, $\pi\,\kappa\,\rho$ for three specific extra-impressions, which those spots connect with the main sensations occasioned by $A\,B\,C$: then the difference between these connected *local signs* $\pi\,\kappa\,\rho$ will be the clue by means of which the sensations falling upon $p\,q\,r$ can be localised in separate places in our perception of space. The associations $A\pi\,A\kappa\,A\rho$ will signify three *similar* impressions which have fallen on the *different* spots $p\,q\,r$ of the organ of sense, and which are prevented by this very difference in their local signs from being fused into one sensation, a fusion which could not have been prevented if the three A's had been perfectly identical[1]; since, where no distinctions exist, no activity of consciousness can make them. The associations $A\pi\,B\kappa\,C\rho$, on the other hand, will signify three *dissimilar* impressions which affect those three *different* spots in the organ at the same time; these impressions, owing to their qualitative difference, need nothing further to prevent their fusion into one sensation, and all that $\pi\,\kappa\,\rho$ give them is their spatial arrangement. Lastly, $A\kappa\,B\kappa\,C\kappa$ would be the same three *dissimilar* stimuli, acting on one and the *same* spot q in the organ of sense, and therefore, as we seem obliged to suppose, appearing *successively* at the same point in our perception of space.

280. I have no desire to conceal the difficulties which arise when these considerations are pursued further. As long as we abstain from considering the differences between the organs of sense, and only try to fix in a general way the requirements we have to satisfy, it is possible to form many different views respecting the nature and genesis of local signs. The simplest would be one I have mentioned in passing, that the extra-process destined to accompany the main impression takes place directly, and at first as a physical excitation, in the same nerve-fibre which is affected by an external stimulus. In that case it would depend on the form of excitation which was found to be the general

---

[1] [I. e. if $A\pi$, $A\kappa$, $A\rho$ had been simply A, A, A or $A\pi$, $A\pi$, $A\pi$.]

mode of activity in the nerves, whether it could permit the simultaneous conduction, without intermixture, of two different processes: and even if we found that this was not possible in the case of two excitations of the same kind, still it might be so when one of the two processes was the extra-excitation which accompanies the main movement issuing from the stimulus, but is not of the same kind with it. However, the whole supposition of a double conduction fails to attain its object. For it involves the tacit presupposition that two processes, which, without being otherwise connected, proceed along the same nerve-fibre, thereby acquire a permanent association: and this presupposition rests in the end on a mode of thought which we were unable to accept, on the notion, I mean, that the mere fact of the excitations existing side by side in space is sufficient to give rise to the idea of their intrinsic connexion. On a former occasion I compared consciousness, by way of figure, to a single vessel; and the various excitations, which were conducted to this vessel and flowed into it through different pipes, were supposed at last to meet in it and mix indiscriminately together. We need not keep to this figure; but however we like to picture the transition into consciousness, the mere fact that A and π, B and κ, C and ρ *were* together in space, will give consciousness no token that it is to connect them exactly in this way instead of joining A to κ, B to ρ, and C to π.

Accordingly, the other supposition seems to me more natural than this of a double conduction,—the supposition that the main impression and the extra-excitation really give rise in each fibre to one total state, which is conducted as a total state and occasions nothing but one total sensation. If this sensation remained by itself alone, we should feel no occasion to distinguish different elements in it, any more than violet, if we knew nothing but it, would suggest to us to separate red and blue from one another in it. But many different stimuli are in process of time connected with one and the same extra-process; and it may be that the comparison of these cases would arouse an activity of separation which would analyse the total impressions into their component parts, but which would at the same time learn to refer the local sign, thus separated, in each case to that qualitative impression from which it was parted in thought and in thought alone. It is possible to find instances in which this actually occurs. The effect produced by a tone must be apprehended as an excitation which is at first one and total, in the sense above described: but not only does the comparison of many successive tones enable us to distinguish the quality from the height of each, but further, when we hear several tones at once, we are able to attach each quality to the height of the note from which it was thus separated. The artificiality of this point of view may make us distrust it, but we shall not find it easy to escape this artificiality by taking another road.

Let us put aside altogether, what is quite unessential, the image of the soul as a point at which all the impressions conducted to it discharge themselves. Let us suppose, what we shall afterwards find confirmed, that the soul perceives the physical nervous processes directly at the spot where they reach the final form in which they are destined to be objects of its perception. Still there remains the question we would so gladly avoid: supposing the soul has apprehended many impressions in this way, either at the same time or one after the other, it can analyse each of them into the components described above; what determines it then not to allow these components to fall asunder but to hold them together in a way corresponding to the connexion from which it has previously disjoined them? We see, then, that the artificiality lies in the fact itself, or in that view of the fact which alone remains open to us now,—in the enigmatical nature of associations generally. I reminded the reader in a former passage that in using this name we are merely designating a fact we are obliged to assume, without being able to give any account of the means by which it is brought about. And now it seems to me that the source of the doubts that beset us here is that we cannot persuade ourselves to renounce our search for a mechanism which would bring about this connexion of states after the analogy of physical processes. Such a construction we shall certainly never find. On the other hand, if we are tempted to regard associations as a peculiarity of the psychical activity, to which there is no analogy elsewhere, we are held back by the undoubted fact that we do not yet possess any intelligible general point of view which would exhibit the *ratio legis* in every case, and which would explain not only the connexion at this point but its absence at that point: instead of this we are forced in each particular case to make assumptions which appear artificial because they are always constructed *ad hoc*. I believe then that the hypothesis I have been speaking of here, that of the origin of the local sign in the stimulated nerve itself, might be maintained; but, later on, I shall substitute for it another hypothesis, according to which the extra-production of the local sign is less direct: and my reason is not that the second hypothesis is free from the difficulties of the first, but that it offers other advantages. At present we will proceed for a moment with our general remarks.

281. If the local signs $\pi \kappa \rho$ merely differ generally in quality, it is true that they would suffice to prevent three perfectly similar stimuli from coalescing, and to make them appear as three instances of the same felt content. But the only result would be an impulse to hold the sensations apart in a general way; there would be nothing to lead us on to give to the sensations thus produced a definite localisation in space. It is this that is left unnoticed by those who regard the isolated conduction of three impressions by three fibres as a sufficient reason, taken by itself, for their being perceived as spatially separate. Even if (in the absence of the extra local signs) this isolation were a sufficient condition of the three impressions being distinguished as three, yet the question whether they were to be represented at the corners of a triangle or in a straight line, could only be decided by a soul which already possessed that capacity of localisation which we are trying to understand. In this case the soul would stand, as it were with a second and inner vision, before the open key-board of the central nerve-terminations, would see them lying ready side by side, and doubtless would very easily refer the arriving excitations to the places occupied by those keys on which they produce some observable motion. If this is impossible, as it is, just as little would it be possible for the local signs given along with sensations to produce a real localisation of the sensations, if these local signs simply differed without being also *comparable*. If they are to lead to this localisation they must necessarily be members of series or of a system of series, in each of which there must be some general characteristic in common, but within its limits a difference, measurable in some way, of every individual from every other. If

$$\kappa = \pi + \Delta, \rho = \pi + 2\Delta, \text{ or } \kappa = \rho - \Delta,$$

then, but only then, can these signs be the reason why a perception, which can and must apprehend these arithmetical differences in some spatial way or other, should place $B\kappa$ nowhere but in the middle between $A\pi$ and $C\rho$. And if more than one series of this kind is involved, so that the general character of the local signs in the one is qualitatively distinguished from that of the other, still even in the transition from series to series this alteration of quality must somehow proceed by measurable differences; otherwise we should not know how great, in terms of space, is the declination of some of the impressions from the straight line which is the shape others are to take in the perception.

282. This postulate is closely connected with the settlement of another question. Wherever the local signs may arise, there is no doubt that, to start with, they are physical excitations which arise, on occasion of the stimulus, in the stimulated spot, this spot having an individuality or special nature of its own. We have gone on to assume as self-evident, that they then produce sensations, states of consciousness, just as the main impressions do which they accompany; and that, from a comparison of the associations which have thus arisen, a referring activity decides what relative position each impression is to take among the rest. Now is this necessary? Or does it suffice to regard $\pi \kappa \rho$ simply as physical processes which do not themselves appear in consciousness, and merely determine the direction in which consciousness guides each impression to its place in the perceived space? Now, supposing we adopt the second of these alternatives, the difficulty remains that it will be just as necessary for the unconscious faculty of localisation as it was for the conscious, that the local signs should stand in the reciprocal relations we have indicated; otherwise this faculty will have nothing to determine it to the definite directions spoken of. This will at any rate be necessary if we are to hold in this case to that general rationality of the phenomena which alone gives any interest to attempts to explain them: for of course it is possible to take a purely fatalistic view, and to say, It simply is the fact that, if the spot p is stimulated the ensuing sensation must take the place x, and if the spot q is stimulated the ensuing sensation must take the place y; and there is no *rule* or reason why the existence of one of these relations should involve that of the other. On this assumption any further hypotheses as to the nature of the local signs would be superfluous: but then on this assumption *all* investigation would be superfluous, for there would be nothing to investigate. If however that general rationality of phenomena is admitted, then I find no sufficient clearness in the theory that our determination of place in perception is conducted unconsciously. For this reason: according to the theory there is something which determines the position to be given to each single impression in the space perceived. This something, this ground of determination, must remain conjoined with this single impression and with it alone (for it holds good of it and of no other impression). It cannot be merely a prior process determining the future localisation; it must be a permanent definite mark attached to that idea whose localisation it is to further. And, since the idea now appears in consciousness, it is difficult to imagine how the grounds of determination can leave such an after-effect attached to the idea, as would operate in consciousness and yet not *appear* in that same consciousness.

Here again there lie more general difficulties which interrupt our course. It is, once more, because we are accustomed to observe the external world, that we naturally separate any occurrence produced by causes into a preceding impression on the one side, and a subsequent reaction on the other. In a chain of processes, in which each link is the sufficient reason only of the next, we may make this distinction between the first link a and the last link z; but it is useless to interpose between the next neighbours a and b another impression, which it is supposed that a must have already made before it can call forth b as a reaction. We are separating what is really a unity, the occurrence which is at once reception of an impression and reaction against it; and it is this false separation which in the present case makes it seem natural that the external stimulus should first produce in the soul an impression which is not yet consciousness, and that the conscious sensation should afterwards follow on this impression as a reaction. But it is easy to see that this interposition can be carried on *ad infinitum*. On such a view, the activity of sensation, in its turn, could not react in consequence of the unconscious impression till it had been stimulated by it—if, that is, the impression had produced in it a second unconscious state:

and it would be only to this second stimulation that the activity of sensation would respond with its conscious manifestation. On this point I accept Herbart's opinion: a conscious idea is *directly* an act of self-preservation against a disturbance. This disturbance does not first appear apart, and then call forth the idea as a reaction. The disturbance only threatens, its threat is only effective, it itself only exists in so far as it asserts itself in the idea itself which, but for it, would not have existed. But I will not pursue these doubts. They cannot be definitely set at rest. We have assuredly no right to interpose some mere lifeless impression between two adjacent links of a causal connexion: but still it remains undecided whether, as a matter of fact, the physical excitation in the nerve, and the psychical process of sensation, do form such adjacent links of a chain. It is not necessary that the sufficient ground for the arousal of a sensation or idea should consist in the connecting link of an unconscious state of the soul; but it is possible that it may consist in this. Accordingly I do not put forward my view as anything more than the hypothesis that I prefer. It may be stated thus: if the physical processes $\pi \kappa \rho$ are the local signs directly used by a referring activity when it determines the position of the sensations in the perceived space, they are so used not as physical processes, not through the instrumentality of unconscious impressions aroused by them in the soul, but in the shape of conscious sensations resulting from them. I shall return to the objections which stand in the way of this supposition, and consider them in detail.

283. These then are the general postulates to which the local signs have to conform. And it is these postulates alone that I regard as a necessary metaphysical foundation for our spatial perceptions. Shortly expressed, they come to the one requirement, that all the spatial relations of the stimuli acting on us should be replaced by a system of graduated qualitative tokens. In adding some instances in fuller detail I am quite aware of the many abiding difficulties which could only be removed by an accurate consideration of all the experience that is available to us, or that may become so. Nothing but experience can disclose to us the means by which the local signs we require are really produced; and I do not think this production takes place in the same way in the case of the two senses which have to be considered.

In the first case, that of sight, the first of the suppositions mentioned appeared to me improbable, I mean the supposition that the local signs arise directly in the spot stimulated. Even supposing that the same kind of light L, falling on various points of the retina, produced sensations of colour somewhat differing from each other, C in the point p, and c in q, still there will always be another kind of light l, which occasions in q that same sensation C which L excites in p. Accordingly it cannot be this difference of quality in the impression that gives the reason for referring that impression to a definite spot p or q. On the other hand, there seemed to me to be a real importance in the fact that, from the yellow spot on the retina—for our purposes let us say, from the central point E of the retina—where the sensitiveness is greatest, there is a gradual diminution of irritability in all directions, until at the edges of the hemispherical distribution of the nerves this irritability entirely disappears. This fact, again, taken by itself is not sufficient for our purpose: for a weak stimulation of a spot lying near the point E would necessarily have the same effect as a stronger stimulation of a spot at a greater distance from E. But if a stimulus in the way of light falls on one of these side-spots p, it also makes the eye turn to such an extent and in such a direction that the ray meets, instead of p, the point of clearest vision E. This direction of the glance, as it is commonly called, is accompanied by no idea of the end it actually serves, or of the means by which it is brought about. It must therefore be regarded, at any rate originally, not as an intentional act, but as an automatic movement, a physical effect due to the stimulus and unknown to the soul. Accordingly the following hypothesis seemed to be admissible: in the central organs the single fibres of the optic nerve are mechanically connected with the motor nerves of the muscles of the eye in such a way that the stimulation of each of the former is followed by a definite excitation of the latter, from which it results that the eye is turned in a particular way. How this mechanical connexion of the sensory and motor nerves is effected, is a question which does not touch our present object; and the settlement of it may be left to Physiology, which has to raise the same question in regard to many other reflex motions.

284. The motions just described would satisfy the requirements to be fulfilled by the local signs. If p is the point stimulated, $p\,E$ would be the arc which has to be traversed in order that the point of clearest vision E may be stimulated instead of p; if q is stimulated, the corresponding curve is $q\,E$; these motions will be different in every case, but the difference between them will be merely one of magnitude and direction. But then, on my hypothesis, it was not these motions themselves, but the sensations excited by them, which were to be directly used as the signs $\pi\,\kappa\,\rho$ of the spots $p\,q\,r$. Now a movement, in occurring, occasions a sensation or feeling of our present state, which is different from the feeling of the non-occurrence of the movement: and we even when at rest distinguish the momentary position of our limbs, produced by former movements, from that position which is not now present: these are facts which need no proof, however simple or however complicated may be the conditions which give rise to these feelings. But a further assumption is necessarily involved. We must suppose that the perceptible differences of the feelings in question correspond in their turn to the slightest differences of those movements which the eye needs in order to turn its glance from one point of the field of vision to its next neighbours: and this hypothesis may arouse graver doubts. These doubts, however, really apply, I think, only to a point which is of no decisive importance here. No doubt, as a matter of fact, we notice those minimal movements, which the glance has to make in passing from one point of the field of vision to the next point, and from that again to the next; but to our immediate *feeling* they seem merely a greater or smaller alteration of our state, a greater or smaller degree of a change which does not alter its character. We cannot here, any more than in the case of our other sensations, reduce the magnitude of these steps to comparable arithmetical values, so as to judge that one of them is double or half as great as another. The reason why this becomes possible is that the movements described bring a number of distinguishable points one after another to the spot of clearest vision, and the images of these points, instead of at once disappearing again, remain for sensation side by side with one another: and it is only the number of these distinguishable points which enables us to interpret the differences in our feelings of movement as expressive of equal or unequal spaces traversed, or of definite differences between these spaces. Thus if the eye were shut or did not see, it would doubtless be aware, from the immediate feeling of movement, that the curve $p\,E$ is smaller than the curve $q\,E$ (which it would describe if it continued the same movement), and that $q\,E$ is smaller than $r\,E$; but these feelings would not enable it to determine the co-ordinates of that point x in the field of vision which would meet its glance if it were opened or began to see. It is only the series of images which pass before the seeing eye while it moves, and which remain side by side for some time so that they can be compared, that enable us to give an accurate quantitative interpretation to the different sections of a series of feelings of movement. If we follow with our eyes from beginning to end a line of one colour drawn before us, doubtless we are conscious of a continuous and homogeneous movement of the glance; but suppose there is a stroke drawn across the line near the beginning, marking off a small part of it, we cannot guess how many more fractions of the same size the rest of the line will contain: it is only by marking them off that we can tell their number and be sure that they are equal. How is it again that we learn this last fact, the equality of the distinguished parts? Is it by keeping the head fixed and turning the eye in such a way that these parts of the line, from a to z, are brought one after the other into the direction of clearest vision? And do we then judge that the movements $b\,c, c\,d, d\,e$, up to $y\,z$, in each of which the eye starts from a different position, and which really would not be equally great, *are* equally great, and therefore that the parts $a\,b, b\,c \ldots y\,z$ are also equal? We cannot ascertain their equality in this way. Any attempt to do so accurately is really made thus: in looking at the starting-point a, b, c of each line $a\,b, b\,c, c\,d$ we place the eye so that the direction of its glance forms in every case the same angle with the direction of the piece to be judged, e. g. a right angle: the movements which the eye has then to make in order to go from a to b, b to c, y to z, are not only equal in magnitude (supposing the lines to be equal), but they are identical, since the position from which they start is in each case the same, and the position in which they end is in each case the same. If, on the other hand, the lines are unequal, one of the movements is readily felt in a general and inexact way to be smaller or greater than another, since the position of the eye, at any rate at starting, is the same in each case.

Thus, as with all sensations, our original capacity of estimating impressions quantitatively would (apart from the results of practice) rest on the possibility of generally recognising what is exactly like *as* like, and what is different *as* different. And I do not think that for our purposes any more delicate sensibility is required. I do not mean that the two local signs $\pi = pE$ and $\rho = rE$[1] would enable the soul forthwith to set the two sensations A and B connected with them at definite points in a circular field of vision: it suffices that these signs secure to the impressions their positions in relation to one another; that, for example, they make it necessary to set B *between* A and C and nowhere else. With these explanations as to details, I think we may hold to the theory that the feelings of movement $\pi \kappa \rho$ are the direct local signs of the sensations. But each of these feelings themselves is at bottom a series of momentary feelings of position answering to the various places traversed by the eye in its movement. In order to keep the signs as simple as possible I merely mention this here, and shall use π to indicate the whole series of the successive sensations $\pi_0, \pi_1, \pi_2 \ldots$, which follow each other as the eye turns along the curve pE.

285. The further application of these ideas will be as follows. If we assume that the first impression of light felt in our lives affected the lateral spot p, it will follow that there succeeded an actual movement pE, and that, during this movement, there took place the series π of successive feelings of the position of the eye. If the *same* impression is repeated, the same movement will ensue; and the fact that an identical stimulation has occurred in the past will make no difference to the present one. But the case will be otherwise if at the moment of their second stimulation *another* stimulus affects the spot q, and solicits, with a force equal to that of the first stimulus, a movement of the eye directly opposite to that which is required by p. The result here will be that the eye remains at rest: but at the same time the two impulses to movement, which in their effects cancel one another, will not on that account be a mere zero; as excitations of the nerves they will remain, just as the force of gravity in two

---

[1] [The letters on the right hand stand now not for the movements themselves but for the feelings answering to them.]

masses remains, although those masses counterbalance one another in the scales and therefore do not move them. The operation of that force consists in the bending of the beam and in the pressure exerted on the point of suspension. And I see no reason why, in the case before us, the two excitations, which are prevented from producing an effect in the way of movement, should not still be represented in the soul by two definite feelings, so that the equipoise of opposed forces would be something different from the repose due to the mere absence of excitation.

No doubt, if this is so, we must once more reform our idea of π or κ. So far we have regarded them as feelings which arise from the movement set up; thus they will not occur unless the movements do. But I do not doubt that the stimulation of the spot p, apart from the actual movement connected with it, can arouse a feeling by its mere existence and occurrence, and that by means of this feeling the presence of a thwarted impulse may be indicated to consciousness and so distinguished from the mere absence of the impulse. This feeling we should now regard as the first link π_0 in that series $\pi = pE$, which is produced during the movement pE, and of which each link π_m will now stand for a momentary feeling of position and also for the momentary remnant of a thwarted impulse to movement. Now, taken by itself, π_0 will be simply a feeling, a way in which we are affected, and it will not of itself point to its causes or its possible effects. But then in that first experience the whole further series π connected itself with the first link; this series is associated with π_0 and, on the repetition of π_0, it also will be reproduced. Accordingly, though there is no movement of the eye, there arises the recollection of something, greater or smaller, which must be accomplished if the stimuli at p or q, which arouse only a weak sensation, are to arouse sensations of the highest degree of strength and clearness. This is what happens at first; but if the soul has learnt that the movements of the eye, reported by its feelings, *are* movements,—are, that is, alterations of the relation in which the organ of sensation stands to a number of what may be treated as fixed simultaneous objects; and if finally the soul both can and must apprehend the differences between such relations in a spatial form,—in this case the idea of that something to be accomplished will be transformed into the idea of a greater or smaller spatial distance between the impressions falling on p and q and that middle point of the perceived space which corresponds to the point E in the eye. If, lastly, we add that to each of the many stimuli which at one and the same time excite the spots $p\,q\,r\ldots$ of the retina, there is now conjoined the corresponding series $\pi\,\kappa\,\rho$ of reproduced feelings, the result will be that owing to movements once performed and now remembered, the eye, even when at rest, will be able to assign to each impression its position among the rest.

286. I should be very prejudiced if I felt no alarm at the artificiality of these ideas. But my intention was not to recommend the hypothesis at all costs, but honestly to recount all the presuppositions it involves; and, further, I do not know that it is possible to reach the end we aim at in any simpler way, or that the artificiality lies anywhere but in the facts themselves. The fact itself is strange enough—and it cannot be got rid of—that we can see an unnumbered mass of different-coloured points at once, and can distinguish them. It must be possible, therefore, that what we require should be effected: it must be possible for a large number of impressions to be in consciousness without mingling together; there must be in each of them something, some 'reason,' which makes it appear now at one point in space, and now at another point; and these various 'reasons' again, which are present simultaneously, must operate without intermixture, each of them in exclusive relation to the definite impression it belongs to. In other words, the same complicated relations which we assume between the feelings of movement, must exist between any other possible elements which we might substitute for those feelings. The only question, therefore, is whether internal experience witnesses to the truth of our hypothesis, or whether any other source of knowledge opposes to it objections which are insuperable.

As to the first point, of course, I cannot tell whether others find in themselves what I find in myself. If I ask what meaning an impersonal knowledge (if the phrase may be used) would attach to the words 'two elements p and q are at a distance from one another,' I can imagine an answer by means of the idea of a universal space in which I myself have no fixed position. But for my sensuous perception of the seen points p and q, the only possible meaning of the statement that these points are at a distance from each other is that a certain definite amount of movement is necessary if I am to direct my glance from the one to the other; the different positions of the single points are felt by me simply and solely as so many solicitations to movement. But then I can base nothing on this experience. My individual disposition cannot be communicated. I cannot therefore contradict those who tell me that they observe nothing of these feelings of movements, however much I may be convinced that they deceive themselves and, though they really have the feelings, do not recognise them for what they are. I must content myself therefore with pointing out to them that, in my view, the spatial perception of the world is not something suddenly given us by nature as soon as we open our eyes, but is the result of successive experience and habituation; only this habituation goes on at a time in our lives of which we have no distinct recollection. The skill of the piano-player, once acquired, seems to us a natural gift that costs no trouble; he glances at the notes, and complicated movements of the hand immediately follow: in this case we know what a laborious process he has gone through, and with what difficulty practice has set up these associations of ideas with one another and with the movements we see,—mere links of connexion which no longer show themselves in the consciousness of the practised artist. Exactly the same thing may happen in the case under discussion; and there need be no distinct recollection in consciousness of the actual movements through which we once learnt to localise our sensations. But, it will be answered, this may be a probable account of the slow development of a child, and as a matter of fact we see that its eyes turn towards any light that is brighter than usual: to an animal on the other hand the spatial knowledge of the world comes with so little trouble that we cannot in its case believe in such a prolonged process of learning. To this I reply that in reality we do not at all know what it is that an animal sees directly it is born, nor what sort of perception of space it has. In order merely to account in general for the early use it makes of its limbs we have to assume a number of mechanical reflex movements. It is therefore conceivable that the unhesitating way in which it makes for an object lying in the direction of its glance may really rest merely on a reflex movement set up by the stimulus; and the fact that many of its other earliest movements are unsuccessful would then go to show that it, like man, only gradually acquires an ordered knowledge of that remaining part of the spatial world which lies outside the direction of its glance. Again, the small amount of experience we possess respecting the rise of an optical idea of space in persons born blind and afterwards operated on, will not suffice to decide the question. In all cases the patient has already learnt, through touch and movement, to find his way in the spatial world. Doubtless the ideas of space thus developed may be very unlike the space that manifests itself to a man who can see: for a touch can apprehend only a few points at once, and can only approach distant objects by means of considerable movements; and therefore the space of the blind man may be not so much what we mean by space, as an artificial system of conceptions of movement, time and effort: and, as a matter of fact, the few reports we possess tell us of the astonishment with which the blind man, after a successful operation, learns what the appearance of space or the spatial world is. Still, in spite of such differences, we cannot tell to what extent this previous practice may assist the formation of the visual perception which ensues: in any case it cannot be analogous to the first formation of *all* ideas of space; and finally, there is even a difficulty in discovering what it really is that is seen at first, since the patient who is just beginning to see, cannot express his first experience in the language of sight.

287. There are many questions which psychological optics would have to settle respecting the further development of the spatial ideas: but it is not the business of metaphysic to discuss them. I will only briefly remark that there is no foundation for any of those views which ascribe to the soul an original tendency to project its impressions outwards, and that in one particular way and in no other; all this has to be learnt through the combination of experiences. How it is actually learnt piece by piece we cannot discover; how it *may* be learnt, it is easy to understand in a general way; but there are particular points in the process which cannot at present be understood at all. What we have accounted for so far is nothing more than the arrangement of the points in the field of vision, the internal drawing of the total image; but this image itself as a whole has as yet no place and no position, for the perception of the total space, in which its place and position are to be, is still entirely wanting. The movements of the eye as it opens, shuts, and turns, make the seen image appear, disappear, and change. We therefore naturally associate this image with the eye in such a way that we conceive it as lying in any case in front of us—to use the later language of the developed perception of space: what is behind us—an expression which at this stage has really no meaning—does not exist at all, and has no more to do with space than the general feeling we have in the hand or foot has to do with clearness or dimness. And so it would remain, if we could not move our bodies and could only turn our eyes to a very slight extent. But as soon as we have learnt to turn on our axis and to refer the consequent feelings of movement to their true cause, the movement, we discover that our first field of vision abc, instead of suddenly disappearing altogether, passes successively into bcd, cde ... xyz, yza, zab, and abc. The unbroken series of images which returns into itself awakes in us the idea of a complete circular space with no gaps in it; and this idea, by the help of similar movements of the eye in other directions, soon passes into the ordinary perception of the spherical space that surrounds us on all sides.

At the same time, this idea could neither arise nor attain any clearness unless the idea of the third spatial dimension, that of depth, were being simultaneously formed. In its own nature the soul has certainly no impulse to project its visual impressions outwards; it does not yet know this 'outside;' and in any case it could not project anything merely *generally* outwards, it could only project impressions into a definite distance; and that definite distance it has as yet no means of determining. Just as little is it possible, as has been supposed, for the soul to represent its impressions as lying directly on the eye; for this again means simply the negation of distance, and distance must be known if it is to be negated. The simple fact is really that the impressions are there, and are seen, but they have no assignable position in the third spatial direction, for this is still unknown. That there is such a third direction, we learn only from experience; and we learn it most easily from our finding ourselves moving *through* the images we see, and from the fact that, in consequence of this movement, the single images undergo various displacements, some of them being hidden, and others which were hidden coming into view. And this greatly increases the difficulty of applying the general idea we have thus acquired, in estimating the degree of distance in any particular case; a problem which we leave to physiology and the special psychology of sense-perception.

Lastly, I will touch very briefly on one vexed question; why do we see objects upright, although the image of them on the retina is upside down? We must remember that we do not observe the image on our eye with a second eye, which further could compare its own position with the position of the object. There is nothing before us but the image itself; all the geometrical relations of the picture on the retina utterly disappear as it passes into consciousness; and, in the same way, the fact that as a whole it has a certain position in the eye does not in the least prejudge the question how it is to appear later in a spatial perception gained through some further means. We are absolutely dependent on this other perception. If there were only a *seen* space, we could give no answer at all to the question what is above and what is beneath in that space. These expressions have a meaning only if we presuppose another idea of space, an idea for which these two directions are not merely generally opposed to one another, but are uninterchangeably different. When we have this idea, and not till then, we can say that that in the visual world is 'above,' the image of which we find or have to seek in the fixed direction towards the 'above' of the other space. It is our muscular feeling or general sense which (even when unaided by the sense of sight) instructs us respecting the position of our body, that gives us the other perception of space. For, the body being in its usual upright position, the downward direction means the direction of weight, and when we oppose our forces to it the result is a number of feelings of effort; and by these feelings the downward direction in this other, non-visual, perception of space is uniformly and uninterchangeably distinguished from the upward. Consequently, if *a* and *b* are places in the field of vision, *b* appears to us as beneath *a*, when the sight or touch of *b* is attained through a movement which, in the language of the muscular sense, is a downward movement; or when (our body being upright) the image of *b* always enters the field of vision along with the images of the lower parts of our body, and never along with those of the upper. This last requirement is satisfied by what is commonly called the reversed position of the image on the retina, since the imaging surface of the eye lies behind the centre of rotation; and it would equally be satisfied by an upright position of the image, if that image arose in front of the centre of motion and on the anterior convex surface of the eye. Thus there is a contradiction between the reports of the eyes and of the muscular sense when we use an inverting telescope which gives an upright position to the image on the retina. In such a case, even if we have no other visual image to compare with the telescopic one, we at once notice an opposition to the reports of the muscular sense: we feel that in order to reach the tops of the trees we see, we should have to move our hand in a direction which, for that sense, is downward.

288. I have still to mention that localisation of impressions which we obtain through the sense of touch. Here again the basis of our view is given by *E. H. Weber's* attempts to fix experimentally the conditions under which we can distinguish two impressions on the skin, which are qualitatively alike but locally different. The skin is lightly touched with the two blunted points of a pair of compasses: and the experiments showed that the extent to which the two points have to be separated in order to be distinguished as two, is very different at different parts of the body. For the finger-ends, the edges of the lips, the tip of the tongue, a distance of half a line suffices: while at many parts of the arm, leg, and back, one of twenty lines is necessary. An explanation seemed to be offered at once by the structure of the nerve-fibres. The sensory nerve-fibre, though isolated and unramified during its conduction, separates at its peripheral end into a number of short branches, and so distributes itself over a small space of the skin for the purpose of receiving stimuli from without. It was thought, then, that all the excitations which affect one of these nerve-ends simultaneously would, through the unity of the fibre which has to conduct them further, be destined to form one resultant, and to be incapable of being distinguished from one another. If, again, these excitations occurred one after the other, they might be distinguished in their qualitative character, but would give no ground for local distinctions. On the other hand it was supposed, if two impressions fell on two different nerve-spaces, this alone would not make it possible to distinguish them as two: this possibility arising only if, between the two stimulated spaces, there lay one or more of such spaces which remained unstimulated. This last supposition is in any case inadmissible; for at every moment there are a great many unstimulated nerve-fibres; if any particular ones among them are to be used for the purpose of distinguishing two impressions a and b, there must be something in them which shows that they lie between the two stimulated nerve-spaces; and this presupposes the possibility of accomplishing what has to be explained, the localisation of the sensations.

In other respects too the point of view described fails to give a sufficient basis for this localisation. Nor was this exactly its purpose: it was intended only to explain why two impressions can sometimes be distinguished and sometimes not. But even in this point I found myself unable to accept it. Two points of the compasses which when they touch the skin simultaneously give only one impression, often leave two distinguishable impressions when they are laid against the skin in turn; and their two impressions appear as locally distinct, though no accurate estimate of the distance can be given; moreover, within one radius of sensation the onward movement of a point can be distinguished from its continued pressure on the same spot. Lastly, the conduction of the excitations by the same or by different nerve-fibres did not seem to me to decide anything; the partitions of the fibres are not continued into consciousness, and there all the impressions must in the end come together, qualitatively distinguishable, if they were different, and indistinguishable if they were not. But neither for the like impressions nor for the unlike did the theory assign any ground of local separation, still less any clue by means of which each of them might have its own place given to it.

289. Thus I found myself obliged in this case, no less than in that of the impressions of sight, to look for local signs, abiding certificates of local origin; these local signs would be attached, in the form of qualitatively distinguishable extra-impressions π, κ, ρ, to all excitations A, B, C, according to the particular spots p, q, r of the skin which they affect. Let us suppose that a stimulus, strictly limited in its local extent—say the prick of a needle—affects the spot p. Owing to the connexion between different parts of the skin it is impossible that the operation of this stimulus should be confined to a point destitute of any extension: whatever alteration it produces directly at the point of contact will produce in the neighbourhood of that point a number of little stretchings, pressings, and displacements. Now, though there is a general uniformity in the structure of the skin, it is by no means exactly alike at all parts of the body. The epidermis is thicker at one place, finer at another; when the skin is attached to the points of bones it is stretched, at other places the extent of its possible displacement is greater. It differs again not less widely according to the nature of its substratum: it is not the same when spread over a cushion of fat as when it is stretched over bones, flesh, or cavities. Lastly, at different places in the body these various situations may pass into one another either suddenly or slowly. We may therefore perhaps assume that at any point p in the body the wave π of little extra-agitations, called forth by the stimulation of that point, will differ from any other wave κ which accompanies the stimulation of a spot q. But these extra-excitations would avail us nothing if they simply occurred without becoming objects of our perception; and this last requisite will depend on the distribution of the nerve-fibres. Let us suppose a case. Within the field of distribution of one and the same fibre, let $p\ q\ r$ be the single ends of that fibre: then the local sign π of the spot p will consist in the sensations of those extra-impressions which the direct stimulation of p calls up in its neighbourhood, and the conduction of which to consciousness is secured by the nerve-terminations q and r that receive them. Now if the structure of the skin within this field of distribution were perfectly uniform, the nerve-fibre which unites $p\ q\ r$ would reach precisely the same final state whichever of these terminations were the place directly stimulated: the impressions could not be distinguished, whether they were simultaneous or successive. But if the structure of the skin varies within this field, the stimulation of p will produce different extra-excitations in q and r from those which the same stimulation of q will produce in p and r. Accordingly, if one and the same impression A affects different places in succession, the uniting fibre will bring this impression to consciousness in company with *different* local signs $\pi\ \kappa\ \rho$; and we shall have a motive for the separation of three sensations, although as yet no motive for a definite localisation of them. If the impressions are simultaneous, the uniting fibre may either conduct them side by side without intermixture, or it may be only capable of conducting a single resultant of their influences: which of these alternatives is correct is a question we cannot discuss.

Let us now return to the other idea. Let $p\ q\ r$ stand for three different nerve-fibres; but let the stimulus A act on a spot of the tissue where there is no nerve-termination: then the effect produced must distribute itself until it finds a nerve-termination on which it can discharge itself. Now if in the whole field of $p\ q\ r$ the structure of the skin was uniform, I should say that it matters nothing whether it is one or two of these fibres that receive the like impressions, which would be accompanied by like local signs; for in no case could the impressions be distinguished, and the only use of the multiplicity of the fibres would be the general one of securing the entrance of the stimuli into the nervous system; for there can be no doubt that the excitation of the tissue could not propagate itself to any very considerable distance. On the other hand, if the texture and state of the skin within this whole field varies rapidly, the different local signs which arise at point after point would be useless unless there are a great number of closely congregated nerve-terminations, each of which can receive the wave of excitation of a small circuit, before that wave has lost its characteristic peculiarity by meeting with others which began at different places and spread over the same field. It seems to me that these suppositions answer to the results of observation. On the back and trunk there are long stretches where the structure of the skin is uniform, and here impressions can only be distinguished when they are separated by wide distances. In the case of the arm and leg, the power of distinction is duller when the stimuli follow another in the direction of the longitudinal axis of those limbs—the direction of the underlying muscles; it is sharper when the stimuli are arranged round the limb, in which case the skin is supported alternately and in different ways by the swell of the muscles and the spaces that intervene between them.

290. The name local signs, in its proper sense, cannot be given to these extra-excitations themselves, but only to the sensations they occasion. Now it strikes us at once that there is one of our postulates which those sensations altogether fail to satisfy. It is true that they differ in quality, while at the same time they admit of resemblances; for example, if we touch any part of the skin that is stretched above a bone, whether it be the forehead, the knee-cap, or the heel, feelings are distinctly aroused which have a common tone. But these feelings are not quantitatively rateable members of a series or system of series. They cannot therefore serve directly to fix the locality of their causes; and, besides, what we require in this case is not the localisation of the sensations within an absolute space, but within that variable surface of the body, to the various points of which they are to be referred. We must have learnt the shape of this surface beforehand, and have discovered through observation to what point p in it that impression A belongs, which is characterised by the local sign π: until this is done we cannot refer a second stimulus $B\,\pi$ to the same point in the surface of the body. This can be done easily enough if we can use our eyes; but how is it to be accomplished by the blind man, who, beyond these feelings, has nothing to help him except movement? Without doubt the help that movement gives him is of decisive importance; but how it is possible to use this help is not so easy to understand as is often supposed. While the movement is going on, we have of course a certain definite feeling which accompanies it; but then this feeling is in itself nothing but a manner in which we are affected; it itself does not tell us—we have to guess—that it is caused by a movement of the limbs. This discovery, again, is easy when we can use our eyes, and so notice that our hand is changing its place while we are experiencing the muscular feeling; but the blind man has to make out in some other way that the alteration of his general feeling is not a mere change of his internal state, but depends on the variable relation into which he or his bodily organs enter towards a series of permanent external objects.

Now it seems to me that the condition which makes such a knowledge as this attainable, consists in this,—that the skin, like the eye, has a number of sensitive and moveable points. If an organ of touch in the shape of an antenna possessed in its tip the sole point at which the skin of the whole body was sensitive; and if its capacities were strictly limited at every moment to the power of bringing one single object-point A to perception, the result would be that, when a movement of this organ led from A to B, the perception of A would altogether disappear and the wholly new perception of B would take its place. No doubt while this was going on a muscular feeling x would have been experienced; but how could it occur to us to interpret that feeling as the effect of a spatial movement? However often we passed from A to B and from B to A, and experienced the feelings $\pm x$, we should never discover what those feelings really signified; this transition would remain a perfectly mysterious process, of which all we knew would be that it transformed our idea A into B. On the other hand, if the hand, like the eye, can feel the three impressions $A\ B\ C$ at once; if this image of pressure changes during the movement by regular stages into $B\ C\ D$, $C\ D\ E$; and if by a movement in the opposite direction we can again reach the parts that have disappeared, or grasp them with one hand while the other moves away from them, these facts must certainly tend to suggest the idea that the muscular feelings which accompany the succession of sensations arise from a variable relation of ourselves towards independent objects— that is, from movement. As soon as this is discovered, it is possible—in a way which I need not further describe—for the limitless variety of combination between the sensations of that part of the body which touches, and the not less sensitive part which is touched, to conduct us to a knowledge of the surface of our body, and to the localisation and arrangement of our single sensations in that surface.

CHAPTER V.

The Physical basis of Mental Activity.

In passing on to consider the forms in which soul and body act on one another, I must observe that there are a number of special questions for the answers to which there is not as yet any sufficient foundation; and of these I do not consider it my duty to treat. All that can be considered proper to this metaphysical discussion are the fundamental conceptions used by various theories in interpreting the facts. We may leave out of sight an infinity of so-called experiences, all of which are not by any means equally well attested, and which alter every day with the progress of observation. They will gradually define the object of some future theory, but, so far at least, they do not contribute to the criticism of these metaphysical foundations.

291. It has been said that the soul is the same thing ideally that the body is really; or that the two are the different sides of a single whole. Such wide expressions will not give us what we want. When once we have distinguished body and soul as two parties between which manifold interactions take place, we need ideas more definite and more capable of being pictured, in order to conceive the processes through which these reciprocal influences make themselves felt. And among the questions which require a clear and unambiguous answer is that concerning the spatial relations of the soul—the question, to adopt the current phraseology, of the *seat of the soul.* There was a time when some philosophers looked down with pity on the maladroitness supposed to be involved in the very asking of this question. Nevertheless, unprejudiced persons will always raise it afresh; and therefore it must be answered and not ignored. I might attempt to answer it at once, by connecting it with the preceding discussions; but I prefer to leave them out of sight, and to repeat the considerations by which on other occasions I have attempted to indicate my view. Let us take, then, the various ideas which are really intelligible to us respecting the spatial relations of anything capable of action, and which we are in the habit of applying to them, and ask which of them answers to the special case of the human soul.

292. To be in a place means simply and solely to exert action from that place and to experience the actions or effects that reach that place: if we put these two powers out of sight, it is impossible to attach any meaning to the assertion that a thing is at this place p and is not at that other place q, where, as at p, it neither exerts nor experiences any action. Now it is possible to conceive an existence standing in a direct, and at the same time an identical, relation of interaction with all the other elements of the world. There is one case in which this is a current idea; it expresses what we mean by the omnipresence of God. No element of the world needs to travel a long road, or to call in the help of other things in order to bring its own state to the presence and knowledge of God; nor have the divine influences to make a journey in order to reach distant things: the interaction here is perfectly direct. But then it is also one and the same in all cases, and has not different degrees; at any rate there is no measure of distance, according to which the interaction is necessarily stronger or weaker; the only reason why its work may be greater in one case than in another is that the meaning of things, or of what goes on in things, gives a reason for an interaction of greater weight in one instance and of less weight in another. In this alone consists our conception of omnipresence; the infinite spatial extension which forms the theatre of that omnipresence we are far from ascribing to God as an attribute of His nature; and on the other hand we see no contradiction between the plurality of the points at which His activity manifests itself, and the perfect unity of His nature.

Now the attempt has often been made to ascribe this omnipresence to the soul, within the limits, that is, of the body in which it resides: and the cause of this mistaken idea is most commonly to be found in the æsthetic impression which makes it seem as though the whole of the body were penetrated by a psychical life, and every part of it were the immediate seat of sensation and a direct organ of the will. But there are some simple physiological facts which show us that this beautiful semblance of omnipresence is the result of a number of intermediating agencies; that the soul knows nothing of the stimuli that reach the body, and loses its power of setting up movements the moment the continuity of the conducting nerve is broken; that therefore the space within which body and soul act directly on one another is limited, and must be found somewhere, though we cannot yet define its limits, within the central portions to which all impressions are conducted, and from which all impulses to voluntary movements start. We may refuse to believe this; we may answer that a natural feeling tells us all that the soul feels directly in the touching hand, and that this natural feeling cannot be created by such intervening agencies. But the objection will not help us. There are certain peculiar double feelings of contact which arise when we touch an object with an instrument held in the hand; but we do not consider ourselves justified in concluding from this that the soul can occasionally prolong its activity to the end of a stick or a probe. And yet we fancy that we have a direct feeling at that point of their contact with a foreign body.

293. The natural sciences have familiarised us with the idea of another interaction, which is direct, but also graduated. This is our notion of the attractive and repellent fundamental forces of masses. These forces need no intermediation; they send their action to infinite distances, whether the space traversed by that action is full or empty; but the intensity of the action diminishes with the increase of the distance. If we applied this notion to the present case, we should conceive of the seat of the soul as a point, or at least as a limited district of the brain, on which the interactions of the soul with the surrounding parts would be at the maximum of intensity, while the further they left it behind the more they would diminish in strength, although actually extending to infinity. But a sober observation finds no witness to this outward activity. The slightest intervening space that separates things from our senses makes them simply non-existent to us, except where there are verifiable processes through which we act on things indirectly, and they on us, and which therefore help us over this spatial interval. Any amount of freedom being permitted in suppositions of this kind, the assumption might be suggested that the force of the soul diminishes in the ratio of a very high power of the distance; in this case it might exert no observable influence upon the lengths of nerve which extend even a slight distance from its mysterious seat. All that is certain is that, however close to the root of the nerve a breach of its continuity may be, the outgoing force of the soul is never able to produce on the other side of this breach the effects which it commonly produces in the nerve. But, be this as it may, to assume that there is a fixed limit—whether the surface of the body, or the smaller zone within which the roots of the nerves lie—at which the outgoing force ceases to operate, is simply equivalent to a surrender of this whole point of view. There is nothing in one spherical surface of empty space that can make it, rather than any other such surface, the limit at which an activity ceases to diffuse itself. If there is any such limit, the reason of its existence must lie in the fact that the force does not stream outward aimlessly through empty space, but that there are other real conditions on which its activity and the absence of its activity depend.

294. But it is not worth while to pursue any further this idea of limited action at a distance. There is a more decided view, which has always been preferred to it, and to which many natural processes bear witness. According to this view, action never takes place except in contact, and therefore we must assume one single seat of the soul, fixed or variable, in the form of a point; and apart from other reasons a local habitation of this kind appeared most suited to that which is immaterial and a unity. Yet this idea was at once found to involve a crowd of difficulties. Let us first suppose the seat of the soul to be, not changeable but fixed. In this case we must assume either that all the nerve-fibres join at this point of intersection, or else that there is a formless space—whether parenchyma or cavity—into which all nervous excitations discharge themselves, and are able to reach the soul which resides at some point of this space. But as to the point of intersection, anatomy, instead of discovering it, has simply made its existence incredible; and as little is it possible to discover a formless space, having edges where all the nerve-fibres terminate, and offering a field within which the excitations of these fibres can spread until they reach the soul. It might possibly be the case that the soul needs no such primary assembly of all the primitive fibres, but stands in direct interaction with a few of them, which would be, as it were, the delegates of the rest: but, so far, we know of no anatomical fact which makes this probable. Secondly, then, we may suppose that the place where the soul resides is not fixed but moveable. This idea leads us back to the notion of limited action at a distance. At any given moment the soul would have to be at the particular spot, where an excitation is arriving—an excitation which cannot become a sensation unless the soul is there; and if it is to be at this spot, it must have been already acted upon *from* this spot and so induced to move to it. Finally, if the soul is to impart an impulse to the root of a motor nerve, it must move to the spot from which it can exert this impulse: but as the motor nerve is not yet active it cannot solicit the soul to move to this spot, and therefore the soul must itself choose its line of movement and follow it: and this implies a knowledge of locality which no one will admit.

But is all this really necessary? Is it really necessary to assume any one of these alternatives?—either that the activity of the soul penetrates indiscriminately the whole body or that it penetrates, again indiscriminately but with decreasing intensity, space simply as space; or finally that the soul is confined to one point and acts only in contact? The root of all these difficulties seems to be a confusion in our idea of the nature of an acting force and of the relation of this force to space. And there is no lack of other examples which will enable us to arrive at a more correct conception.

295. Any force arises between two elements out of a relation of their qualitative natures; a relation which makes an interaction necessary for them, but only for them and their like. It is altogether a mistake to regard a force as a hunger for action, spreading itself throughout a space and seizing indiscriminately on everything it finds in that space. We should do better to think of the magnetic force, which within the provinces over which it extends operates on no bodies but those which can be magnetised, and remains indifferent to those with which, though they lie within the same space, it has no elective affinity. Or we may think of the chemical reagents which, when poured into a fluid, pass without acting by the substances which are indifferent to them, while they supplement those with which their chemical nature makes it necessary for them to join. These examples prove nothing, and the idea they are meant to illustrate is intelligible without them, but they enable us to picture it. It is not their spatial position that compels the elements to act on one another or makes such interaction impossible; but it is their own natures and the relations between them that make some elements indifferent to each other and impel others to a vigorous copartnership. If we apply this general idea to the present case, our first assertion must be this: wherever the soul may have its local habitation (for it may be still held that we must assume that it has such a habitation), the extension of its activity will not be determined by its position there: this position will not confine the soul to an interaction with those nerve-elements which surround and touch that habitation: nor will its activity start from this centre, and, like a physical force acting *in distans*, extend with a decreasing intensity to all the elements which are grouped at an increasing distance around that centre. On the contrary, wherever there are elements with which the nature of the soul enables and compels it to interact, there it will be present and active; wherever there is no such summons to action, there it will not be or will appear not to be.

Now doubtless it is pleasant to the imagination to represent the elements that stand in this sympathetic relation to the soul as in spatial proximity to one another, and, where this is possible, to picture a small extended province of the brain, best of all, a single point, where they are all assembled. But there is no necessity in real earnest for this hypothesis. We have reached the conviction that spatial positions and spatial distances are not in themselves conditions of the exercise or non-exercise of forces, and that they form such conditions only because they themselves are the manifestation of forces[1] which

[1] [Cp. §§ 116 and 203.]

are already active and determine the continuance and progress of the action. We have seen that to be in a place means nothing but to exert action and to be affected by action in that place, and that the sufficient grounds of this action and affection lie nowhere but in the intelligible relations of existences in themselves non-spatial. With this conviction of this insight we can now take up again, in a better defined shape, the idea of that omnipresence of the soul in the body which, as we explained in dealing with it, we could not help rejecting. The soul stands in that direct interaction which has no gradation, not with the whole of the world nor yet with the whole of the body, but with a limited number of elements; those elements, namely, which are assigned in the order of things as the most direct links of communication in the commerce of the soul with the rest of the world. On the other hand there is nothing against the supposition that these elements, on account of other objects which they have to serve, are distributed in space; and that there are a number of separate points in the brain which form so many seats of the soul. Each of these would be of equal value with the rest; at each of them the soul would be present, with equal completeness, but not therefore without any distinction; rather we might suppose that at each of them the soul exercises one of those diverse activities which ought never to have been compressed into the formless idea of merely a single outgoing force. In using the current conception of omnipresence we refused to attribute to God, as a predicate of His nature, the infinite cubic extension which His activity fills; and we could see no danger to the unity of His nature in the infinite number of distinct points which form the theatre of that activity: and there is just as little conflict between the unity of the soul and the multiplicity of its spatial habitations. Each of them is simply an expression, in the language of our spatial perception, for one of the manifold relations in which the soul as taking part in the intelligible connexion of things is at one and the same time involved. Our imagination naturally and unavoidably symbolises this unity, no less than the variety, in a spatial way. We shall therefore be inclined to oppose to these many places a single one which is really and truly the seat of the soul. Perhaps it will be the fixed geometrical central point of all the rest; perhaps it will be a variable central point, and then we must conceive it to be determined not geometrically but dynamically as the joint result of the spatial co-ordinates of the distinct places on the one hand and the intensities of the psychical activities going on in them at the given time on the other. Such ideas do no harm and they act as supports to our perception: but they have no objective meaning; for the point arrived at by such a calculation as the above, would not express a real fixed position of the soul in that point at the given moment, nor would it give us grounds for determining anything whatever as to the behaviour of the soul in the next succeeding moment.

296. But our view has to meet an objection coming from another side, and will therefore have to undergo another and a final revision. Observation discloses no such differences among the elements of the brain as would give some few points in it the exclusive privilege of forming the seat of the soul. And yet we have to suppose the existence of such a special qualification. For if we were to widen our idea into the supposition that the soul can stand in the direct relation of interaction, above described, with *all* the constituent parts of the brain, the laboriously intricate structure we find in it would become wholly unintelligible. But is it necessary, is it even possible, to suppose that a real existence A stands once for all in the relation of interaction with other real existences B and C, simply because B is B and C is C, while it stands in no such relation with D and E, just because they are D and E?

In the first place, what is it that makes B to be B and C to be C but this: that under different conditions (these conditions forming a series) B experiences the states $\beta_1 \beta_2 \beta_3 \ldots$, and not $\gamma_1 \gamma_2 \gamma_3 \ldots$, whereas under the same conditions C experiences the latter states and never the former? And, in the second place, we have to suppose that at one time an interaction takes place between A and B, and at another time does not take place; and yet what would this interaction mean, if A and B were simply A and B, and if A did not undergo certain variable states a_1 or a_2, which formed signals to B to realise forthwith β_1 or β_2, and no other of the states possible to it? Without doubt, then, our conception was still incomplete, when we sought to place the soul S in a direct and ungraduated connexion of interaction with different nerve-elements $B\,C\,D$, considered simply as such. Things cannot stimulate one another in respect of their unchanging natures; they can only be stimulated in respect of what goes on in them, and that reciprocally. Accordingly it is the events $\beta\,\gamma\,\delta$ which occur in $B\,C\,D$ that, in virtue of their occurrence, make these points and no other points the seats or localities of a direct interaction with the soul.

Starting from this point of view, then, we should be led in consistency to the following metaphysical conception of the significance of the central organs. The interlacing of the nerve-fibres serves two ends. First, it has to act upon the excitations which arrive from without through the organs of sense, so to connect, separate, and arrange them, that as the result there arise those final states $\beta\,\gamma\,\delta$, which now for the first time, and in their present shape, are in a condition to be brought to the knowledge of the soul, or by which alone it is capable of being stimulated. The second function is the converse of this. The excitations which come from the inner nature of the soul, have to be transformed into physical occurrences in such an order and arrangement, that their centrifugal action on the moveable members of the body will allow of an influence, answering to a conceived end, on the shape of the external world. At the point where these duties are fulfilled, lies a seat of the active soul, the locality of one of the different functions, in the connected whole of which its life consists. In an earlier passage I spoke of this point of view as one of the hypotheses which might be framed in accordance with the facts to be explained: it will now be seen that it is only the continuation of our ontological views. We have left far behind us the theory which conceived the world as based on a number of elements, beings, or atoms, which simply 'are' and form a primary fact, and between which we then suppose actions to take place, the nature and occurrence of these actions being thus of necessity grounded in something external to the fixed existence of the primal elements. We found that there is nothing in the fullest sense actual but the one reality which is in eternal motion, and in the development of which any member of the whole is connected with any other only in accordance with the meaning of the whole, and stands in no such connexion where the meaning of the whole does not warrant it. It is only this connexion of events that gives to single stable conjunctions of these manifold occurrences the appearance in our eyes of beings with an independent existence; in reality these conjunctions are only the meeting points, or crossing points, of in-going and out-going actions, which the significance of the course of events keeps in being, and they form actual beings or existences only when, like the soul, they do not simply appear to others as such centres, but really make themselves such centres by opposing themselves, in consciousness and action, to the external world.

297. From the preceding account of the functions of the central nervous organs we might conclude that their only business is to bring about the commerce of the soul with the external world; the internal activity of the mind would seem not to need their co-operation. Taken as a whole, I do not disclaim this inference, though it must be limited in essential respects; rather I regret that no further explanation is possible regarding those other operations, in which it is agreed on all hands that the help of the body is needed. There are a very large number of cases in which unfortunately we are not simply unable to point out the means which would render the required service, but we do not even know exactly what services are required. And I mean this admission to apply not only to my own view, but to many others which would be very unwilling to make a like confession. We studied the retina of the eye, and the nerve-terminations found in it: dioptrics revealed to us the passage of the rays of light, and their point of meeting on the nerve-terminations: What more did we want? Were we not in complete possession of all the conditions (so far as they can be fulfilled in the eye) implied in the occurrence of visual perception? And yet further investigation has discovered new layers of a strange structure in the retina, of the use of which we know nothing, and which yet can scarcely be useless. It is certain then that we made a mistake in supposing our knowledge to be complete, when we cannot tell the function of what is afterwards discovered: and yet even now we cannot guess what part it was we overlooked in the work the eye has to perform. Now in the case of the brain we are equally at a loss: it is not merely that in the greater part of its structure we find everywhere arrangements of the most remarkable kind, and yet cannot tell their purpose: but even where experience has disclosed to us with sufficient certainty the existence of relations between psychical functions and particular parts of the brain, we cannot get further than this very general result: no one can specify the exact physical function their elements have to perform in order that this or that definite expression of psychical activity may be possible. Thus we talk in a highly perfunctory way of organs of this or that mental faculty, without knowing very well what there is to prevent the soul from manifesting itself without this organ, what intelligible properties there are which enable this organ to supply the conditions lacking to the soul, and lastly in what way the soul is enabled to make use of this organ as its instrument. This last idea indeed, the idea of an instrument, is the most unsuitable of all that could possibly be applied to the case. We may call the limbs of the body instruments: for though we do not know *how* they follow out our ideas, we are at any rate able consciously to connect the movements, which we do not understand in detail, so that they form the means of carrying out an intention. But when we are told that man cannot think with a frozen brain, it is only the obliging preposition 'with' that gives these words the appearance of meaning something; for it seems to indicate that we are able to understand how gloriously thought goes to work with an *un*frozen brain as its instrument. If for the preposition we substitute the conditional sentence which forms its real meaning,—'*if* the brain is frozen, man cannot think,'—the words remind us only of what is perfectly familiar, the many conditions on which life in general and therefore every mental activity depends, but they tell us absolutely nothing of the *nature* of the service which these conditions render to the realisation of these activities. Nothing can help us over this state of ignorance, but the multiplication of exact observations: all that remains for us to do here is to touch on the few general ideas which we should wish not to be neglected when the new knowledge we hope for comes to be interpreted.

298. The older psychology used to speak of a *sensorium commune*: but it was not able to point it out, and the motive for assuming its existence was probably only an indefinite desire for a place where all sensations could be collected into a common consciousness. It may be that in this matter we are in the position described in the last section: perhaps there really is some function we have overlooked, which is necessary to this end, and has to be performed by the physical organs. But all that is certain is that we do not know of any such function. So long, therefore, as we cannot point to definite processes of modification, to which all impressions must submit before they can become objects of consciousness, we have no ground at all for supposing such a place of assembly for these impressions.

Modern physiology has sometimes spoken of a *motorium commune*, and supposed it to be found in the cerebellum. But the movements of the body show the utmost degree of variety; and their classification under the head of movements connects them no more closely with one another than with other functions of the mind to which they are conjoined in the economy of our life. We may suppose that the manifold excitations of the muscles, which each species of animal needs for its characteristic kind of locomotion, and for the preservation of its equilibrium in different positions of the body, are really dependent on a central organ, which compels them to occur in company, and grouped in a way that answers this special purpose. But I know no reason why we should make the same centre a condition of all the other movements, which are excited for other purposes and by other occasions in the various limbs of the body. Thus the idea of this general motory organ, again, seems to me to owe its origin to a logical division of the psychical activities, and not to a consideration of the connexion in which these activities have to stand in supporting each other for the purposes of life. It is much more likely that sensory and motor nerves are combined with one another in various ways, so as to form central points for whole complexes of exertions dependent on one another. Even the motorium to which we ascribed the preservation of the equilibrium, would be unable to perform its task unless it received at every instant an impression of the threatening position which it has to counteract by a compensating movement. And even if it is possible for this movement to be carried out in a perfectly mechanical way, and without the participation of the soul, it is, in the ordinary course of events, at the same time an object of our perception. It seems to me probable, therefore, that this organ, too, consists in a systematic connexion of sensory and motor fibres; although the former do not always communicate their excitations to consciousness, but sometimes simply produce a movement by transferring their excitation to motor fibres. Now among the organs which I should suppose to be formed in this way, I should place first an organ of the perception of space: and I am completely satisfied, although utterly unable to prove it, that in all the higher kinds of animals this organ, dedicated in each case to a function which appears everywhere the same, forms a considerable part of the brain. If the hypotheses I have ventured respecting the local signs of the sensations of sight be correct, the function of this organ would be to connect the optical impressions with the motor impulses of the eye. But how this function can be performed, and in what form the efficient connexion of the sensory and motor nerves is established,—these are questions on which I will offer no conjecture.

299. In the second division of the functions of the central organs—those functions which consist in the physical working out of the internal impulses of the soul—there is one process with respect to which the observations of the most recent times seem to have led to a secure result. It has been proved with sufficient certainty that an organ of language is to be found at a particular spot in the large hemispheres of the human brain. In order to understand the office of this organ, let us glance at the different modes in which our movements in general arise. I put aside the purposeless twitchings which occur in particular muscles, owing to internal irritations for the most part unknown to us: but even with respect to the movements which we produce at will in accordance with our intentions, we must confess that we do not understand how they take place. We do not know by nature either the structure of the limbs which gives the movement its form, or the position of the muscles and nerves which carry it into execution. Even if we did, there would remain a further question as to which we are still in darkness, and which science also is not at present able to answer: what is it exactly that we have to do, if we are to give to the nerve that first impulse which produces in all this preparatory mechanism the desired state of activity? It takes the newly-born animal but a short time to acquire that control over its limbs which characterises the genus to which it belongs; and this fact compels us to assume, not merely a succession of chance experiences which gradually teach the animal that its limbs can be used, but also internal impulses which call these experiences into being. On the one hand, the external stimuli, by transferring their excitations to motor nerves, will at once call forth connected groups of movements combined in conformity with their common end; on the other hand, the central apparatus, on which this combination depends, may be stimulated to activity from within by variable states of the body. The sensory excitation then will produce in consciousness a sensation of the stimulus, and at the same time the movement that occurs will produce in consciousness the sensation of its occurrence, and the perception of its result; and in this way the soul, playing at present the part of a mere spectator, will have acquired the different elements of an association which it can reproduce at a later time with a view to its own ends. The soul cannot always produce of itself the efficient primary state that would recreate the movement: sometimes this movement demands, for its repetition, the complete reproduction of the corporeal stimulus from which it sprang originally as a true reflex movement. For example, up to a certain point one can imitate coughing and sneezing at will, but one cannot bring about an actual sneezing or vomiting without a fresh operation of their physical excitants. Even the movements which depend on states of emotion are only to a slight extent conjoined to the renewal of the mere ideas of a pain or pleasure; they depend on the renewal of the pain and pleasure themselves. I refer to the familiar facts of bodily expression and gesture—an endowment due to nature, and not to our invention—involuntary manifestations of its internal psychical states, which the soul simply witnesses without willing them, and, for the most part, without being able to hinder them.

300. But what is the starting-point which the soul must produce in order that the motor mechanism may execute exactly that movement which at the given instant answers to the psychical intention? I speak simply of a starting-point, because we certainly cannot suppose that the soul exerts an independent and conscious control over the details of the process, and metes out to the particular nerve-fibres, which must be called into action in the given case, those precise quantities of excitation which will secure the direction and strength of the desired movement. In place of thus generating homogeneous impulses, and merely giving them different directions in different instances, it has to produce for different movements A and B qualitatively different internal states a and β; and these, instead of being guided by it, seek and find their way for themselves, simply because they are themselves and no other states. Let a and b be two different motor central points, of which a connects into a whole the single excitations necessary to A, and b those necessary to B: then a will find its efficient response only in a, β only in b, while to other nerves they will remain indifferent. If, again, both movements A and B depend on the same central point, only that they depend on different degrees of its excitation, then the strength of

a and β will determine also the strength of this excitation. If, lastly, one movement requires the simultaneous activity of both organs, then the internal state γ, which is to set up that activity, must contain the two components a and β, and these two components will determine the share taken by a and b in the joint-result they have to produce. This view of the origin of movement corresponds but little to ordinary notions; it leads us back to the often-repeated idea, that the ultimate ground or reason of every action or effect lies in the fact that the two elements which stand in this relation of interaction exist for one another directly—that they stand, if the word may be used, in a direct sympathetic *rapport*, which makes each receptive to the moods of the other. There may be many intermediating processes producing the conditions on which this *rapport* depends, or removing the hindrances to it, but they are all mere preparations for the action; the action itself, which comes when they are finished, cannot be explained in its turn by a similar machinery, between every pair of whose parts this immediate sympathy would again be necessary. Our theory presents difficulties to the imagination only if we take in literal earnest the expression in which the internal state a or β is described as finding its way to a or b. The internal state has not really any way to traverse; for the soul in which it arises is not placed at some distant spot in space, from whence it has to send out its influence in search of the organs that are to serve it. The soul, without its unity being on that account endangered, is itself everywhere present where, in the connexion of all things, its own states have attached to them the consequent states of other elements.

301. When the soul then reproduces within itself these starting-points, they proceed, without any further interference or knowledge on its part, and in obedience to a mechanism which was not invented by us and remains concealed from us, to produce as a final result the actual

movement. We now naturally ask the further question in what precisely do these starting-points consist? A very close approach has already been made to our view when it is asserted that, if the movement is to become actual, we must will, not the movement itself, but the end of it, and that then the movement will take place of itself. But the question is, What is this willing of the end? The imitative movements with which the devout spectator accompanies the actions of the fencer or skittle-player, or by which an unskilful narrator tries to portray the objects he speaks of, might convince us that, in the absence of hindrances, the mere idea of a movement passes of itself into the actual movement. And if we take this point of view, we may really leave the influence of the will out of account. For whatever else it may consist in, and whatever positive contribution, over and above the mere absence of resistance, it may make to our movements, still its function in reference to a given movement a, distinguished from another b, will consist essentially in this,—that it favours the definite ground or reason a or β, which leads to the one or the other of these movements; and the nature of this starting-point or ground is precisely the question we were concerned with. On the other hand, I certainly do not think we need look for this starting-point in the idea, at any rate not in the visual ideas of the movement; although innumerable little acts of our daily life are directly conjoined, without any consideration or resolution of the will, to the ideas arising in us of a possible and desirable movement; and though they even seem to be conjoined, without the intermediation of an idea at all, to the mere perception of the object with which the act may deal. Taken by itself the visual idea would signify nothing more than the somewhat abstract fact that a moveable limb is at this moment at the spot p in space, and at the next moment at the spot q; but it would contain none of the concrete interest for us which is given to this fact by the circumstance that *we* are the cause of the visual idea and that *our* limbs are the object, whose spatial positions are in question. Thus the starting-point or state, which the soul has to reproduce in itself in order that, conversely, the actual movement may be conjoined to that state is not, I conceive, the idea of the movement, but rather the feeling which we experience during the execution of the movement and in consequence of its execution. It is common in physiology now to speak of feelings of innervation, but I should not choose that name to describe what I mean. The case is not, I think, that there is an act, consisting in an influencing of the nerve, and directed now here and now there, but in other respects always of the same nature; and that this act is on the one hand what we feel, and on the other hand what according to the direction given to it produces this movement a or that movement b. The case is rather that this feeling itself, its mere unhindered existence, constitutes that internal condition of the soul which effects an innervation proceeding from it and affecting in all cases a particular complex of nerves. There are some very simple facts of experience which seem to me to confirm this view. A beginner finds it difficult to hit a certain musical note or a given uttered sound, and then there is this special difficulty that the necessary movements are not completely visible; but we also find that any other movement which is at all complicated, continues, even though it be fully measured by the eye, to be difficult to us until we have once succeeded in it. Then we know how we must *feel* if we wish to repeat it, and that feeling π,—or, to state the matter as we did in the case of the local signs, that first link π_0 in the series of momentary muscular feelings which followed one another during the actual movement,—has to be reproduced if the movement is to be repeated; and we consider the movement to be successful, and to answer our intention, if the repeated series π is identical with the series we remember.

302. If, taking these results as our presuppositions, we now return to the organ of language, our account will be as follows: the idea of that which we wish to designate awakes the idea of the sound of its name, and this idea awakes the idea of the muscular feeling π which is necessary to the utterance of the name; and to this last idea is conjoined the movements of the organs of speech. But here we come to a standstill; we cannot determine what contributions the organ has to make to this end. Since the feeling π arose from the physical excitations experienced by the muscles when first the movement was executed, it seems a tenable hypothesis that the reawakening of this feeling in the soul must produce (to begin with) a general state of physical excitation in the organ, and that this state then, in conformity with the structure and internal states of the organ, divides into the various components which give their particular impulses to the executing nerves and muscles. The morbid phenomena produced by an injury to the organ, as well as many simple phenomena of daily life— those of passion, intoxication, and others—show that this chain of processes may be interrupted at various points; there may be a correct image of the object, though the idea of sound united with it is false; or the latter may be still distinct to us, but we are annoyed to find that the spoken word does not correspond with it. But these disturbances again give us no exact information respecting the function of the organ in its healthy state. It is easy to talk of telegraphic conductions and perverted connexions of them, but this is nothing but a way of picturing the observed facts; and images are useless unless one can confront every single line of them with the real process which corresponds to them point for point. The other movements of the body are subject to similar disturbances; but these I must leave to the pathological works in which interesting descriptions of them may be found. Whatever anatomical basis is given to that feeling which instructs us respecting the position, the movement, and the amount of exertion of our limbs, the fact remains that, wherever this *feeling* is diminished or disappears, we find it difficult or impossible to execute movements, the *idea* of which is none the less present to consciousness, as the idea of a task to be accomplished.

303. Phrenology has attempted to connect with corporeal bases the activities commonly ascribed to the higher faculties of the mind. We cannot say that the observations on which this attempt rests have no significance; but phrenology should have confined its efforts to talents whose nature is unambiguous, such as can scarcely conceal themselves where they really exist, and never can be simulated where they do not. It was of little use to speak offhand of peculiarities of disposition and character, respecting which our knowledge of mankind is easily deceived, and which, where they are actually present, may owe their existence to the co-operation of very various influences of life and education. If this limitation were observed, an accurate comparison might then give us, not indeed an explanatory theory, but trustworthy information establishing a connexion between particular facts of bodily and of mental development. These facts would then have to be interpreted; and we cannot tell what the result of a conscientious attempt to interpret them would be. But at any rate it is quite impossible to put any faith in the cherished notion that every one of the capacities and inclinations enumerated in the phrenological plans has a local subdivision of the brain assigned to it as its particular organ: for each of these peculiarities, considered psychologically, is the final outcome of the co-operation of a number of more general psychical functions, and any one of them is distinguished from any other by the different proportions in which the manifestations of these more general activities co-operate. It is only in the case of these general activities that phrenology can hope to discover a dependence on the structure of the brain or skull; and even this hope depends on the very doubtful assumption that fundamental faculties, whose business is a constant and close interaction, would find their needs answered by a localisation of their organs at different spatial positions.

But I pass from these questions, for no one can decide them; I may hold it to be in general a natural assumption that, supposing a material mass to be necessary to the manifestation of a mental function, that manifestation will be more intense according to the size of the mass; but for the higher mental life I believe much more importance is to be attached to the quantity, multiplicity, and intensity of the stimuli afforded by the body to the excitation of an activity, which in its innermost nature or work seems neither to need nor to be accessible to any further physical help. But the contributions which the bodily organisation thus makes to the vivacity and colouring of the psychical life, need not consist exclusively in structural relations of the brain. They may come from all parts of the body; from those delicate mechanical and chemical differences of texture which are not less real because we imperfectly describe them as contrasts between tense and lax fibres; from the architecture of the whole which allows to one organ a more extensive and to another a less extensive development. For all these peculiarities of the solid parts give a special stamp to the play of the functions and the mixture of the fluids, and in this way they are continually bringing to consciousness a large quantity of small stimuli, the total effect of which is that dominating tone or general feeling, under whose influence the labour of the mental forces is always carried on. A part of these bodily influences we know by the name of the temperaments, which need not be described here, and the definite assignment of which to physical bases has never yet been achieved. As peculiar forms taken by our internal states, in accordance with which the excitability of our ideas, emotions, and efforts, is greater or smaller, one-sided or many-sided, passing or continuous, and their changes are slower or more rapid, the temperaments condition in the most extensive way the whole course of mental development. And although the body does not by the physical forces of its masses directly create the faculties of the soul, it forms in this indirect manner one of the powers which control their exercise.

304. We in no way share the view which conceives the activities of the soul materialistically as an effect of its bodily organs, and, as a matter of fact, every attempt hitherto made to connect its higher functions with given substrates has proved fruitless: yet there are many facts which require us to consider the general dependence of *consciousness* on states of the body. The name consciousness cannot now be withdrawn from use; but it has this inconvenience, that it seems to represent as an independent existence something which is really only possible in inseparable union with those variable states which we conceive as occurrences happening to it. We all know that consciousness[1], or being conscious, means only being conscious in oneself of something; the idea of consciousness is incomplete if we omit from it either the subject, or the something which this subject knows or is conscious of. But in handling special questions we often forget this, and lapse into various fancies; sometimes we imagine a bodily organ, which prepares consciousness in general for the use of a soul which is to employ it, in application to a content that may come into it; sometimes we dream of a special faculty of the soul itself which produces the same curious result; or at any rate we figure consciousness itself as the natural and constant state of the mind—a state which is not, properly speaking, unreal and inoperative even when it is completely prevented from appearing. In opposition to these ideas we are ready to admit that it is only in the

---

[1] [The German word *das Bewusstsein*, which we translate 'consciousness,' means literally 'conscious-being,' or 'the being conscious.']

moment of a sensation that consciousness exists as that activity of the soul which directs itself to the content felt; and that it forms a continuous state only in so far as the multiplicity of simultaneous or successive exertions of this activity does itself, as before described[1], form the object or exciting cause of a new act of representation—an act by which we form an idea of this multiplicity. Accordingly we should agree that a soul which never experienced a first stimulus from without, would never, as we say, awake to consciousness: but the question remains whether, when once the play of this internal activity has been started, it can carry on an independent existence, or whether it remains as dependent on bodily causes for its continuance as it was for its excitation.

Now the states of unconsciousness offered to observation by natural sleep, swooning, diseases, and injuries of the central organs, have made the conclusion seem probable to many minds that nothing but the constant continuance of physical processes contains productive conditions of consciousness. By this we need not understand that the activity, in which consciousness at every moment of its actual presence consists, is the private and peculiar product of a bodily organ; the functions of this organ may be no more than stimuli which, but for the particular nature of the soul, would be unable to win from it an activity which is possible to it alone: yet, even so, this activity will still be the production of the organ, so long as its exercise has for its indispensable cause the excitation of that organ. Now on a previous occasion[2] I thought it necessary to remind my readers that the cessation of an activity previously in a state of exercise can, generally speaking, be explained in either of two ways; it may be that the productive conditions of its appearance are absent, or, again, that there is a hindering force which opposes its exercise. None of the

[1] [Sect. 271.]
[2] [See Lotze's *Medicinische Psychologie* (Leipsic, 1852), § 388 ff.]

phenomena mentioned above seemed to me to preclude the second of these ideas. When a sudden fright interrupts consciousness, the physical impression made on the senses by the fact that causes terror may be perfectly harmless, and the reason of our disquietude lies in the interpretation which our judgment puts on the perception: in this case we can see no reason why this psychical movement should not be the direct cause which makes the soul incapable of a continuance of its consciousness, no reason for the supposition that the bodily fainting, which can have its cause only in itself, must intervene and produce, as a secondary effect, the loss of mental activity. When disease slowly clouds over the consciousness, this final result is commonly preceded by a series of feelings of discomfort in which we can see the beginning of the check that is going on, just as in health trifling depressions of mind make a continuance of mental activity distressing though not impossible. But it is not, we may generally say, necessary that the influences which check consciousness should at the beginning of their hindering action be themselves an object of our consciousness. We must remember that of that which is going on in our nerves and of the mode of their influence on the soul we experience nothing: it is only the final result of these processes, the sensation, or the feeling of pleasure and pain, that appears in consciousness; and, when it does appear, it tells us nothing of the mode in which it was brought about. In the same way then, when bodily excitations, instead of producing consciousness, check it, it is possible for their action to remain unnoticed until unconsciousness suddenly supervenes. Injuries of the brain, lastly, can hardly be defined with any probability as the clean disappearance of an organ and the excitation dependent on it; they will probably always include positive changes in the organs that remain, and in the activity of those organs, and from these organs they will develope forces that check consciousness.

These were the general remarks on which I formerly relied; but at bottom they only had a significance in opposition to the view which took consciousness to be the direct product of the work of a bodily organ, and they have not much to say against the other view which conceives activities, in their own nature mental, to be evoked anew in every moment by the constant excitation of the nerves, and to be capable of continuance in this way alone. Many facts, which have been more accurately observed in late years, favour this idea. We know that animals can be sent to sleep, if a compulsion, lasting some little time but causing no pain, deprives them of all movement, and if at the same time all external sense-stimuli are shut out, and so any new sensation prevented: it follows that the internal changes conditioned by the transformation of substances by tissue-change, and by nutrition, are not sufficient to preserve in them the waking state which preceded the experiment. It is not quite safe to argue from brutes to men; but in any case it is certain enough that men too fall asleep from ennui, and quite lately a remarkable case of prolonged anaesthesia (Dr. *Strümpell*, Deutsches Arch. f. Klin. Med. XXII) has proved that in the case of men also the same experimental conditions that were applied to animals can rapidly produce sleep. Nevertheless it remains doubtful whether all these facts tell us anything new, or whether they only present, no doubt in highly remarkable circumstances, what we knew before. With regard to the animals successfully experimented on, we do not know whether there is any impulse in them tending to extend the course of their ideas in any considerable degree beyond the contents of their sensuous perception; in the case of ennui, we know that for the moment this impulse is absent, while the sensations of the special senses are not absent, and it is only the lack of interest in them that removes the stimulus to follow up what is perceived with an attention that would find relations in it. Thus we seem to have found nothing but what needs no explanation: where the external and internal impulses which stir the soul to activity are absent, this activity is absent, and the lack of it may form the point of departure for that further depression of nervous irritability by which at last sleep is distinguished from waking.

305. Before I attempt to give some final view on this subject, I have still to mention that alternation of consciousness and unconsciousness which is presented to us in the forgetting of ideas and their recollection. Everyone knows the views which regard memory and recollection as possible only by means of a corporeal basis; according to this view some physical trace of every perception must have remained in the brain, a trace which, it would be admitted, would gradually disappear altogether if no occasion for its renewal occurred. It would be unjust to require a closer description of these abiding impressions; but a consideration of the precise requirements they must fulfil does not, as it seems to me, reveal the advantages which this hypothesis is thought to possess when compared with a theory which regards these processes as merely psychical. I raise no objection to the idea that the simultaneous stimuli traversing the brain in extraordinary numbers, leave behind them an equal number of traces which do not intermix: that for a moment, at least, these traces can remain unintermixed is proved by the fact that they help us to form an equally large number of separate perceptions; but this very fact at the same time proves that the unity of the psychical subject holding these perceptions together in its consciousness, is, no less than the brain, capable of a simultaneous multiplicity of states which remain apart from one another. This, however, was the very point respecting which these theories at starting expressed mistrust: a material system, consisting of a large number of parts, seemed to them better adapted to the purpose of receiving and preserving a number of impressions than the indivisible unity of an immaterial substance. But the theory does not get rid of the necessity

of ascribing these capacities to such a substance, as well as to the brain; unless indeed we are prepared to return to the old mistake of confusing a multiplicity of impressions distributed in the brain with the perception of this multiplicity. As we proceed, the duties demanded alike of brain and soul are multiplied at the same rate for both. If we approach an object, there is only one point of it—that which our glance continuously fixes—that throws its image constantly on one and the same element of the retina; all the other points, as the apparent size of the object increases with our approach to it, make their impression from moment to moment on fresh spots in the nerve. Thus, if this one object is to be perceived, countless images must be represented within a short time, and that in such a manner that every part a of the object leaves traces in countless elements $p\,q\,r\,\ldots$ of the brain, while each of these elements again receives such traces impressed upon it by all the parts $a\,b\,c\,\ldots$. An intermixture of these latter images would be of no service to the act of representing the object; each single material atom will in its turn have to preserve countless impressions without intermixture—the very same task which this theory refused to entrust to the unity of the soul—and on both sides the functions to be performed multiply immeasurably when, instead of one object, there are many to be perceived.

But the important point was not this preservation itself, but the service it can render to memory when only a part $a\,b$ of a composite image is given by a new perception, and the parts $c\,d\,e$ which belong to it have to be supplied. If we suppose that the new impression $a\,b$ now affects the same nerve-elements p and q which it affected before, it is conceivable that the trace of it still remaining may be somehow called to life again in those elements; but how does it come about that p and q renew in other nerve-elements, r and s, the traces of the impressions c and d which formerly affected *them*—these impressions c and d being precisely those which united with a and b will form the image that has to be recollected? It may be answered that the psychological view of the matter equally demands that a peculiar connexion should be established between those impressions which occur simultaneously, or, if successively, with no intervening link: that the very same solidarity obtains between the abiding remnants of the nerve-excitations; that, if time be conceived as a line of abscissa's those of equal abscissa form such an associated group. And this stratified deposition of the impressions, supposing it admitted, might indeed explain why their reproduction would take the direction from $a\ b$ only to $c\ d$, and not to any $p\ q$ belonging to another stratum; but the mechanical possibility of the process itself which takes this direction would remain in obscurity. For we cannot misuse the metaphor to such an extent as to regard the simultaneous states of all the nerve elements as a connected stratum, the continuity of which produces the result that a vibration of one point sets all the rest vibrating in those forms in which they formerly vibrated in this stratum, and not in those forms in which they vibrated in other strata. It could be nothing but the nature of the impressions a and b that in its turn revives the others c and d which are connected with them: and since there is no reason why a by itself or b by itself should reproduce c or d any more than many other impressions, it can be nothing but the concurrent existence of a and b that limits the selection to those impressions that really belong to them. This implies not only that the single nerve-elements in which a and b are revivified, interact on each other, so that the fact of the concurrent existence of those two impressions is transformed into an efficient resultant, by which the reawakening of c and d can be brought about; but, over and above this, those nerve-elements which are now to contribute c and d, can only add this definite contribution to the whole, if the fact of the previous simultaneity of their impressions c and d with a and b has left behind in them, too, a permanent disposition to answer this and no other solicitation with this and no other response.

I will not pursue the investigation further. Its final outcome seems to me clear: the hypothesis must transfer to every single nerve-atom precisely the same capacity of an ordered association and reproduction of all successive states which the psychological view claims for the soul. How these two occurrences (this association and reproduction) come about we have confessed that we do not know; but it is utterly vain to hope that a physical construction can enable us to understand them without presupposing that the same enigmatical process is repeated in every element of matter.

306. These considerations would all be useless, if interruption of memory occasioned by bodily suffering admitted of no explanation whatever in consonance with our views. Unfortunately I cannot maintain that what I have been saying makes such a satisfactory explanation possible; but this does not seem to me to diminish the impossibility of those other views which localise particular groups of ideas or particular remembrances off-hand at definite places in the central organs. All that we can, properly speaking, be said to observe is not an absence of memory, but merely the incapacity to reproduce ideas, which, according to the ordinary view, may nevertheless still be present as unconscious ideas, only that the associations are wanting, by help of which they might be restored to consciousness. This account, apart from a further definition, would do no more than explain the total forgetting of ideas of which there is nothing whatever to remind us; whereas in the cases of morbid interruption of memory, the sensuous perceptions frequently go on unhindered, and bring with them a quantity of impressions, associated in manifold ways with the forgotten ideas: and yet the restoration of these ideas to memory does not take place.

There is only one supposition that I can suggest, and I

am not sure myself whether it does not push to exaggeration a conception which in itself is valid. Ideas are connected not only with one another, but also in the closest way with the general feeling g of our total state at the moment of their origin. If g changes into γ, and it is impossible to us to experience g again, the way is barred which might lead our memory back to the ideas connected with g: in whatever numbers single ideas among these may be reproduced by new perceptions, still the common bond is absent, which connected them together as our states, and thus made those contents of theirs, which in themselves were reciprocally indifferent, capable of reciprocal re-excitation. It is in this way that I should attempt to interpret the facts that, when we have recovered from severe illness, we do not remember what we experienced while it lasted, or while, before its outbreak, our general feeling was already changed; that, when we are free from the paroxysm of fever, we do not remember sets of ideas which accompany it, and that in particular cases these sets of ideas are carried on when the next paroxysm occurs, owing to the return of the morbid general feeling: that unusual depression sometimes brings long-forgotten things to remembrance, while in other cases of the same kind things familiar to us affect us so little that they seem like something new, unknown, and unconnected with the whole of our life. It is far harder to apply this explanation to those defects of memory that occur with regard to a certain definite subject-matter of our ideas; e. g. the forgetting of proper names, of a series of scientific conceptions, of a foreign language. But here again what other course is open to us than to refer these cases, so far as they are confirmed by observations, to similar causes? It is impossible to conceive of the activities which are here impeded as assigned to different organs; they could only be assigned to different ways of working on the part of the organs: we should have to come back to a general depression of the organs, preventing them from executing a group of functions, which, though they belong to one another, do not disclose even such a similarity of physical work as would correspond to their intellectual connexion, and would make it a matter of course that they should all be interrupted together. In that case there would be no greater impossibility in the further supposition, that this physical depression has for its consequence a mental general feeling, different from and superseding that which ordinarily accompanies these mental operations. For that which moves and forms connexions in us is not abstract truths: the course of our thoughts is always a course of *our* states, and every particular form of our intellectual activity gives us the feeling of a peculiar mental posture, which reacts again on the bodily general feeling. If a change originally set up in this latter feeling makes its mental echo impossible, the mental activities will be checked in their turn by the conflict of the tone of feeling which they find in existence with that which should normally accompany them.

307. Efforts to assign to the soul a sphere in which its activity should be independent of the body, commonly proceed from the desire to secure its substantiality, and thereby its endless continuance; though in reality the certainty with which we can infer the latter from the former is strictly proportionate to the energy with which at starting we have chosen to identify the two. No such motives have guided our present investigation: indeed what use would there be in securing to the soul all the rights of substance, if the exercise of these rights is not equally unrestrained? But no theories can change the facts. Whether we see in the central organs the creative causes of mental activity, or only, on occasion, the causes which impede it, in either case the facts remain, that a state of perpetual wakefulness is impossible to us; that the exhaustion of the body brings with it the total cessation of mental life; that, conversely, this life, in some way, whatever that way may be, consumes the forces of the body; that diseases and injuries of the brain either cripple particular faculties, or sink us in a complete mental night. When, then, we joined in the efforts alluded to, it was not with the hope of finding in the intrinsic substantiality of the soul any warrant for an independence of which so little does as a fact exist; but in the certainty that, even if exact observation should prove the activity of the soul to be still more closely bound up, than it is now proved to be, with the body and its agitations, still this dependence could in no way alter the essence of our conviction; and that essential conviction is that a world of atoms, and movements of atoms, can never develope from itself a trace of mental life; that it forms, on the contrary, nothing more than a system of occasions, which win from another and a unique basis the manifestation of an activity possible to that basis alone.

But even this expression of our view must after all be once more modified. We found it impossible to conceive the world as built up out of a disconnected multiplicity of real elements of matter: just as little, on the other side, have we considered the individual souls on which this system of occasions acts, to be indestructible existences; both they and these occasions meant to us simply actions of the one genuine being or existence, only that they are gifted with the strange capacity, which no knowledge can further explain, of feeling and knowing themselves as active centres of a life which goes out from them. Only because they do this, only in so far as they do this, did we give them the name of existences or substances. Still we have so named them; and now the question arises whether it would not—but for the exigencies of imagination—be better to avoid even that name and the inferences into which it will never cease to seduce men. Beginning by speaking of the souls as existences, we go on to speak of their states, and we even venture to talk of such states as betray nothing whatever of the essential nature of that to which we ascribe them. Thus we have not scrupled, any more than any psychology has so far scrupled, to use the supposition of unconscious ideas, or of unconscious states, which ideas have left behind, and which become ideas again. Is it really necessary that they should so be left behind, and can we gather any intelligible notion from these words unless we take refuge, as men always naturally and inevitably have done, in the crassest metaphors of impressions that have altered a spatial shape, or of movements that are not conceivable except in space? There was nothing to compel us to these suppositions but the observed fact that previous ideas return into consciousness: but is there no other way in which that which once was can be the determining ground of that which will be, except by continuing to be instead of passing away? And if the soul in a perfectly dreamless sleep thinks, feels, and wills nothing, *is* the soul then at all, and what is it[1]? How often has the answer been given, that *if* this could ever happen, the soul *would* have no being! Why have we not had the courage to say that, *as often as* this happens, the soul *is* not? Doubtless, if the soul were alone in the world, it would be impossible to understand an alternation of its existence and non-existence: but why should not its life be a melody with pauses, while the primal eternal source still acts, of which the existence and activity of the soul are a single deed, and from which that existence and activity arose? From it again the soul would once more arise, and its new existence would be the consistent continuation of the old, so soon as those pauses are gone by, during which the conditions of its reappearance were being produced by other deeds of the same primal being.

[1] [Compare *Medicinische Psychologie*, § 123.]

Conclusion.

I have ventured on these final hints because I wished to give a last and a full statement of that requirement which I believe we must lay on ourselves,—the total renunciation of our desire to answer metaphysical questions by the way of mathematico-mechanical construction. There can be no need for me to express yet again the complete respect I feel for the physical sciences, for their developed method and their intellectual force; the efforts of Metaphysic cannot in any way compare with their brilliant results. But it has sometimes befallen the investigation of Nature itself, that, at points which for long it thought itself warranted in using as the simplest foundations of its theories, it has discovered a whole world, new and never surmised, of internal formation and movement; and in this world it has at the same time discovered the explanation of occurrences, which had previously been connected, in a bare and external way, with these seemingly simple points of departure. It is a like discovery that Metaphysic has always sought, only the distance which separated its goal from anything that can become the object of direct observation was still greater. It sought the reasons or causes on which the fact depends, that we are able to pursue with confidence throughout the whole realm they govern the fundamental conceptions of the natural sciences, and which at the same time would determine the limits of this realm. It is a true saying that God has ordered all things by measure and number, but what he ordered was not measures and numbers themselves, but that which deserved or required to possess them. It was not a meaningless and inessential reality, whose only purpose would have been to support mathematical relations, and to supply some sort of denomination[1] for abstract numbers: but the meaning of the world is what comes first; it is not simply something which subjected itself to

---

[1] [Cp. § 214, end.]

the order established; rather from it alone comes the need of that order and the form in which it is realised. All those laws which can be designated by the common name of mathematical mechanics, whatever that name includes of eternal and self-evident truths, and of laws which as a matter of fact are everywhere valid,—all these exist, not on their own authority, nor as a baseless destiny to which reality is compelled to bow. They are (to use such language as men can) only the first consequences which, in the pursuit of its end, the living and active meaning of the world has laid at the foundation of all particular realities as a command embracing them all. We do not know this meaning in all its fulness, and therefore we cannot deduce from it what we can only attempt, in one universal conviction, to retrace to it. But even the effort to do this forces upon us a chain of ideas so far-reaching that I gladly confess the imperfections which, without doubt, can be laid to the charge of this attempt of mine. When, now several decades since, I ventured on a still more imperfect attempt, I closed it with the dictum that the true beginning of Metaphysic lies in Ethics. I admit that the expression is not exact; but I still feel certain of being on the right track, when I seek in that which *should* be the ground of that which *is*. What seems unacceptable in this view it will perhaps be possible to justify in another connexion: now, after I have already perhaps too long claimed the attention of my reader, I close my essay without any feeling of infallibility, with the wish that I may not everywhere have been in error, and, for the rest, with the Oriental proverb—God knows better.

INDEX.

'Absolute motion,' 370 ff.
'Accidental views' (Herbart), 180 ff.
Action (at a distance), ii. 28.
Albumen, ii. 131.
'Allgemeine Physiologie des körperlichen Lebens' (Author's), ii. 128.
Anaesthesia, ii. 309.
Antinomies (Kantian), 240 ff., 321 ff.
Aristotle, 24, 74, 78, 106, ii. 129, 141.
Articular surfaces, ii. 135.
Association of Ideas, ii. 226.
Atomism, ii. 38.
Attention, ii. 239, 242.
Attraction, ii. 23, 67, 70.
Avogadro, ii. 127.

Baer (K. E. von), ii. 142.
Binary combinations, ii. 131.
Brain, injuries of, ii. 308.

Categories, 24.
'Causa transiens,' 135.
Cause (opp. 'Reason'), 126.
Cause (and effect), 138.
Cellulose, ii. 131.
'Cessante Causa—,' 367.
Checking of Ideas by Ideas, ii. 219, 229.
Chemistry, ii. 127.
Comparison, conditions of, ii. 232.
Conceptions (universal), ii. 242.
Consequent, 108 ff.
Conservation (of Mass), ii. 89.
— (of Force), ii. 93 ff.
Constancy (of Mass), ii. 56.
— (of the sum of motions), ii. 91.
Contact, 132 ff.
Content ('*Inhalt*'), 23 *note*.

Continuity, Law of, 357.
Contradiction, Law of, ii. 12.
Cosmology, 27.

Darwin, ii. 159.
Depth, Idea of, ii. 274.
Descartes, 268, ii. 4.
'*Deutsches Archiv für Klin. Med.*' quoted, ii. 309.
Dialectic method, 21.
Difference (quantitative) Idea of, ii. 234.
'Dim' Ideas, ii. 221, cp. 244-5.
Disappearance of Sensations, ii. 217.
Distance (and force), ii. 67, 81.
Distinction, of points by Touch, ii. 276.
Drobisch, 279.
δύναμις, 106.

Effect (and Cause), 138.
Electricity, ii. 125.
'*Elemente der Psychophysik*' (Fechner), ii. 196.
Emotions (and the Interest of Ideas), ii. 224.
ἐνέργεια, 106.
Epicurean Physics, ii. 129.
Equality, *note*, 62.
Equality of Cause and Effect, 138.
Equivalence, ii. 56, 101.
Euclidean Geometry, 275.
Experience, 3.
Extra-impressions, or Local Signs, ii. 255.
Eye, how we estimate movement of, ii. 265.

Fechner, '*Atomenlehre*,' ii. 40, 174.
— '*Elemente der Psychophysik*,' ii. 196 ff., 187.

INDEX.

Fechner and Weber, ii. 210.
Feeling ('*Gefühl*'), in the reproduction of Ideas, ii. 229.
— in initiation of action, ii. 302.
— and Memory, ii. 314.
Fichte, 221.
Force, ii. 15.
— (and Distance), ii. 67.
— (and Time), ii. 83.
— (a single), ii. 101.
— (vital), ii. 129.
Formulae, for consciousness, ii. 236.
Freedom, 206, 293.

Generic Idea, ii. 141.
Geometry, 275, 293.
Geulinx, 157.
Gravitation, ii. 70, 275.
'Grund,' 126.

Hegel, 173, 204, 270 ff., ii. 10.
Helmholtz, 293 ff.
Heraclitus, 106, 112, 157.
Herbart, 47 ff., 57, 69–72, 132, 180, ii. 48, 72, 151, 219, 235, 238.
ὕλη, 79.

Idea ('*Vorstellung*'), usage defined, ii. 220.
— (universal), ii. 234, 242.
Idealism, 95, 211 ff.
Identity, 62 *note*, 63.
— Law of, 104.
— Idea of, ii. 234.
Impulse ('*Trieb*'), ii. 130.
Infinite divisibility, 244.
Infinity (of world in space), 241.
'Innervation,' ii. 302.
'Interest' of Ideas, ii. 224, 244.
Irritability, ii. 135.

Kant, 24, 268 ff., 315, 321, ii. 9 ff., 61, 244.
— (Trans. Aesth. *quoted*), 238.
Kinds, ii. 150.

Lambert, ii. 12.
Law, 5 ff.
Leibnitz, 150 ff., 183, ii. 48, 61.

Lichtenberg, ii. 98.
'Life and Vital Energy' (Essay by Author), ii. 128.
Life, a Principle of, ii. 133
Like, 62 *note*.
Likeness, idea of, ii. 233.
Local Signs, ii. 255.
— in Vision, ii. 264.
— in Touch, ii. 276.
Logic (Author's), 187, 367.
Lucretius, ii. 41, 137.

Machines, ii. 135.
Mass, ii. 56, 89.
Mechanism, ii. 115.
'*Medicinische Psychologie*' (Author's), ii. 165, 187, 307.
Memory, alleged physical basis of, ii. 310.
— Interruptions of, ii. 313.
μὴ ὄν, 83.
Metaphysic, 2, 8.
'*Mikrokosmus*' (Author's), 228, ii. 157, 165, 175.
Monads, 183.
Monism, 217.
Motions (the sum of), ii. 91.
'*Motorium Commune*,' ii. 295.
Muscular sense, ii. 275.
Mythology, mathematical, ii. 236.

Natural Kinds, ii. 150.
Nature, our idea of, ii. 53, 138.
Nerve-fibres, Isolation of, ii. 250, 253.
Nervous organs, central, ii. 293.
Necessity, 206.

Objective, cp. 23 *note*.
Occasional causes, 129.
Occasionalism, 147.
Ontology, 27.
Opposite ideas, association of, a fiction, ii. 227.
Organ of Space-perception, ii. 297
— Language, ii. 297.
Organic Life, ii. 158.
Organs, special in Brain, ii. 295.
οὐκ ὄν, 85.

Pain, *see* Pleasure.

Parallel lines, 291, 297.
Parallelogram of Motions, 386 ff.
'Parmenides' (of Plato), 174.
Parsimony (Principle of), ii. 104.
Perception of Space, 377 ff., ii. 240.
Persistence, law of, 363.
Phrenology, ii. 304.
Plato, 1, 79, 95, *quoted* 174.
Pleasure, affects course of Ideas, ii. 225.
Pluralism, 217.
Poisson, *quoted*, 384, 386.
'*Position*' ('*P. oder Setzung*'), 42 *note*, 83.
Predicates in Plato, 95.
'Pre-established Harmony,' 150.
Psychical Mechanism, ii. 235.
Psychology, 18, 27, ii. 163, (Herbart's) 237.
Psycho-Physical Mechanism, ii. 187.

'Qualitative Atomism,' ii. 48.
Qualities, Herbart's 'simple Qualities,' 57 ff.
Quality, ii. 15.
Quaternary Combinations, ii. 131.

Radiation (of force), ii. 67 ff.
Ratio (*sufficiens*), 115.
Rational Psychology, ii. 163.
Reactions of the soul, grades of, ii. 241.
Realism, 95, 217.
Reason (and Consequent), 108 ff.
Reason (opp. Cause), 126.
Reflex motion of Eye, ii. 264.
Relation, or Reference, an act of mind, ii. 232, and *note*.
Relativity, 374.
Reproduction of Ideas in order, ii. 228.
Repulsion, ii. 23, 67.
'*Res cogitans*,' ii. 4.
'*Res extensa*,' ii. 4.
Riemann, *quoted*, 311-2.

Satisfaction, of force (Herbart), ii. 72.
Schelling, 206, 268, ii. 8.

Self-maintenance (Herbart), of things, 69-71.
— of soul, ii. 237.
Sensation, 32-3.
'*Sensorium Commune*,' ii. 295.
Similars, association of, ii. 227.
Socrates, 174.
Solidity (Lambert), ii. 12.
Sophists, 95.
Soul, the Seat of, ii. 283.
— Interrupted existence of, ii. 317.
Spatial image, reproduction of, ii. 230.
Space-perception, 377, ii. 240.
— of blind, ii. 272.
— organ of, ii. 297.
Specific energies, ii. 205.
Spinoza, 120, 267, ii. 5.
Square of distance, ii. 67, 80.
Stahl, ii. 139.
Stimuli of Sense, ii. 199 ff.
Stream of Time, 316.
'*Streitschriften*' (Author's), *quoted*, ii. 237.
Strength of Ideas, ii. 220, 244.
Strümpell, Dr. (*quoted*), ii. 309.
Subjectivity of Sensation, ii. 204.
Substance, 100.
'Substantial Forms,' ii. 129.
Substantiality of Soul, ii. 315.
Successive Synthesis, 324.
Sufficient Reason, 107.

Ternary Combinations, ii. 131.
Thing (for use of 'Ding' and 'Sache,' v. 23 *note*), 23, 75, 222.
$\tau i \ \tilde{\eta} \nu \ \epsilon \tilde{\iota} \nu \alpha \iota$, 78.
Time, Idea of, ii. 240.
$\tau \grave{o} \ \tau i \ \grave{\epsilon} \sigma \tau \iota$, 78.
Touch, localisation by, ii. 276.
Transeunt action, 114 ff.
'*Transiens*' (*Causa*), 135.
Treviranus, ii. 130.
Triangle (sum of its angles), 291.
Type, ii. 141.

'Unconscious' Ideas, ii. 224.
Unconsciousness, ii. 307.
Unity of the soul, ii. 192.
Universal conceptions, ii. 242.

'Up' and 'Down,' relative to Gravity, ii. 275.
'*Ursache*,' 126.

Vision, erect, ii. 275.
Vital Force, ii. 129.
'Vocation of Man' (Fichte), 221.
Von Baer, ii. 142.
'*Vorstellung*' (Idea), defined, ii. 220.

Wagner (Rudolph, Hand-Dictionary of Physiology), ii. 128.

Weber's Law, ii. 210.
Weber on Localisation by sense of Touch, ii. 276.
Weisse, 206, 271.
Whole, parts of same associated, ii. 227.
'*Wirkung*,' 126.

Yellow spot of Retina, ii. 263.

Zeno, 174, 385.
'*Zusammen*' (in Herbart), 132.

THE END.

www.bookjungle.com *email: sales@bookjungle.com fax: 630-214-0564 mail: Book Jungle PO Box 2226 Champaign, IL 61825*

The Codes Of Hammurabi And Moses
W. W. Davies

QTY

The discovery of the Hammurabi Code is one of the greatest achievements of archaeology, and is of paramount interest, not only to the student of the Bible, but also to all those interested in ancient history...

Religion   **ISBN:** *1-59462-338-4*   **Pages:132**
MSRP $12.95

The Theory of Moral Sentiments
Adam Smith

QTY

This work from 1749. contains original theories of conscience amd moral judgment and it is the foundation for systemof morals.

Philosophy   **ISBN:** *1-59462-777-0*   **Pages:536**
MSRP $19.95

Jessica's First Prayer
Hesba Stretton

QTY

In a screened and secluded corner of one of the many railway-bridges which span the streets of London there could be seen a few years ago, from five o'clock every morning until half past eight, a tidily set-out coffee-stall, consisting of a trestle and board, upon which stood two large tin cans, with a small fire of charcoal burning under each so as to keep the coffee boiling during the early hours of the morning when the work-people were thronging into the city on their way to their daily toil...

Childrens   **ISBN:** *1-59462-373-2*   **Pages:84**
MSRP $9.95

My Life and Work
Henry Ford

QTY

Henry Ford revolutionized the world with his implementation of mass production for the Model T automobile. Gain valuable business insight into his life and work with his own auto-biography... "We have only started on our development of our country we have not as yet, with all our talk of wonderful progress, done more than scratch the surface. The progress has been wonderful enough but..."

Biographies/   **ISBN:** *1-59462-198-5*   **Pages:300**
MSRP $21.95

www.bookjungle.com *email: sales@bookjungle.com fax: 630-214-0564 mail: Book Jungle PO Box 2226 Champaign, IL 61825*

The Art of Cross-Examination
Francis Wellman

QTY

I presume it is the experience of every author, after his first book is published upon an important subject, to be almost overwhelmed with a wealth of ideas and illustrations which could readily have been included in his book, and which to his own mind, at least, seem to make a second edition inevitable. Such certainly was the case with me; and when the first edition had reached its sixth impression in five months, I rejoiced to learn that it seemed to my publishers that the book had met with a sufficiently favorable reception to justify a second and considerably enlarged edition. ..

Reference   ISBN: *1-59462-647-2*   Pages:412 MSRP *$19.95*

On the Duty of Civil Disobedience
Henry David Thoreau

QTY

Thoreau wrote his famous essay, On the Duty of Civil Disobedience, as a protest against an unjust but popular war and the immoral but popular institution of slave-owning. He did more than write—he declined to pay his taxes, and was hauled off to gaol in consequence. Who can say how much this refusal of his hastened the end of the war and of slavery ?

Law   ISBN: *1-59462-747-9*   Pages:48 MSRP *$7.45*

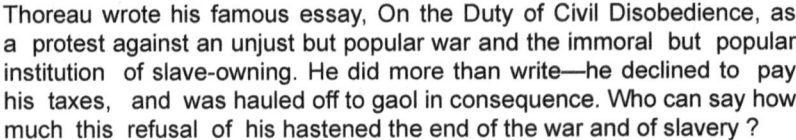

Dream Psychology Psychoanalysis for Beginners
Sigmund Freud

QTY

Sigmund Freud, born Sigismund Schlomo Freud (May 6, 1856 - September 23, 1939), was a Jewish-Austrian neurologist and psychiatrist who co-founded the psychoanalytic school of psychology. Freud is best known for his theories of the unconscious mind, especially involving the mechanism of repression; his redefinition of sexual desire as mobile and directed towards a wide variety of objects; and his therapeutic techniques, especially his understanding of transference in the therapeutic relationship and the presumed value of dreams as sources of insight into unconscious desires.

Psychology   ISBN: *1-59462-905-6*   Pages:196 MSRP *$15.45*

The Miracle of Right Thought
Orison Swett Marden

QTY

Believe with all of your heart that you will do what you were made to do. When the mind has once formed the habit of holding cheerful, happy, prosperous pictures, it will not be easy to form the opposite habit. It does not matter how improbable or how far away this realization may see, or how dark the prospects may be, if we visualize them as best we can, as vividly as possible, hold tenaciously to them and vigorously struggle to attain them, they will gradually become actualized, realized in the life. But a desire, a longing without endeavor, a yearning abandoned or held indifferently will vanish without realization.

Self Help   ISBN: *1-59462-644-8*   Pages:360 MSRP *$25.45*

www.bookjungle.com *email: sales@bookjungle.com fax: 630-214-0564 mail: Book Jungle PO Box 2226 Champaign, IL 61825*

QTY

☐ **The Rosicrucian Cosmo-Conception Mystic Christianity** *by Max Heindel*   ISBN: *1-59462-188-8*   **$38.95**
The Rosicrucian Cosmo-conception is not dogmatic, neither does it appeal to any other authority than the reason of the student. It is: not controversial, but is: sent forth in the, hope that it may help to clear...   *New Age/Religion Pages 646*

☐ **Abandonment To Divine Providence** *by Jean-Pierre de Caussade*   ISBN: *1-59462-228-0*   **$25.95**
"The Rev. Jean Pierre de Caussade was one of the most remarkable spiritual writers of the Society of Jesus in France in the 18th Century. His death took place at Toulouse in 1751. His works have gone through many editions and have been republished...   *Inspirational/Religion Pages 400*

☐ **Mental Chemistry** *by Charles Haanel*   ISBN: *1-59462-192-6*   **$23.95**
Mental Chemistry allows the change of material conditions by combining and appropriately utilizing the power of the mind. Much like applied chemistry creates something new and unique out of careful combinations of chemicals the mastery of mental chemistry...   *New Age Pages 354*

☐ **The Letters of Robert Browning and Elizabeth Barret Barrett 1845-1846 vol II**   ISBN: *1-59462-193-4*   **$35.95**
by Robert Browning and Elizabeth Barrett   *Biographies Pages 596*

☐ **Gleanings In Genesis (volume I)** *by Arthur W. Pink*   ISBN: *1-59462-130-6*   **$27.45**
Appropriately has Genesis been termed "the seed plot of the Bible" for in it we have, in germ form, almost all of the great doctrines which are afterwards fully developed in the books of Scripture which follow...   *Religion/Inspirational Pages 420*

☐ **The Master Key** *by L. W. de Laurence*   ISBN: *1-59462-001-6*   **$30.95**
In no branch of human knowledge has there been a more lively increase of the spirit of research during the past few years than in the study of Psychology, Concentration and Mental Discipline. The requests for authentic lessons in Thought Control, Mental Discipline and...   *New Age/Business Pages 422*

☐ **The Lesser Key Of Solomon Goetia** *by L. W. de Laurence*   ISBN: *1-59462-092-X*   **$9.95**
This translation of the first book of the "Lernegton" which is now for the first time made accessible to students of Talismanic Magic was done, after careful collation and edition, from numerous Ancient Manuscripts in Hebrew, Latin, and French...   *New Age/Occult Pages 92*

☐ **Rubaiyat Of Omar Khayyam** *by Edward Fitzgerald*   ISBN:*1-59462-332-5*   **$13.95**
Edward Fitzgerald, whom the world has already learned, in spite of his own efforts to remain within the shadow of anonymity, to look upon as one of the rarest poets of the century, was born at Bredfield, in Suffolk, on the 31st of March, 1809. He was the third son of John Purcell...   *Music Pages 172*

☐ **Ancient Law** *by Henry Maine*   ISBN: *1-59462-128-4*   **$29.95**
The chief object of the following pages is to indicate some of the earliest ideas of mankind, as they are reflected in Ancient Law, and to point out the relation of those ideas to modern thought.   *Religion/History Pages 452*

☐ **Far-Away Stories** *by William J. Locke*   ISBN: *1-59462-129-2*   **$19.45**
"Good wine needs no bush, but a collection of mixed vintages does. And this book is just such a collection. Some of the stories I do not want to remain buried for ever in the museum files of dead magazine-numbers an author's not unpardonable vanity..."   *Fiction Pages 272*

☐ **Life of David Crockett** *by David Crockett*   ISBN: *1-59462-250-7*   **$27.45**
"Colonel David Crockett was one of the most remarkable men of the times in which he lived. Born in humble life, but gifted with a strong will, an indomitable courage, and unremitting perseverance...   *Biographies/New Age Pages 424*

☐ **Lip-Reading** *by Edward Nitchie*   ISBN: *1-59462-206-X*   **$25.95**
Edward B. Nitchie, founder of the New York School for the Hard of Hearing, now the Nitchie School of Lip-Reading, Inc, wrote "LIP-READING Principles and Practice". The development and perfecting of this meritorious work on lip-reading was an undertaking...   *How-to Pages 400*

☐ **A Handbook of Suggestive Therapeutics, Applied Hypnotism, Psychic Science**   ISBN: *1-59462-214-0*   **$24.95**
by Henry Munro   *Health/New Age/Health/Self-help Pages 376*

☐ **A Doll's House: and Two Other Plays** *by Henrik Ibsen*   ISBN: *1-59462-112-8*   **$19.95**
Henrik Ibsen created this classic when in revolutionary 1848 Rome. Introducing some striking concepts in playwriting for the realist genre, this play has been studied the world over.   *Fiction/Classics/Plays 308*

☐ **The Light of Asia** *by sir Edwin Arnold*   ISBN: *1-59462-204-3*   **$13.95**
In this poetic masterpiece, Edwin Arnold describes the life and teachings of Buddha. The man who was to become known as Buddha to the world was born as Prince Gautama of India but he rejected the worldly riches and abandoned the reigns of power when...   *Religion/History/Biographies Pages 170*

☐ **The Complete Works of Guy de Maupassant** *by Guy de Maupassant*   ISBN: *1-59462-157-8*   **$16.95**
"For days and days, nights and nights, I had dreamed of that first kiss which was to consecrate our engagement, and I knew not on what spot I should put my lips..."   *Fiction/Classics Pages 240*

☐ **The Art of Cross-Examination** *by Francis L. Wellman*   ISBN: *1-59462-309-0*   **$26.95**
Written by a renowned trial lawyer, Wellman imparts his experience and uses case studies to explain how to use psychology to extract desired information through questioning.   *How-to/Science/Reference Pages 408*

☐ **Answered or Unanswered?** *by Louisa Vaughan*   ISBN: *1-59462-248-5*   **$10.95**
Miracles of Faith in China   *Religion Pages 112*

☐ **The Edinburgh Lectures on Mental Science (1909)** *by Thomas*   ISBN: *1-59462-008-3*   **$11.95**
This book contains the substance of a course of lectures recently given by the writer in the Queen Street Hall, Edinburgh. Its purpose is to indicate the Natural Principles governing the relation between Mental Action and Material Conditions...   *New Age/Psychology Pages 148*

☐ **Ayesha** *by H. Rider Haggard*   ISBN: *1-59462-301-5*   **$24.95**
Verily and indeed it is the unexpected that happens! Probably if there was one person upon the earth from whom the Editor of this, and of a certain previous history, did not expect to hear again...   *Classics Pages 380*

☐ **Ayala's Angel** *by Anthony Trollope*   ISBN: *1-59462-352-X*   **$29.95**
The two girls were both pretty, but Lucy who was twenty-one who supposed to be simple and comparatively unattractive, whereas Ayala was credited, as her Bombwhat romantic name might show, with poetic charm and a taste for romance. Ayala when her father died was nineteen...   *Fiction Pages 484*

☐ **The American Commonwealth** *by James Bryce*   ISBN: *1-59462-286-8*   **$34.45**
An interpretation of American democratic political theory. It examines political mechanics and society from the perspective of Scotsman James Bryce   *Politics Pages 572*

☐ **Stories of the Pilgrims** *by Margaret P. Pumphrey*   ISBN: *1-59462-116-0*   **$17.95**
This book explores pilgrims religious oppression in England as well as their escape to Holland and eventual crossing to America on the Mayflower, and their early days in New England...   *History Pages 268*

www.bookjungle.com *email: sales@bookjungle.com fax: 630-214-0564 mail: Book Jungle PO Box 2226 Champaign, IL 61825*

			QTY
The Fasting Cure *by Sinclair Upton*	ISBN: *1-59462-222-1*	**$13.95**	☐

In the Cosmopolitan Magazine for May, 1910, and in the Contemporary Review (London) for April, 1910, I published an article dealing with my experiences in fasting. I have written a great many magazine articles, but never one which attracted so much attention... New Age/Self Help/Health Pages 164

Hebrew Astrology *by Sepharial* ISBN: *1-59462-308-2* **$13.45** ☐

In these days of advanced thinking it is a matter of common observation that we have left many of the old landmarks behind and that we are now pressing forward to greater heights and to a wider horizon than that which represented the mind-content of our progenitors... Astrology Pages 144

Thought Vibration or The Law of Attraction in the Thought World ISBN: *1-59462-127-6* **$12.95** ☐

by William Walker Atkinson Psychology/Religion Pages 144

Optimism *by Helen Keller* ISBN: *1-59462-108-X* **$15.95** ☐

Helen Keller was blind, deaf, and mute since 19 months old, yet famously learned how to overcome these handicaps, communicate with the world, and spread her lectures promoting optimism. An inspiring read for everyone... Biographies/Inspirational Pages 84

Sara Crewe *by Frances Burnett* ISBN: *1-59462-360-0* **$9.45** ☐

In the first place, Miss Minchin lived in London. Her home was a large, dull, tall one, in a large, dull square, where all the houses were alike, and all the sparrows were alike, and where all the door-knockers made the same heavy sound... Childrens/Classic Pages 88

The Autobiography of Benjamin Franklin *by Benjamin Franklin* ISBN: *1-59462-135-7* **$24.95** ☐

The Autobiography of Benjamin Franklin has probably been more extensively read than any other American historical work, and no other book of its kind has had such ups and downs of fortune. Franklin lived for many years in England, where he was agent... Biographies/History Pages 332

Name	
Email	
Telephone	
Address	
City, State ZIP	

☐ Credit Card   ☐ Check / Money Order

Credit Card Number	
Expiration Date	
Signature	

Please Mail to: Book Jungle
PO Box 2226
Champaign, IL 61825
or Fax to: 630-214-0564

ORDERING INFORMATION

web: *www.bookjungle.com*
email: *sales@bookjungle.com*
fax: *630-214-0564*
mail: *Book Jungle PO Box 2226 Champaign, IL 61825*
or PayPal *to sales@bookjungle.com*

Please contact us for bulk discounts

DIRECT-ORDER TERMS

20% Discount if You Order Two or More Books
Free Domestic Shipping!
Accepted: Master Card, Visa, Discover, American Express

www.ingramcontent.com/pod-product-compliance
Lightning Source LLC
Chambersburg PA
CBHW080530170426
43195CB00016B/2519